THE EVOLUTION OF INTERNATIONAL BUSINESS 1800–1945

The Evolution of International Business 1800–1945
Selected and with a new Introduction by Mark Casson

Rippy, J.F. – *British Investments in Latin America, 1822–1949*

Spence, C.C. – *British Investments and the American Mining Frontier, 1860–1901*

Jackson, W.T. – *The Enterprising Scot: Investors in the American West after 1873*

Cameron, R.E. – *France and the Economic Development of Europe, 1800–1914*

Bagchi, A.K. – *Private Investment in India, 1900–1939*

Southard, F.A. Jr – *American Industry in Europe*

Phelps, D.M. – *Migration of Industry to South America*

Hou, Chi-ming – *Foreign Investment and Economic Development in China, 1840–1937*

Other titles in the series, *The Rise of International Business 1200–1800*

The Emergence of International Business 1200–1800
Selected and with a new Introduction by Mark Casson

Dollinger, P. – *The German Hansa*

de Roover, R. – *Money, Banking and Credit in Medieval Bruges*

Rabb, T.K. – *Enterprise and Empire*

Chaudhuri, K.N. – *The English East India Company*

Davies, K.G. – *The Royal Africa Company*

Davis, R. – *Aleppo and Devonshire Square*

Klein, P.W. – *De Trippen in de 17eeuw*

The Hegemony of International Business 1945–1970
Selected and with a new Introduction by Mark Casson

Dunning, J.H. – *American Investment in British Manufacturing Industry*

Islam, M. – *Foreign Capital and Economic Development*

Safarian, A.E. – *Foreign Ownership of Canadian Industry*

Brash, D.T. – *American Investment in Australian Industry*

Kidron, M. – *Foreign Investments in India*

Vernon, R. – *Sovereignty at Bay*

Stonehill, A. – *Foreign Ownership in Norwegian Enterprises*

Stubenitsky, F. – *American Direct Investment in the Netherlands*

THE EVOLUTION OF INTERNATIONAL BUSINESS 1800–1945

Volume 7

Migration of Industry to South America

Dudley Maynard Phelps

London and New York

First published 1936 by McGraw-Hill Book Company
This edition reprinted 2000 by Routledge
2 Park Square, Milton Park, Abingdon, Oxon OX14 4RN

Simultaneously published in the USA and Canada
by Routledge
711 Third Avenue, New York, NY 10017

Transferred to Digital Printing 2002

Routledge is an imprint of the Taylor & Francis Group

© 1936 McGraw-Hill Book Company

Typeset in 10/12pt Times by Graphicraft Limited, Hong Kong

First issued in paperback 2013

All rights reserved. No part of this book may be reprinted or
reproduced or utilised in any form or by any electronic, mechanical,
or other means, now known or hereafter invented, including
photocopying and recording, or in any information storage or
retrieval system, without permission in writing from the publishers.

British Library Cataloguing in Publication Data
A catalogue record for this book is available from the British Library

Library of Congress Cataloging in Publication Data
A catalogue record for this book has been requested

ISBN13: 978-0-415-19014-2 (hbk)
ISBN13: 978-0-415-51053-0 (pbk)

Publisher's Note
The publisher has gone to great lengths to ensure the quality of these
reprints, but wishes to point out that certain characteristics of the
original copies will, of necessity, be apparent in reprints thereof.

Disclaimers
The publishers have made every effort to contact authors/copyright holders
of works reprinted in *The Evolution of International Business, 1800–1945*.
This has not been possible in every case, however, and we would welcome
correspondence from those individuals/companies we have been unable to trace.

MIGRATION OF INDUSTRY
TO
SOUTH AMERICA

BY

DUDLEY MAYNARD PHELPS, Ph.D.

Assistant Professor of Marketing
School of Business Administration
University of Michigan

FIRST EDITION

McGRAW-HILL BOOK COMPANY, Inc.
NEW YORK AND LONDON
1936

PREFACE

The field of international trade has been studied diligently by economists and others in both its theoretical and its practical aspects. International investments have likewise received the attention of able investigators. Here we are dealing with the subject of "industrial migration," which in its modern form—the establishment of subsidiary manufacturing plants—partakes of the nature of both foreign trade and foreign investment and has, in addition, certain characteristics of its own. In recent years the migration of industry has usually been an outgrowth of a trade relationship between two nations. It has developed, most often, when the mere exporting of products became an inadequate means of cultivating the foreign market. Industrial migration involves not only the exportation of physical products and of capital but also the transfer of managerial abilities and industrial techniques. It may be considered a hybrid of foreign trade and foreign investment, with a greater measure of managerial supervision and control.

The migration of industry is not new. It has merely become more noticeable in recent decades. Capital, business experience, and individuals with particular business abilities have for many centuries passed over national borders and started functioning elsewhere. Frequently an industry has been developed in a new country by individuals who settled there for other than economic reasons. Thus, the English textile industry probably owes its beginning to the Huguenots and other groups who in the latter part of the seventeenth century took refuge in England from the religious persecution to which they were subjected in continental Europe. Because of their skill in weaving, these refugees were welcomed in England and were even aided by the government. This was before the days of machinery, and skilled labor was the primary requisite for an industrial system. The emigration of the Huguenots even involved, to a slight degree, the transfer of capital, for some of the weavers brought their looms with them. Again, the development of an industry has sometimes been the work of individuals who migrated with the specific intention of starting a new industry. Industrial history has recorded many instances in which an individual, having learned the business of his father, emigrated to another country and there started a like business for himself. Probably some capital and undoubtedly some business experience were taken with him.

While these examples were typical of the migration of industry, one feature which characterizes the modern version was usually lacking. All ties with the parent organization were cut, and the new industrial enterprise lacked connection with the old. At least, this was true of most manufacturing operations. Financial and trading companies commonly extended their activities to other countries and retained control over them. One reason for the tendency of new industrial enterprises to be completely separated from the old was the unwillingness of the older industrial nations to permit exportation of either their manufacturing equipment or any information pertaining thereto. In England, during the latter part of the eighteenth century, laws were passed prohibiting the exportation of any plans or drawings of the machinery used in manufacture, and efforts were made even to prevent the emigration of factory workers or others who had knowledge of the construction of factory machinery. Despite these restrictions, textile manufacturing was started in the United States between 1775 and 1800, but if there was any connection between the American industry and its British counterpart, it was necessarily a surreptitious one. In later years, with the adoption by England and other countries of a policy of free trade, the handicap of legal restrictions on the export of equipment was removed, and thus the establishment of subsidiary operations in new countries was made possible. Furthermore, the growth of corporate industry, as contrasted with the family type, has facilitated interconnection between home and foreign activities, so that now the unity of an industrial enterprise often transcends national borders.

When trade passes freely between adjoining countries unhampered by numerous restrictions, there is little reason for the existence of similar manufacturing activities in both countries, unless the product manufactured is very bulky in relation to its value. But the spirit of nationalism, which has been accentuated by the progress of science in partially eliminating the barriers of time and space, has dictated an increasing measure of self-sufficiency. Nations evidently fear proximity and dependence on others. Trade barriers have been created, and international exchange of goods has been stifled. With this has come the migration of industry, which enables the old industrial country to circumvent artificial trade barriers. At the same time, it enables the less-developed country to attain a higher degree of industrial self-sufficiency. It is true that the newer countries are fearful of economic dominance by people of other nations, who are frequently considered as intruders and are the object of ill will. Hence the development of economic opportunities by foreign concerns is permitted somewhat grudgingly, being considered the price which must be paid for economic expansion and self-sufficiency. In such cases, foreign participation in the economic life of a nation is evidently considered more desirable, or at least less undesirable, than dependence upon an import-export relationship.

During the last three decades, many of our large corporations have established subsidiary manufacturing facilities in South America. The activities of these companies in Argentina, Chile, Brazil, and Uruguay constitute the subject of this study, which may be considered a pooling of the business experience of United States concerns in these countries. The bringing together and analyzing of this experience should be of value not only to the concerns already represented in South America but also to those which may enter South American markets in the future. The subject is treated from the standpoint of business policy, but it is believed that many of the facts and observations presented also have a bearing on the broader subject of international relations.

The material upon which this study is based was secured in 1932–1933 under a fellowship grant from the Social Science Research Council of New York. Without this grant, which permitted extensive travel in South America, the study could not have been made. Much assistance has likewise been received from other organizations and numerous individuals. The members of the Chamber of Commerce of the United States of America in the Argentine Republic were unfailingly courteous and answered innumerable questions. The author is particularly indebted to Dr. Alexander V. Dye, formerly United States Commercial Attaché in Argentina, now Director of the Bureau of Foreign and Domestic Commerce; Mr. Charles R. Cameron, American Consul-General in São Paulo, Brazil; Mr. Harry McLerie of the Swift International Company; Mr. Leland C. Ball of the International Printing Ink Corporation; Mr. M. L. Shoemaker of the National Lead Company, S.A.; and Mr. Sterling Thompson of the Du Pont Cellophane Company, Inc.

It was originally intended that this study should be published through the Bureau of Business Research of the University of Michigan. Its director, Clare E. Griffin, Dean of the School of Business Administration, has been interested in the study throughout its preparation and has given invaluable assistance. Special acknowledgment is due, also, to Valborg Emde, Research Associate in the Bureau, who has given able assistance in the preparation of the manuscript.

DUDLEY MAYNARD PHELPS.

ANN ARBOR, MICHIGAN,
April, 1936.

CONTENTS

PREFACE... v

CHAPTER 1
EXTENT OF MIGRATION 1
Activities of Migrating Companies—Time of Migration—Amount of Capital Invested—Number of Employees.

CHAPTER 2
THE GENERAL SETTING FOR INDUSTRIAL MIGRATION 27
The Background of Migration in the United States—Economic Changes in South America—The Influence of Nationalism.

CHAPTER 3
SPECIFIC REASONS FOR MIGRATION 43
The Influence of Raw Material Resources—Production Incentives to Migration—The Effect of Competition—The Tariff Incentive—Marketing Inducements to Migration—Summary.

CHAPTER 4
DIFFICULTIES ENCOUNTERED BY MIGRATING COMPANIES 90
Lack of Information on Which to Base Decisions—Distance from the Home-office Organization—Prejudice against Foreign Capital—Race and Nationality Factors—Lack of Stability in Government—Currency Depreciation—Inadequacy of Commercial Law.

CHAPTER 5
TARIFFS AND TAXATION 127
Changes in Tariffs and Port Charges—Reasons for Tariff Changes—Illogical Tariff Classifications—Administration of the Customs—Interstate and International Tariffs—Taxation.

CHAPTER 6
GOVERNMENTAL CONTROL OF BUSINESS ACTIVITIES 165
Regulation of the Packing Industry—Regulation of the Petroleum Industry—Regulation of Other Industries—Social Legislation—Means of Protection against Governmental Regulation.

CHAPTER 7
OPERATING DIFFERENCES AND DIFFICULTIES 231
Machinery and Equipment—Raw Materials and Supplies—Labor—Executive Personnel.

CHAPTER 8
POLICIES OF MIGRATING COMPANIES.................271

CHAPTER 9
RESULTS OF INDUSTRIAL MIGRATION...............288
   Mortality among Branch Plants—Profits—Effect of Migration upon Industry in the United States—Effect of Migration upon the Economic Development of South America.

CHAPTER 10
SUMMARY—FAVORABLE AND UNFAVORABLE INFLUENCES.......307

APPENDIXES
I. NORTH AMERICAN COMPANIES WHICH HAVE MIGRATED TO VARIOUS SOUTH AMERICAN COUNTRIES............325
II. CLASSIFICATION BY INDUSTRIES OF NORTH AMERICAN COMPANIES WITH PRODUCTION FACILITIES IN SOUTH AMERICA........328
III. AVERAGE ANNUAL EXCHANGE RATES BETWEEN VARIOUS SOUTH AMERICAN MONETARY UNITS AND THE DOLLAR, 1900–1932 . . 330

INDEX...............................331

MIGRATION OF INDUSTRY TO SOUTH AMERICA

Chapter 1

EXTENT OF MIGRATION

Prior to a detailed analysis of questions of policy, which will appear in later chapters, it is necessary to present some data on the extent of industrial migration. Certain questions need to be answered to prepare the reader for later sections of the study. To what extent have North American concerns placed production facilities in Argentina, Brazil, Chile, and Uruguay?[1] What types of concerns have migrated, and what are the activities in which they are engaged? When did this movement take place, recently or some time ago? How much capital has been invested by these companies? How many men do these concerns employ within the foreign areas? An answer to these and similar questions will serve a threefold purpose. It will provide the needed orientation to the study. It will indicate the breadth of business experience from which the ideas and information of this study were drawn, as practically all of the executives of the subsidiary organizations were interviewed. Finally, such factual information has intrinsic value, for it has not been published previously, and knowledge in regard to the extent of our interest in the industrial life of other nations may prevent individual concerns and government agencies from taking ill-considered and thoughtless action which would jeopardize business relationships.

[1] Argentina, Brazil, and Chile will hereafter be referred to as the ABC countries.

The procedure might be followed of presenting information separately for each concern. In this manner a complete picture would be given. But reasonable regard for the length of this section prohibits such a detailed method; also, some of the data, particularly the information in regard to investment, were given as confidential. Therefore a concise, summarized statement will be given of the extent of our industrial migration to these countries.

Activities of Migrating Companies

First, let us note what concerns have established some form of production facilities. In Appendix I is given a complete list of these concerns, classified by the countries in which their production facilities are located. In Argentina, thirty-seven concerns are listed, and a few others engage in production activities intermittently. In Brazil there are twenty-five concerns, and in Uruguay there are six. In Chile, eighteen companies are listed, but all were not operating when the material for this study was secured in 1932–1933. Some of the companies had withdrawn from the country entirely, others were still operating but on a very restricted schedule. For purposes of record, all companies which were operating as late as 1930 are included. It will be observed that some concerns operate in all four countries, many of them in more than one. If these duplications are eliminated, a total of fifty-two United States concerns are represented in this group. Included in the group are subsidiaries of the three large packing companies, with plants in Brazil, Uruguay, and Argentina; our largest automobile and tire concerns; two large public utility interests; and our chief producers of petroleum products, minerals, pharmaceuticals, and construction materials. The following is a broad classification of the activities of these companies:[2]

[2] A listing of the various companies on the basis of this classification is given in Appendix II. Some companies are mentioned more than once, as their activities may differ between products or between countries.

1. Activities primarily related to the extraction and processing of mineral products and other raw materials
2. Processing products of agricultural or pastoral origin
3. Furnishing services (public utilities)
4. General manufacturing

The first group is exemplified by the Standard Oil Company and the National Lead Company in Argentina, and by the Guggenheim interests in Chilean nitrate; the second group, by the meat-packing concerns in Brazil, Uruguay, and Argentina. For these groups only one subclassification is necessary; that is, the plants may be classified according to the market for their output, which may be foreign or domestic. In the case of the meat-packing companies, operations were started in South America primarily to provide a source of supply for European markets. The Standard Oil Company and the National Lead Company operate in Argentina to supply the domestic market.

The third group covers the activities of public utility concerns, such as the American and Foreign Power interests in Brazil, Argentina, and Chile; the Brazilian Traction, Light & Power Co., Ltd., in Brazil; and the International Telephone and Telegraph Corporation interests in the ABC countries. Some of the companies furnish transportation or communication service, others furnish such products as electric current or gas.

The fourth group, that of general manufacturing, requires greater attention. Further classification is difficult because of the variations in the methods by which companies handle their business in South America. There is variation even among those concerns which manufacture like products. The relative newness of the situation and a feeling of uncertainty—the outgrowth of less accurate information—lead to less uniformity in operations. One basis for classification is the agency which performs the manufacturing operation. Manufacturing may be carried on by the North

American company itself or by native concerns under a contractual relationship. More will be said of this later. Another basis is the extent of manufacturing activities or, stated more exactly, the extent of participation by the foreign subsidiary in the manufacturing process. On this basis, the dividing line between concerns is far from clear-cut, as is evident from the following classification:

1. Complete production of a commodity in the branch plant
2. Production of some assembly units, importation of others, and assembly in the branch plant
3. Minor production, assembly, and service operations in subsidiaries of public utility companies
4. Assembly of parts imported from abroad
5. Minor assembly and service operations in subsidiaries primarily devoted to merchandising operations
6. Packaging of commodities imported in bulk

While this classification is largely self-explanatory, still reference to specific concerns and products may be advisable. The nature of the product often demands complete production. Cement is a good illustration. The International Cement Corporation has plants in Brazil, Uruguay, and Argentina. Other examples are the production of yeast and corn products, the former by Standard Brands, Inc., of Brazil, and the latter by the Corn Products Refining Company in both Brazil and Argentina. In these instances the branch plant is largely an autonomous unit. As we proceed further in our classification, interrelationships between the parent organization and the subsidiary assume more importance.

The activities of the Otis Elevator Company exemplify the second group. Here we have a combination of assembly and production. The lifting apparatus is mostly imported, but the cabins, doors, shafts, and even signal systems are produced in Buenos Aires. Minor units are also purchased, and finally the various parts, some foreign, some domestic in origin, are assembled into the finished product. In this instance probably half of the entire production process is performed in the branch plant.

The servicing of equipment, which often includes the manufacture of assembly parts, makes production facilities necessary for the public utility concerns. The best example is the shops of the Brazilian Traction, Light & Power Co., Ltd., on the outskirts of Rio de Janeiro. This is one of the largest foreign-owned manufacturing plants in South America. Steel, brass, and aluminum castings are made, coils for motors and armatures are assembled, copper wire is reduced and insulated, and such items as bolts, screws, nuts, and various repair parts for trucks, busses, and street cars are manufactured. Other public utilities do not engage in manufacturing activities to a like extent, but all do some service work. Production in this third group is dissimilar to that in the previous group, in that the range of manufacturing activities is greater, products are made and assembled for use by the utility company, and service work is included.

Few companies confine themselves strictly to assembly operations. Practically all produce some parts, or change the form of the product in some manner. The automobile assembly plants of the Ford Motor Company and General Motors Corporation approach "assembly only" most closely. Some work is done on sheet metal, leather, and glass, but there is little dependence on the branch plant for the production of parts. The cost of assembly relative to the total cost of the product varies, but in the case of automobiles it constitutes about 20 to 25 per cent of total cost. This is a rough measure of the importance of the branch in the manufacturing process.

The fifth group is exemplified by a number of important concerns, among which are the National Cash Register Company, Singer Sewing Machine Company, International Harvester Company, and United Shoe Machinery Corporation. Each concern owns and occupies large quarters, has an appreciable investment, and employs many individuals.

Branch establishments are maintained in a number of cities by the Singer and International Harvester companies. These establishments are primarily merchandising institutions, but each performs some assembly operations and services its products. For trucks and tractors the activities of the International Harvester Company are similar to those of the automobile companies. The United Shoe Machinery Corporation in Buenos Aires, although designating itself as an importing rather than a manufacturing concern, maintains a shop for the service and rebuilding of its machines, in which it employs thirty to forty men. For this group, the contribution of the branch plant to the manufacture of the product is slight, probably less than 10 per cent.

The last group of our classification involves the packaging of commodities imported in bulk. It is confined largely to pharmaceutical products. In addition, mixing operations are often needed to prepare the product for the retail trade. Although these activities are necessary, still the contribution of the branch plant to the total preparation of the product is slight. Yet the inference should not be taken that the branch plants of the pharmaceutical companies do nothing but mix and package the product. Some products are completely manufactured. Any specific company may thus break over the lines of this classification. It is not a classification of companies but one of activities.

Attention has been called to the fact that some North American companies do not own or operate a branch plant but have their products manufactured through a contractual relationship with native concerns. Although the procedure differs, the essential fact remains that the product is manufactured within the foreign country under the direction of the North American company. Such arrangements account for the fact that the product is manufactured locally. Therefore it is migration of industry and comes within the scope of this study.

This procedure is followed by a number of concerns. Contracts are given to native companies for the manufacture of cabinets for radios and refrigerators. Likewise, a native concern is used for the manufacture of road-building forms involving metal pressing and the production of castings. In this latter instance the United States company had decided to establish a branch factory in Argentina but found upon investigation that local firms could do the work satisfactorily and at an appreciably lower total cost. No one local firm was equipped to perform all the necessary operations. Nor would it have been advisable to entrust complete product plans to a native concern, for this would stimulate copying, and legal protection against such action is ineffective. Therefore, a number of concerns were given contracts to produce specific parts, and the product was later assembled.

Pharmaceutical companies use this manufacturing procedure most often. A case in point is the arrangement which has lasted for a number of years between the Colgate-Palmolive-Peet Company and Conen Cía. de Productos, S. A., for the manufacture of Palmolive soap. The latter company is a producer of low-grade soaps, and thus there is no direct competition in products. In the factory a certain section is continuously devoted to the production of Palmolive soap. It is, in fact, a small factory within the confines of a larger one. The equipment, which is partly of German and partly of North American origin, is thoroughly modern for the manufacture of Palmolive soap. Undoubtedly it was purchased at the suggestion of the Colgate company, for other parts of the factory are not so well equipped. The necessary raw materials for Palmolive soap are furnished by the Colgate company. Manufacturing operations are supervised very carefully by representatives of the Colgate-Palmolive-Peet Company to assure adherence to rigid quality standards. The Conen company manufactures the soap and delivers it to the branch establishment of the Colgate-Palmolive-Peet Company for a fixed price per unit.

In other instances, a native concern or perhaps a migrating concern becomes a cooperative manufacturing unit for a number of companies. The native concern has an entirely separate and independent existence, but through arrangement with North American companies manufactures a variety of products. For example, De Valle, Ltd., is an Argentine concern which manufactures for the J. B. Williams Company, Kolynos Company, Lehn & Fink Company, Lily-Tulip Cup Corporation, R. L. Watkins Company, L. D. Vaulk Home Products Company, and A. S. Hinds Company. Cía. Argentine Sydney Ross, Inc., manufactures its own preparations and, in addition, those of the Lambert Pharmacal Company, Forhan Company, Williams Medical Company, and McCoy Laboratories. This type of arrangement is not confined to Argentina. It is also common in Brazil and Chile. Schilling, Hillier and Company and Heyman Rinder and Company in Rio de Janeiro manufacture and sell the preparations of many pharmaceutical companies. Among the products which they handle are Odorono, Cutex, Bromo-quinine, Antiphlogistine, and the line of Daggett & Ramsdell, a subsidiary of the Standard Oil Company. Schilling, Hillier and Company also manufactures for two large German concerns.)

Let us observe briefly the details of arrangements between the native and foreign companies. Uniformity is not to be expected, since the majority of such agreements are of recent date, mostly since 1930. Agreements sometimes involve only the privilege of manufacturing a product under the formula and name used in the United States. For the use of the formula and name, a small royalty on each unit is given. This might more accurately be termed the migration of secret formulas than the migration of industry. In such cases, the United States concern projects its influence into the other country but little.

The opposite extreme is illustrated by the production arrangement for Hinds' Honey and Almond Cream. Under the direct supervision of a representative from the home office, enough of the product is prepared in a few days to satisfy the total annual demand. Production takes place in the factory of De Valle, Ltd., in Buenos Aires, and the product is stored there and shipped as needed. The equipment is owned by A. S. Hinds Company and after use is stored away until again needed. In fact, a part of a factory is simply rented for intermittent production and the storage of product, although payment of the native concern is on the unit basis. In instances such as this, and there are many of them, the North American company exercises a large measure of control over raw materials, equipment, production processes, formulas, and often even the final sale of the product.

There are all degrees of gradation between the two plans previously outlined. The plan adopted in any arrangement depends upon the relative participation of the foreign company and the native company in production and marketing activities, and the extent of control exercised by each. Two arrangements will be sketched in some detail, one in which both activity and control are centered in the native concern, and the other in which the foreign concern exercises greater control. Both arrangements are now in use between pharmaceutical companies here and in Brazil. In the first arrangement, the United States company does not procure a license to do business in Brazil. Operations are conducted under the license procured by the native concern, the owner of which is really a local agent for the foreign company. In this capacity he purchases materials, containers, wrappers, and other needed supplies, and pays taxes and other expenses for the account of his principal. In order to do this, he needs, and is given, the power of attorney. He keeps adequate records and makes periodic reports. Although price is determined by the foreign concern, still the local agent suggests the price that should be charged for the product. His contribution as an independent rather than as an agent consists of performing the manufacturing operations required and, frequently, of selling the finished product. At times he owns the equipment, but it may be the property of the foreign company. His compensation for these various activities as agent, manufacturer, and distributor is a fixed amount per unit of product. The names of both companies appear on the wrapper, usually as follows: "Formula the property of . . . , New York, New York," and lower on the package, "Fabricated by . . . , Rio de Janeiro, Brazil." The name of the local concern, at least, must appear on the package, for the law demands that the producer's name be given, and the foreign concern has no corporate existence within the country.

The second arrangement differs from the first in that the United States company procures a license to operate in Brazil. Its designated place of business is the office or factory of the native company. Because it is thus domiciled and licensed to do business, products can and do appear under the company's name without also having the name of the local concern affixed. Therefore any consumer goodwill which may accrue to the product is associated with the name of the migrating company, and the possibility that the company will lose control of the market is lessened. Native concerns have been known to copy products and to trade on the goodwill secured through previous association with like products of other, especially of foreign, concerns. As in the former arrangement, the owner of the native concern is really the manager of the foreign concern. He is given the power of attorney, but his range of discretion is narrowed. Raw materials may be imported by the foreign company and requisitioned as needed by the local company. Likewise, in regard to the quantity to be produced, the price, and the manner in which the product is manufactured, more rigid control may be exerted.

In order to attain this measure of control, additional expense is assumed. There is the expense involved in securing a license to operate within the country. There are annual taxes on business entities. There are also income taxes and several other licenses and taxes which would not be collected if operations were in the name of the native company. Some companies have thought it necessary to maintain a representative to oversee the activities of the native concern, even though the latter is responsible for both manufacturing and selling operations. Doubtless some pharmaceutical concerns pay heavily for trying to establish their identity in these South American markets. Still the additional control attained may justify the expenditure.

Further questions which may arise in regard to the feasibility of these various arrangements are not of concern at the moment. Our present interest is in the extent of industrial migration. The exposition of the preceding paragraphs should disclose two things in this connection: (1) that industrial migration is not confined to those concerns which set up production facilities abroad; (2) that there are varying degrees to which a migrating concern may engage in manufacturing activities through contractual relationships with native concerns. The migration of industry may be only partial, but it constitutes migration because goods are produced at the instigation and under the control of a North American company.

Time of Migration

The United Shoe Machinery Corporation and the Singer Sewing Machine Company are two of the pioneers in South America. The former was established in Argentina in 1903 and in Brazil in 1905. The latter established a branch in Chile in 1904 and branches in Brazil and Argentina in 1906. The Singer company is probably more widely known throughout the length and breadth of South America than any other company, either foreign or domestic.

While these two companies do some assembly and service work, both are engaged primarily in merchandising operations. It was not until 1907 that the first branch manufacturing plant came under the control of a North American concern. In that year, the La Plata Cold Storage Company was purchased by Swift and Company after negotiations covering many months. Later, Swift and Company started operations elsewhere in Argentina, at Rio Gallegos in 1910, and at Rosario in 1924. In Uruguay, Swift and Company also took the lead by the establishment of a packing plant outside Montevideo in 1911. Two other concerns entered the picture in 1913. Wilson & Company, Inc., had previously acquired an interest in the Sultzburger Company in São Paulo, Brazil, and in 1913 took over active control of the concern. It was in this year also that the Pullman Standard Car Export Corporation built a factory in Rio de Janeiro for the assembly of railroad equipment.

Table 1 provides a complete picture of the time at which branch plants were established. All the companies listed in Appendix I are not here included, for this analysis is confined to those concerns which have set up manufacturing or processing facilities. Public utility companies are excluded, also those concerns which are engaged primarily in merchandising activities. Neither does the list include mining companies, except those which further process the product and sell it within the country of origin. For instance, the subsidiary of the Standard Oil Company in Argentina is included, because crude petroleum is not only extracted but refined for sale by the company within Argentina. The United States Steel Corporation subsidiary company in Brazil is not included, for the manganese ore which is mined is not further processed before export to the United States. In instances where a concern produces for a number of North American companies, only the date at which production was started for one of the more important concerns is included; in other words, the branch plant is here treated as the classification unit. There is one exception to this, however; namely, that only ten packing plants are listed, whereas there are a total

TABLE 1.—DATE AND PLACE OF ESTABLISHMENT IN SOUTH AMERICA— BRANCH PLANTS OF NORTH AMERICAN COMPANIES

Year	Argentina	Brazil	Chile	Uruguay	Total
1907	1	..	..	..	1
1908	..	..	..	..	..
1909	..	..	..	..	..
1910	..	..	..	..	..
1911	..	..	..	1	1
1912	..	..	..	..	..
1913	..	2	..	..	2
1914	..	..	..	..	..
1915	1	..	..	..	1
1916	2	..	..	1	3
1917	1	1	1	..	3
1918	2	..	..	..	2
1919	1	2	..	..	3
1920	..	..	..	..	..
1921	..	1	..	..	1
1922	..	1	..	..	1
1923	..	..	..	..	..
1924	4	..	2	..	6
1925	2	1	..	..	3
1926	1	2	1	1	5
1927	2	..	..	..	2
1928	2	2	2	..	6
1929	1	1	1	2	5
1930	3	2	2	..	7
1931	3	2	2	..	7
1932	3	2	..	..	5
1933	2	..	..	..	2
Total	31	19	11	5	66

of sixteen operated by North American companies in these countries. Of the six not included separately, three are small ones operated only intermittently in the state of

Rio Grande do Sul, Brazil, and the other three are sheep-killing plants in Patagonia. They are not listed separately because they are in the same countries and under the same managements as those listed.

There are a total of sixty-six branch plants in this more restricted group: thirty-one in Argentina, nineteen in Brazil, eleven in Chile, and five in Uruguay. There was only one previous to 1910; fifteen were established in the 1910–1919 decade, twenty-nine in the following decade, and twenty-one since the beginning of 1930. In the last two decades covered in this table, only the years 1914, 1920, and 1923 failed to witness the decision of some company to migrate to this area. Thus, we see that migration is not, as is commonly thought, a phenomenon of the 1920–1929 decade. There were sixteen branch plants prior to 1920, of which nine were meat-packing plants. After 1923, however, the movement was accelerated and has continued unabated to the present time.

Let us observe how these sixty-six branch plants divide on an industry basis. In Table 2 such a division is given under eight groupings. There is approximately an equal number of plants producing construction materials and pharmaceuticals. There are ten meat-packing plants and one plant processing bones. Automobile and tire companies have established nine plants. The food group consists of two factories of the Corn Products Refining Company and one yeast manufacturing plant of Standard Brands, Inc. The miscellaneous group includes a variety of branch plants such as the carbon bisulphide plant of E. I. du Pont de Nemours & Company in Argentina; Cía. Sud-America de Explosivos in Chile, which is partly owned by the du Pont company; the plant of the General Electric Company in Brazil, which manufactures light bulbs and many other products; the shops of the Brazilian Traction, Light & Power Company, Ltd., in Rio de Janeiro; and the aeroplane assembly plant of the Curtiss-Wright Corporation in Santiago, Chile.

From an examination of this table it becomes evident that the various industries tended to migrate at different

TABLE 2.—DATE OF ESTABLISHMENT IN SOUTH AMERICA—BRANCH PLANTS OF NORTH AMERICAN COMPANIES CLASSIFIED BY INDUSTRY
(Argentina, Brazil, Uruguay, Chile)

Year	Automobile and tire	Construction	Food	Meatpacking	Petroleum	Pharmaceutical	Phonograph and radio	Miscellaneous	Total
1907	..	..	..	1	..	..	..	..	1
1908	..	..	..	..	..	..	..	..	..
1909	..	..	..	..	..	..	..	..	..
1910	..	..	..	..	..	..	..	..	..
1911	..	..	..	1	..	..	..	..	1
1912	..	..	..	..	..	..	..	..	..
1913	..	..	..	1	..	..	..	1	2
1914	..	..	..	..	..	..	..	..	..
1915	..	..	..	1	..	..	..	..	1
1916	..	1	..	2	..	..	..	..	3
1917	..	..	..	2	..	..	..	1	3
1918	1	..	..	..	..	..	..	1	2
1919	..	..	..	1	1	1	..	..	3
1920	..	..	..	..	..	..	..	..	..
1921	1	..	..	..	..	..	..	..	1
1922	..	..	..	..	..	..	..	1	1
1923	..	..	..	..	..	..	..	..	..
1924	1	1	..	1	..	1	1	1	6
1925	1	..	..	..	..	2	..	..	3
1926	2	2	1	..	..	..	..	..	5
1927	..	..	..	..	..	1	1	..	2
1928	..	2	..	..	..	..	1	3	6
1929	1	1	..	..	..	..	2	1	5
1930	..	..	1	..	1	3	..	2	7
1931	2	2	..	..	..	2	..	1	7
1932	..	2	1	..	..	1	..	1	5
1933	..	..	..	..	..	1	1	..	2
Total	9	11	3	10	2	12	6	13	66

times. The periods of migration for the different industries appear to have been roughly as follows:

Meat-packing plants—prior to 1920
Automobile assembly plants—1921 to 1926
Tire factories—1931
Construction materials—since 1924—four plants since 1930
Pharmaceuticals—from 1925 on—seven plants since 1929
Miscellaneous—over a period of two decades—eight plants since 1927

Amount of Capital Invested

In considering the amount of capital invested by migrating concerns, we must recognize the fact that all investment data are largely estimates, for they are based on evaluations and these are the product of someone's judgment. The accounting figures given out by a business enterprise may be either very conservative or too optimistic. There may be hidden assets or heavy depreciation which is not recognized in the accounts. Oftentimes the data which are published relative to the financial standing of business organizations tax the interpretative power of the investigator, and even after careful and painstaking analysis he finds that some questions cannot be answered with any degree of certainty.

The difficulties encountered are especially great when one attempts to determine the investment of business enterprises of one country in the economy of another country, for many problems arise which are entirely unrelated to the analysis of domestic investment. For instance, the exchange problem enters in. Investment data published in this country, to be meaningful, must be in terms of dollars rather than in pesos or milreis. For the purposes of this study, data furnished in pesos or milreis had to be converted into dollars, and conversion could be made at any one of several exchange rates. The average exchange rate of the year in which the investment was made could be used. But this rate would be difficult to apply without a wealth of information about each company, for, in the majority of instances, the investment had been built up over many years, either directly through new capital importations or through the use of profits to extend operations. Again, the average exchange rate of the year in which the data were collected could be used—that is, in this case, 1932-1933—but such a procedure would seriously distort the investment picture, for the exchange rate at that time was very low. The figure thus secured would be closely akin to liquidation value, and, since liquidation was not contemplated, we should not be justified in using such a rate to evaluate a relatively fixed investment. Finally, the par exchange rate could be used. The chief objection to the use of this rate is that some investments were made after 1930, when the peso and milreis were relatively cheap compared to the dollar. At par, the Argentine peso is worth $0.4245. In 1932 the average value of the peso in terms of the dollar was $0.2571.[3] It is now approximately $0.33 (summer of 1935). Some firms, motivated in part by the exchange situation, established branch operations in Argentina and Brazil in 1932 and were able to do so at low cost. However, since the greater number of concerns made their initial investments when exchange was around par, the investment data secured in terms of milreis and pesos have been converted at par exchange. Some indication will be given of the difference which would have resulted in the figures for total investment if conversion had been made on the basis of the average exchange rate of the year in which the initial investment was made.

Other complications arose in the interpretation of investment data as a result of the time at which the data were secured. In 1932-1933, all the countries included in this study were rigidly controlling exchange, and permits to buy exchange could be obtained only with difficulty. Because of the scarcity of exchange and its arbitrary allocation, many concerns had balances of pesos or milreis which

[3] *Commerce Yearbook*, 1933, U. S. Department of Commerce, Vol. II, p. 172.

were not needed for current business operations but which could not be sent to the United States. These funds could not be considered a part of normal working capital, but nevertheless, they appeared on the balance sheet of the branch plant. Therefore, in some instances in which these frozen funds were not assigned to the parent corporation, deductions were made to allow for their presence in capital and reserve figures.

Further questions arise in regard to the nature of the investment data which are presented. Should the initial investment be considered, or the investment after earnings have been ploughed back into the business or after losses have been recognized? Should the figures be limited to fixed investment, or to fixed investment plus normal working capital? In this study, the objective has been to secure data which represent the normal amount of capital used, both fixed and working, by those companies conducting branch plant operations. There may be some understatement, because of the fact that the inventories of some companies in 1932–1933 were less than normal. On the other hand, some overstatement may result from the presence of frozen funds. Furthermore, as previously noted, all investment figures are in the nature of estimates, and only approximate accuracy can be hoped for. First we will concern ourselves with the total investment in each country, and later with the investment in each industry for the four countries combined. This procedure must be followed, for otherwise some data given in confidence might be disclosed.

Argentina.—The capital invested in the thirty-one branch plant operations in Argentina totals $164,721,000.[4] Of

[4] Investment data were secured from a number of sources. The Argentine government requires all corporations to submit annual balance sheets, which are published in the *Boletin Official*. Some of the data were taken from these statements. The larger share, however, were furnished directly by the companies, either at the South American branch or at the home office in this country. Only four companies refused to give investment data, and for two of these data were procured from other sources. Estimates were

this amount $55,498,000 represents the investment of two oil companies and another extractor of mineral products.[5] Because the investment of each of these three companies includes refining plants, they are included in the general grouping of branch plant operations. It is recognized, however, that the capital used in such processing facilities is undoubtedly only a minor part of total investment. The information secured does not make possible a division of the total amount between refining plants and other investment. If this $55,498,000 is deducted from the total figure of $164,721,000, the balance, which represents the investment in the other twenty-eight operations, is $109,223,000. This latter figure more nearly represents the amount which North American companies have invested in actual manufacturing operations in Argentina.

In the computation of these investment figures, all investments which were given in pesos instead of dollars were converted at par exchange ($0.4245). Some of the investments, however, particularly those after 1930, were made when the peso was at an appreciable discount. In this group were eight companies, whose combined investment at par would amount to $13,982,000. If the conversion from pesos to dollars was made in each instance at the average exchange rate prevailing during the year in which the investment was made, the amount invested would be $10,039,000, or $3,943,000 less. Since the great majority of investments were made when the peso was approximately at par, the use of the average exchange rate in the year in which the initial investment was made does not alter the total figure appreciably. In order to attain greater exactitude, however, the difference of $3,943,000 should be

---

resorted to in a few instances, but these were carefully checked, and anyway the amounts involved were too small to affect the total figures appreciably.

[5] There is some inexactitude in the figure here given, for it includes the entire investment in an oil company in which a North American company has a substantial interest but not entire ownership. The overstatement would not exceed 10 per cent.

deducted from $109,223,000, leaving a total investment figure of $105,280,000.

The investment of those companies which engage in some minor assembly and service activities, but which are primarily merchandising institutions, totals $26,559,000. These companies might be considered border-line cases between manufacturing subsidiaries and purely selling organizations. One concern assembles trucks, another scales, a third shapes steel sheets into culverts, but in each instance the activity which might be termed manufacturing is greatly subordinate to importing and selling activities.

No attempt is made to state the investment in purely merchandising activities, financial institutions, or governmental or other securities. In public utilities the North American investment, represented by three companies, is approximately $215,000,000. Practically all of this investment was made between 1925 and 1930, when the peso was at par, and therefore conversion at par figures does little violence to the data. In these three classifications—branch factory operations, merchandising institutions performing some service and assembly, and public utilities—the North American investment in Argentina is between $400,000,000 and $425,000,000.

Brazil.—The capital invested in the nineteen branch plant operations in Brazil totals $47,165,000. Since most of the data for Brazil were furnished in terms of dollars, the problem of conversion was faced to a lesser extent than in the case of Argentina. No attempt was made further to refine this figure by making a differentiation between investment at par exchange and investment at the exchange rate prevailing at the time the various investments were made. Those acquainted with the monetary history of Brazil will realize the difficulties of so doing. Par itself has changed a number of times, and for a century the milreis has more or less constantly declined in value in relation to the dollar.[6] The figure given can be considered a reasonably conserva-

[6] See Chart 1, p. 109.

tive one; it is a combination of data secured almost entirely from companies rather than from published sources.

The investment by concerns which are primarily engaged in merchandising, but which do some assembling and service work, is very small compared with that in Argentina. A number of concerns operate in Brazil under policies which require little investment. The International Harvester Company, for instance, which has a heavy investment in Argentina, has little if any fixed investment in Brazil. Other companies which sell through branches in Argentina sell through independent middlemen in Brazil. The Pullman Standard Car Export Corporation falls in the merchandising classification in Argentina, but in Brazil it operates a branch plant and thus is in the first classification. The investment of the companies in the merchandising group totals $2,143,000. The investment of the three North American oil companies operating in Brazil might be included here, since, although they are primarily merchandising institutions dealing with imported products, they do mix and blend oils, and such activities might be considered production rather than marketing. The normal investment of the oil companies, including stocks, is between $15,000,000 and $20,000,000. In public utilities the investment totals approximately $490,000,000. This figure includes the total investment of the Brazilian Traction, Light & Power Co., Ltd., for United States citizens own substantial amounts of the securities of this organization, which furnishes the greater share of all public utility services to Rio de Janeiro, São Paulo, and Santos. Securities of this company are also held in large quantities in Canada and England.

Uruguay.—The capital invested in the five branch plant operations in Uruguay totals $14,534,000. This amount, a combination of figures furnished by the companies operating there, undoubtedly is a conservative one, for conversion of their capitalization figures at par exchange would yield something approaching twenty million dollars. Likewise, the accounting data required by and submitted to the government indicate a greater total investment. In public utilities the North American investment is $3,000,000.[7] According to releases from the Inspector General of Banks and Limited Liability Companies, the total North American investment in branch plants, merchandising companies, public utilities, and banks in 1932 was 27,738,000 gold pesos, which, converted at par ($1.034), would be $28,681,000.[8] The branch plants, however, account for only a little more than 68 per cent of this total. Therefore, if all of the estimates were as conservative as those furnished by the companies operating branch plants, the total investment of the North American companies doing business in Uruguay would be placed at something over $21,000,000.

Chile.—The capital invested in the eleven branch plant operations in Chile is estimated at $8,147,000. This information, however, is presented with much less confidence than similar information for the other countries included in this study. It is based more on estimates and less on published information or direct statements from company executives. Moreover, conditions in Chile in 1932–1933 were so unsettled that operations were practically at a standstill. Stocks of merchandise in the hands of branch organizations became greatly depleted, for Chilean currency had fallen to but a fraction of its former value in terms of the dollar and, furthermore, exchange cover was not procurable for other than bare necessities. The result was that little merchandise of foreign origin was being sold. In the middle of 1933, one of the companies which previously had operated a branch plant was liquidating and turning its business over to an independent concern, two other companies had been closed for many months with reopening a matter of question, and two companies with appreciable investments in manufacturing

[7] These properties were disposed of in 1934.
[8] *Diario del Plata*, Oct. 4, 1932, p. 4.

and assembling facilities were marking time until conditions improved. Practically all concerns had on deposit in Chilean banks frozen peso funds which were worth little at existing exchange rates and which could not be moved to the United States. Under such conditions, any investment figures compiled can mean but little.

At the end of 1928, an estimate was made which gave the investment in manufacturing activities as $11,285,000 and in merchandising activities as $22,500,000.[9] However, five of the eleven branch plant operations were started in 1929 or later, with a capital investment estimated in 1933 as approximately $1,500,000. Therefore, it is probable that the North American investment in branch plant operations in Chile prior to the economic breakdown so evident in 1932–1933 was between $12,000,000 and $15,000,000.

The investment in public utilities, as estimated from published statements of the three companies involved, totals $126,120,000. No independent estimate was made of the investment in mining properties represented by the copper companies and those interested in Chilean nitrates. In 1928 it was estimated that the total investment in these enterprises was $358,000,000.[10] But, since many changes in control and in the valuation which might be placed on mining properties, particularly on those producing nitrates, have appeared since 1928, a reappraisal might yield an appreciably different total at this time.

Investment in Various Industries.—Table 3 presents the combined investment in the four countries under observation in branch plant operations classified by industry. The combined investment total is $234,567,000. Of this total, all can legitimately be considered branch plant investment with the possible exception of the $55,137,000

---

[9] Max Winkler, "Investments of United States Capital in Latin America," *World Peace Foundation Pamphlets* (Boston: World Peace Foundation, 1928), Vol. XI, No. 6.
[10] *Ibid.*

in the oil industry. This, of course, is a joint investment in oil lands, extractive equipment, pipe lines, and refining plants. In all probability, some capitalized developmental expense is also included. The refining activities by which the crude oil is prepared for the local market come within our definition of branch plant operations, and for this

TABLE 3.—NORTH AMERICAN CAPITAL INVESTED IN BRANCH PLANT OPERATIONS, CLASSIFIED BY INDUSTRIES
(Argentina, Brazil, Uruguay, Chile)

Industry	Number of operations	Amount invested
Automobile and tire..........	9	$ 26,500,000
Construction...............	11	21,400,000
Food.....................	3	3,319,000
Meat packing..............	10	94,569,000
Petroleum.................	2	55,137,000
Pharmaceutical.............	12	1,744,000
Phonograph and radio.......	6	2,066,000
Miscellaneous..............	13	29,832,000
Total....................	66	$234,567,000

reason the investment of the oil companies is included. But, as was noted previously, only a small part of the total investment is in such branch operations. If the oil companies' investment is excluded, the total figure is reduced to $179,430,000. Of this latter figure, 53 per cent is the investment of the packing companies, 15 per cent is the investment of the automobile companies in assembly operations and of the two concerns which manufacture tires in Argentina, 12 per cent is the investment of those companies which produce construction materials both for roads and for buildings, and the remaining 20 per cent is the investment of numerous companies producing a variety of products. Among those listed as miscellaneous, the most important are the General Electric Company, the manufacturing and servicing operations of the Brazilian Traction, Light & Power Co., Ltd., and the Pullman Standard Car Export Corporation, all in Rio de Janeiro, Brazil; E. I. du Pont de Nemours & Company, Consolidated Chemical Industries, Inc., and the National Lead Company in Buenos Aires, Argentina; and the manufacturing activities of Grace (W. R.) & Company in Chile. The branch plant investment of these seven companies combined is something over $25,000,000, or approximately 14 per cent of the total figure. The remaining 6 per cent includes the investment of small miscellaneous concerns and of those included in the food, pharmaceutical, and phonograph and radio industries in the classification given.

Number of Employees

The number of men employed by the companies which have established branch plants will provide a final measure of the extent of migration. In many ways, this is the least satisfactory measure, for it varies both from season to season and from year to year. At the time the data were collected in 1932–1933, employment in the plants producing construction materials and assembling automobiles was at a low level. Concerns such as the International Cement Corporation and Otis Elevator Company were operating with about two-thirds of a normal labor force. The automobile assembly plants, because of their inability to secure exchange, were operating with little more than one-third of their usual force. But, in general, industry in South America was not depressed during the period subsequent to 1930, and companies in industries other than construction and automobiles were active.[11] By far the largest employers of labor, the packing companies, were operating with a normal labor force. The oil companies in Argentina also were active and were increasing their output. Accordingly, the total labor force employed by North American companies engaged in manufacturing

[11] D. M. Phelps, "Industrial Expansion in South America," *American Economic Review*, Vol. 25, No. 2 (June, 1935), pp. 273–282.

operations through subsidiaries was not far from normal in 1932–1933. The total figure was between 36,000 and 38,000 persons. Of this total, approximately 22,000 persons were employed in Argentina, 7,500 in Brazil, 6,000 in Uruguay, and the remainder in Chile. The packing industry employs between 20,000 and 22,000 men, the oil companies in Argentina about 5,000, and the companies producing construction materials between 2,500 and 3,000. With a full labor force in the automobile and construction material industries, the total number of employees in branch plant operations would probably reach 40,000.

Chapter 2

THE GENERAL SETTING FOR INDUSTRIAL MIGRATION

We have observed that the penetration of our industries into South America has been a continuing movement over almost three decades. For specific industries the length of the migrating period has been shorter, but there has been no marked concentration in time, as reference to Tables 1 and 2 will clearly indicate. This suggests that the forces behind migration are not confined to any one period in their influence. Furthermore, some of the factors which are influential in decisions as to whether or not to migrate are of general application; that is, they are pertinent to the inquiry for any industry, or for the expansion of industry into any foreign country. Other factors, equally influential, apply to one product only, to one country, or to one point in time, perhaps to only one company in an industry and not to others. Attention will be given to such factors in the following chapter. Our present interest is in basic factors of broad general application which have caused industrial migration to South America.

An inquiry in regard to why a certain company has established a factory in Brazil or Argentina is likely to draw forth a reply that there were possibilities of profitable operation. But such an assertion is of little value, for it is a safe assumption that the profit motive is behind all private business decisions. Further questioning may yield the comment that in no other way could the market be cultivated more profitably. In such manner alternative methods of meeting foreign market demands would enter the discussion. For instance, why does a company discontinue to serve the market by simple exporting and decide instead to produce within the market? Later it might be observed that conditions seemed ripe for industrial migration or perhaps that the company had idle funds and thus was able to make investments abroad. The first assertion raises a multitude of questions. Would such an observation apply to conditions in the country from which, or to which, migration was contemplated, or possibly to both? What is the general setting in the foreign country which makes feasible the establishment of new industry? The second assertion, in regard to the possession of idle funds, would refer specifically to a certain company, but still it has its background in general business conditions in the country from which the company migrated. First we will consider the background of industrial migration from this country and later the economic changes in the ABC countries, without which there would have been little justification for the movement.

The Background of Migration in the United States

The World War created a distinct change in the international economic position of the United States. Participation in the economic affairs of other nations was extended in many directions. This applies particularly to our relationships with South America. Trade and financial interconnections were strengthened materially, and this resulted in a heavy volume of foreign trade. Prior to the war the United States was relatively unimportant as a source of supply for South American markets. European countries were in the ascendancy. But during the war Europe was forced practically to abandon its export markets. There was no alternative, for production facilities were taxed severely to provide for war needs. Accordingly, South American countries began to buy more and more goods from the United States. Traditional supply sources were no longer able to furnish the needed products, and in addition the purchasing power of the South American countries was augmented by approximately 70 per cent through increased prices received for the products exported. Under these favorable conditions, the United States soon attained first position as a source of supply for every important Latin American country and held that position until 1931.

For the first time, our industry became actively interested in commercial interchange with South America. This could not be stated as true for all companies, nor for all industries, but surely for industry as a whole. Prior to 1915, the actual and potential needs of South America for the products of an industrialized economy were little recognized in this country. Later, when exports had increased materially and business executives had begun to recognize the potentialities of the market, it was often stated that Latin America was the "natural" market for American goods. Also it was asserted that the future of our export trade was not in Europe, nor the Orient, but in Latin America. Such broad assertions are rarely more than half-truths, and in this instance they were even misleading. So far as proximity, cultural relationships, racial interconnections, and complementary product needs are concerned, the South American countries as a group are more nearly the "natural" market of Europe than of the United States. But the assertions mentioned, whether correct or not, do show the degree to which trade interest was aroused. It was furthered by loans which were productive of heavier exports. It was carefully fostered by the Pan American Union and other bodies designed to nurture inter-American relations. Under the leadership of Herbert Hoover, who was then Secretary of Commerce, the Department of Commerce enlarged its field forces and exerted every effort to make trade contacts for exporting companies and to furnish executives with needed information about the markets.

Knowledge of South American markets and their potentialities was usually gained while direct exporting was still the prevailing mode of meeting demand. Later, as an outgrowth of the interest and experience previously acquired, many concerns established branch plants within the markets. Therefore, the effect of the World War was to hasten the migratory movement to South America, for otherwise the background of interest and experience would not have been prepared so quickly.

In time our industry probably would have expanded into the ABC countries, even without the international economic adjustments of the war years. Before 1914 a start had been made through the establishment of three subsidiaries by the packing companies, and one by a railroad equipment concern. The beginnings of migration to Canada antedated the war by many years, and it is conceivable that expansion across our borders into Canada was a forerunner of expansion to more distant areas, although the difficulties involved in the former case are fewer in number and more easily dealt with. Surely the migratory movement as a whole cannot be dated by the war. Rather, the impetus behind the movement is to be found in our maturing industrial economy. Concerns which have migrated are, in general, those which occupy a strong if not dominant position in the domestic market. Furthermore, they are the mass-production industries in which there is a constant incentive to increase the volume of output in order to decrease unit costs of production. Often there appeared to be little chance to secure additional business in the domestic market. Hence, foreign markets were cultivated, for they were newer and less saturated, and competition was likely to be less severe.

On first thought, it would appear probable that the establishment of a branch factory abroad would be a substitute for direct exporting and thus would decrease the output from domestic plants. In many instances, the effect was just the opposite, for the product was not completely manufactured in other countries but was only assembled as in the case of automobiles, packaged as for pharmaceuticals, or cut and reshaped as in the case of steel sheets. The result achieved was a lower price to foreign consumers, or perhaps a product which more fully met their needs. Bringing a product within the purchasing abilities of foreign consumers stimulated demand and therefore increased the output from domestic factories, despite the fact that some manufacturing operations were shifted to foreign branch plants. In the instances in which domestic output was thus increased, foreign operations were engaged in to provide for more effective selling of the product, rather than for more effective production.

For products whose manufacture could not be divided between two locations, or for which such division was possible but not feasible, because of other influences, the extent of our industrial development was the essential fact behind migration. Industry must reach a certain stage in its development before expansion abroad is likely to take place. It is quite evident that any specific concern must attain a strong financial condition in order to be able to establish foreign branches. Likewise, a company must attain a strong competitive position as compared with companies manufacturing like products elsewhere if migration is to be successful. If there is no native concern of like type in the country to which migration is contemplated, nor a branch plant from another industrial nation, then sufficient funds may be all that is required. Usually, however, competition soon emerges, and, to maintain its position, the company must rely on the experience gained over many years in its original setting. When foreign subsidiaries of American companies come into direct competition with concerns owned and managed by natives, a noteworthy difference between the two appears. The American concern has the benefit of the experience gained over many years of industrial growth. Therefore, in the majority of cases its branch plant is better managed than the native concern, more modern production techniques are used, more capital is available, and often operations are profitable, whereas the native concern is unable to operate on a profitable basis. This is particularly true in South America. Briefly, it is quite evident that we have certain intangible assets in capital, managerial abilities, and industrial techniques. Under conditions where tangible product cannot be exported, there is the incentive to export these intangible elements through the establishment and operation of manufacturing subsidiaries in foreign countries.

Economic Changes in South America

Now let us turn to a consideration of economic changes in South American countries without which there would have been little likelihood of industrial migration from North America. Prior to the beginning of the century and, for most industries, prior to 1915, there was little incentive to expand to any South American country. The stage was not set for incoming industry. Some migration was taking place across our borders into Canada, but establishment of a branch factory in Canada or in Europe is one thing, in Argentina or Brazil it is quite another. Migration into Canada has various advantages—among them, proximity and therefore easy supervision, a high standard of living, similarity of market demands, and the presence of auxiliary industries. While the establishment of a manufacturing subsidiary in Europe does not possess all of these advantages, yet it constitutes expansion from a newer to an older industrial situation, which is generally considered advantageous. Later, the essential differences between migration to another industrial area and migration to an agricultural or raw-material-producing area will be reviewed. Here it is our purpose to observe somewhat briefly the economic changes which have taken place in the ABC countries during the past two or three decades, changes which have made it much more feasible for our manufacturing concerns to establish branch plants.

Notable among these changes has been an expanded agricultural and mineral output. While this is undoubtedly the main feature of the economic development of these countries, it does not require detailed review. The facts are well known. It is sufficient in this connection to recall that agricultural progress, particularly in the supplying of foreign markets, has come largely during the present century. In a relatively short period of time Argentina has become one of the largest producers and exporters of cereals and meats. Uruguay shares in this forward movement. A like advance has been made by Brazil in the last thirty or forty years, but from Brazil the exports are coffee, cocoa, and other more tropical products. In each of these countries, agriculture has prospered, for newer markets were opening up abroad and older markets were taking additional quantities. It is hardly necessary to emphasize that a prosperous agriculture furnishes an active market for manufacturing industry and thus for incoming branch plants. Much the same comments can be made in respect to Chile. Here it was mineral products—particularly nitrate and copper—around which economic developments centered. Growth in the output of copper has been entirely an event of the twentieth century. Nitrates have been important for a much longer period. In Chile, as on the eastern seaboard, an expanding economy made certain manufacturing operations more feasible.

The profitableness of setting up manufacturing facilities to serve a market depends on the extent of the demand for the goods to be produced. Demand in turn depends on the number of buyers and their desire and ability to purchase. In other words, if population was growing, if buyers wanted the type of products which branch plants would manufacture, and if they possessed the wherewithal with which to purchase, then branch plants might expect to engage in profitable operations. In each of these respects, conditions in South America have become continuously more favorable for incoming industry. Population has increased rapidly, both through a high birth rate and through immigration. Argentina furnishes a good example, and the data are fairly reliable. In 1900 the population was 4.6 million, now it is almost 12 million. The most rapid increase occurred in the earlier years, but in the last twenty years the increase has been over 50 per cent. Urbanization has proceeded apace, the population of the ten chief cities increasing by 54 per cent in the last twenty years. Immigration accounted for 150,000 new inhabitants annually in the decade before the war and for 80,000 annually between 1920 and 1930. In Brazil, Uruguay, and Chile there have been much the same population tendencies, but the changes have not been so noticeable as in Argentina.

TABLE 4.—INDEXES OF EXPORTS FROM ARGENTINA*
(Base period, 1911–1915, equals 100 per cent)

Years	Quantity index	Value index
1911–1915	100	100
1916–1920	90	170
1921–1925	116	170
1926–1930	163	188

* *El Comercio Exterior Argentina en 1931 y 1930*, Boletin No. 209, pp. 6, 27.

TABLE 5.—INDEXES OF EXPORTS FROM CHILE*
(Base period, 1911–1915, equals 100 per cent)

Years	Quantity index, nitrates	Quantity index, copper	Value index, all exports
1911–1915	100	100	100
1916–1920	106	196	163
1921–1925	83	321	135
1926–1930	98	553	172

* *Commerce Yearbooks*, U. S. Department of Commerce, Bureau of Foreign and Domestic Commerce.

There have been favorable changes in the purchasing power of these countries also, particularly since 1915. By reference to the foregoing tables, the extent of the increase may be observed.[1] Purchasing power is measured by changes in the value of exports. These tables show the

---
[1] Tables 4 and 5 are from the author's article, previously mentioned, "Industrial Expansion in South America," and parts of the following discussion have also been adapted from this article.

trend of exports from Argentina and Chile over the past two decades, both on a quantity and on a value basis. The table for Chile illustrates what has happened in an economy in which mineral products dominate, that for Argentina illustrates one in which agricultural products hold the major position. In each case it will be observed that the value of exports increased by more than 60 per cent in the period from 1916 through 1920, as compared with the preceding five-year period. During the following ten years Argentina experienced no reversal toward the former low figure; the value of exports from Chile declined in the first half of the 1921–1930 decade, but reached a new high in the latter half. In each instance, although prices declined, the value of exports was maintained by the exportation of a greater quantity. After 1929 the value of exports declined precipitously, and with it purchasing power. But, for a period of fifteen years, purchasing power, as measured by export value, was at least one-half again as great as it was previous to the war. Of all the economic changes which have a bearing upon the question of industrial migration, this is the most significant. Had there not been this increased ability to buy, it is doubtful whether so many concerns would have placed factories in the ABC countries.

There were many other changes of an economic character which prepared the way for incoming industry. Railroads had been built by British capital in the latter half of the nineteenth century, and additions were made in the early years of this century, partly by foreign interests, partly through direct ownership and operation by the various governments. The expansion of agriculture and of mining and other extractive operations furnished many products that were needed by industrial enterprises. Industrial expansion was made much less difficult by the immigration of trained workers from Europe. The addition of some well-trained workers into the general laboring classes acted as a leaven, and thus the performance of the whole was improved. Native industry had developed and often served in an auxiliary capacity to branch plants. Unless they are a part of a generally expanding industrial situation, branch plants are severely handicapped, for other companies ordinarily are depended upon for a variety of supplies, small equipment, and services. Foreign concerns which were represented in these countries at an earlier date found local industry unable to cope with their needs. At times there simply was no concern which supplied the product or the service required. Stories are rife in which branch plant managers made heroic efforts to avert temporary shutdowns which were threatened because local industry was not equipped to make repairs or furnish supplies. Like conditions still arise now and then, but, in general, auxiliary industry is now able to meet ordinary demands for non-technical equipment, supplies, repair work, and even for many parts to be placed in final assemblies. This is particularly true in São Paulo and Buenos Aires.

The brevity with which this subject of economic changes has been treated should not be allowed to obscure its importance as a motivating force behind industrial migration. A more complete and detailed statement would violate the predetermined limitations of this study. Enough has been said to show that conditions in the ABC countries surely were not such as to warrant migration before the turn of the century, and for most industries not previous to 1915. Obviously, if migration is to take place, the general situation must be such that it presents an inviting picture to those foreign concerns which are contemplating the establishment of a branch plant. Expansion in livestock output in Argentina and Uruguay tempted the packing companies as early as 1905. They needed additional livestock to supply their already developed European markets. Other migration awaited the beginning of the World War. By that time, conditions were much more favorable for industry to enter. Also a phenomenal increase in purchasing power appeared, and demand soon followed for many products previously denied the inhabitants of these countries. In other words, the stage was set for industrial migration from the United States.

The Influence of Nationalism

We have now examined two basic factors which have had a direct bearing on migration: the background of the movement in the United States, and the economic changes in those countries toward which the movement was directed. A third factor has been the influence exerted by nationalistic tendencies throughout the world, particularly in industrial nations—an influence which has induced a greater measure of manufacturing activity in all non-industrial countries and has caused foreign concerns to establish branch plants. This force in its effect upon migration has become increasingly potent since 1920, and has reached unprecedented proportions in the past few years. Perhaps nations will gradually withdraw from their over-nationalistic positions and adopt a policy which limits international trade less drastically. At present there is much talk of reciprocal trade agreements, and reciprocity in international trade presumes that some concessions will be made by both parties. In the event that trade barriers are lowered, the motivation for a greater measure of national self-sufficiency will be correspondingly lessened. But whether nations will about-face and promote rather than discourage foreign trade is conjectural. As yet what evidence there is appears inconclusive. Our immediate task is to show that nationalism in the past has been a motivating force behind industrial migration.

The nationalistic policies of industrial nations stimulated industrial activity as a whole in the ABC countries, and in each country expansion in industry was shared by some North American companies either through the establishment of new plants or through the manufacture of additional products in those previously located. Reference to Table 2 on page 15 will show that twenty-one branch plants were established in the years 1930–1933, inclusive, a period of depression and likewise one in which the force of nationalism was rampant.

From 1920 on, nationalistic tendencies were discernible and to an ever increasing extent hampered South American export trade. The facts presented in Tables 4 and 5 apparently do not substantiate this statement, for the quantity indexes of exports rose during the period covered. But tariff barriers to specific products—notably meats and cereals—were gradually being raised, particularly after 1925. Continental European markets were closed to Argentine cereals and meats to a greater and greater extent through trade barriers of every conceivable type—tariffs, quota systems, and license systems. Tariffs ranging from 85 cents to $1.60 per bushel on wheat so stimulated home production that France, Italy, and Germany became practically self-sufficing. Germany, by using synthetic nitrates in place of those previously imported from Chile, became self-sufficing in cereals and meats, which were previously imported from Argentina and Uruguay. Our own tariff on Argentine chilled beef effectively closed the United States market. The English market, for many years the chief reliance for meat exports, was partially closed by the Ottawa agreements between England and other members of the British Empire. The state of mind in Argentina during the Ottawa Conference was one of great perturbation through fear that the English market for chilled beef would be greatly curtailed. While the action taken was less drastic than many expected, still a quota system was imposed and exportation from South America was limited. Numerous specific examples could be cited of the manner in which the nationalistic acts of industrial countries have hampered the export trade from South America, but it is sufficient to observe that, between 1929 and 1933, the ABC countries were in the forefront in foreign trade decline.

What followed in South American countries in conjunction with the shrinkage in foreign trade is now a matter of record. Depreciated currencies, higher tariffs, exchange control, and moratoriums on debt service constituted the sequence of events between 1929 and 1932. Argentina raised all tariffs a flat 10 per cent. This was in reality a 36 per cent increase, since the average tariff paid on dutiable merchandise in 1930 had been 28 per cent. Tariff increases in Brazil and Chile were even greater. Exchange control was instituted by all three countries in the middle of 1931. Chile declared a moratorium on debt service on July 15, 1931, and Brazil took similar action on September 19. While Argentina, to her great credit, has maintained service on her national external debt, many of the Argentine states and municipalities have been obliged to default. Accompanying the reduction of imports, the depreciation of the currency, the raising of tariffs, and the declaration of moratoriums on debt service, and largely as a result of them, there has appeared a marked stimulation to industry.

Let us first examine the causal factors more closely. First among them in order of time was currency depreciation. In Argentina, for instance, the peso, which has a par value of forty-two cents, depreciated to a value of about twenty-five cents. For many months before the United States went off the gold standard, the official rate established by the Exchange Control Board was 3.88 pesos per dollar, or a peso value of twenty-six cents. With a decrease in the value of the peso in relation to foreign currencies, importers were forced to increase their peso prices to Argentine consumers in order to secure the same amount for their products in dollars, English pounds, or other foreign currencies. Prices of imported commodities would have been increased about 60 per cent, had there been an exact equivalence between peso depreciation and price increase. Local manufacturers were placed at a decided advantage over importers, for their costs of production were increased only to the extent that imported raw materials entered into their finished products. Costs of native raw materials, labor, and overhead costs were little influenced by currency depreciation. Therefore, in spite of the fact that the domestic article was often inferior in quality to the imported one, still importers were unable to compete with domestic manufacturers as successfully as before.

Of like effect were tariff increases. While higher rates were applied primarily to maintain governmental revenues in the face of decreasing imports, still the effect was to stimulate home industry. In Argentina, as noted previously, 10 per cent was added to all existing duties, and this constituted an average increase in duties of about 36 per cent. Some increases were made in basic rates as well, and certain reclassifications had the effect of an increase. Such upward tariff readjustments could not fail to improve the position of local industry, at least temporarily, especially in marginal cases in which the protection previously given was not quite sufficient to permit manufacture on a profitable basis. It should be observed also that raw materials were mostly on the free list of Argentine imports and thus were not affected by the general increase in import duties. Therefore, an advantage was given to the local producer over the importer, even in those industries in which the raw materials were largely imported.

When increased tariffs and depreciated currency were impotent in withholding imports, other forces succeeded in doing so. One of these was the sheer inability to obtain exchange, even though goods could be imported and sold at a profit under existing exchange rates. Exchange control boards in these countries dictated the allotment of exchange, and the importer was at the mercy of these organizations. While there was a floating supply of bootleg exchange, it was limited in amount and there was always doubt whether such exchange could be purchased legally. Many importers would willingly have paid the higher rates of the bootleg exchange market, but the question of legality and the possibility of later action by the government made them hesitant to do so. Therefore, if the exchange control authorities did not grant exchange to an importer, he could not continue to do business except by continuing to sell in the hope that exchange would soon be forthcoming. But the extent to which an importer or a foreign manufacturer will continue to sell goods and accumulate balances in foreign currencies for which there is little immediate chance of remittance is necessarily limited. Representatives of North American companies had many bona fide orders which could not be filled because their parent organizations refused to make further shipments until frozen balances in South American banks were transmitted to New York. The orders were taken at a price which would allow a profit at exchange rates considerably above the official rates established by the exchange control boards. It is thus apparent that the withholding of importations was due, not to the higher price necessarily charged for the imported product because of currency depreciation and tariff charges, but to arbitrary control of exchange.

The exchange control boards prepared preference lists by which they were guided in the allocation of exchange. The object in view was to give preference to those products considered as necessities in the national economy, such, for instance, as certain raw materials needed but not produced within the country. Even for products toward the head of the list it was difficult to procure exchange cover. For products regarded as luxuries, which were in the lower ranges on the list, little if any exchange was granted. Such products, because of their foreign origin, were also particularly subject to increased tariff charges and at times to extra internal taxation. As a result, the manufacture of pharmaceuticals, beauty products, and other small-value consumers' goods has been enjoying what might be termed a boom period during the past few years in both Brazil and Argentina.

The nationalistic policies of the United States and of European countries forced industrial expansion upon South America, which found that, in view of the drastically lowered prices for exportable commodities and not only non-expansible but definitely contracting over-sea markets, self-sufficiency was the only alternative to a decreased standard of living. Therefore, certain policies were adopted, and these policies served as an invitation to foreign concerns to enter the industrial life of the nation by manufacturing therein. The only choice was to manufacture locally or to withdraw from the market entirely, for importation of many products was almost disallowed. Particularly in the case of luxury products and small-value convenience goods, the former alternative was accepted, and branch plants were established. In other instances new products or assembly parts were manufactured in already existing plants.

Another recent incentive for migration which partly accounts for the establishment of new plants since 1929 has been the relative cheapness of so doing. Because of depreciated currencies, dollars possessed by United States concerns contemplating migration could be exchanged for many more pesos or milreis than formerly, approximately twice the former amount. But, while these foreign currencies were devalued in relation to the dollar, they were not devalued for many purchases in their own country. Labor and many raw material costs were no greater in pesos or milreis than formerly, and only about half as great in terms of dollars. Thus our concerns were able to purchase sites and erect buildings at a much lower cost than prior to 1930. While this matter of cost surely would not be the deciding factor in the question of whether or not to migrate, still there can be little doubt that from the cost point of view the past few years have been an opportune time to enter these countries.

Chapter 3

SPECIFIC REASONS FOR MIGRATION

From this analysis of the more general and pervasive influences behind industrial migration, we will now turn to those of a more immediate, less pervasive character. In this, our task of determining the reasons for the movement necessarily becomes a more complex one, for the influences which we are about to examine may apply to one product only, to one country, to one industry, or perhaps, to only one concern within an industry. For instance, the presence of a certain raw material may be of absolutely no significance to one concern, whereas to another it may be the all-important consideration. Moreover, the forces which induce migration are, from time to time, subject to variation in the extent of their influence. The situation is never a static one. At one time a certain aspect of the situation looms up as the most significant, but later it may be dwarfed by something else.

Complexity also is engendered by the number and variety of influences which crowd in upon those executives who have been given the authority to make decisions regarding foreign expansion. There are many factors of varying importance which must be considered, some leading to a negative decision, some to a positive one, and only after a thorough investigation and a careful weighing of the pertinent factors can a wise decision be made. Here we are interested in the motivating influences behind sixty-six favorable decisions extending from 1907 to 1934. Obviously a complete inquiry into the motivation of each concern, or even of each industry, is difficult of achievement. In a previous study, the writer quite fully considered the question as it pertains to the automobile industry.[1] But here our interest is less confined, and the analysis must be less detailed for any one industry. Nevertheless, the chief influences can be noted and some idea given of the manner in which they affected particular industries or concerns.

Usually an immediate change of some sort brought the whole question into focus. This change may have been an alteration of tariff rates, the sudden move of a competitor, failure of the accustomed sources to furnish sufficient raw material, or a rapid expansion in the market demand in some foreign area. When the attempt is made to classify the various changes which furnished the incentive for migration, it is found that some of them pertain to raw material resources, both agricultural and mineral; others to production, the competitive situation, tariffs, and the need for effective distribution of products. Therefore, in the discussion which follows each of these will be considered in turn. The order of treatment will be not from the most to the least influential factor but from the least to the more complex situations. Some overlapping is inevitable but is preferable to a disconnected treatment.

The Influence of Raw Material Resources (Agricultural and Mineral)

While the number of companies which found their chief inducement to migration in the presence of raw material resources is small, the companies themselves are important ones by any test which may be applied, as, for instance, capital investment, the number of employees, or the extent of operations. Of these, the packing companies, which operate sixteen plants in Argentina, Uruguay, and Brazil, are by far the clearest examples of concerns actuated entirely by the presence of needed materials. The facts of the situation appear to be largely as follows. In the latter

[1] D. M. Phelps, "Effect of the Foreign Market on the Growth and Stability of the American Automobile Industry," *Michigan Business Studies*, Vol. III, No. 5.

decades of the nineteenth century, European countries, particularly England, came to rely upon the United States for meat supplies to an increasing extent. This foreign demand was met by the large packing companies, and they found the trade to be remunerative. The shipping distance was short as compared with that for other would-be suppliers, and the quality of the chilled and frozen beef was excellent. Supplies in the United States at that time were liberal. Later, however, because of rapid increases in our population and a tendency toward more diversified agriculture, supplies were less and the domestic demand was greatly stimulated. Consequently surpluses for export were decreased, and, after the beginning of the present century, the foreign trade in meat declined appreciably. "In 1901 British imports of beef from the United States amounted to 3,180,219 hundredweight, whereas in 1910 imports from that source had fallen to 477,147 hundredweight. During the same period, imports from South American countries rose from 811,999 hundredweight to 7,769,200 hundredweight. For the time at least, the beef-export business of the United States had practically disappeared. Her place had been taken by Argentina."[2]

The change pictured in this quotation called for a far-reaching decision on the part of those packing concerns which were engaged in the export trade to Europe. Supplies for that trade apparently were no longer available in the United States. Therefore, either new supply sources would have to be tapped, or withdrawal from the European markets was in order. But to withdraw would have meant not only to relinquish future profits from the trade but even to sustain serious losses. The valuable considerations which the packing companies had in the situation were well-developed distributive organizations and facilities to handle semi-perishable meat products in Europe. Moreover, they exercised a certain control over the markets through their

[2] George E. Putnam, *Supplying Britain's Meat* (London: George G. Harrup & Co., 1923), pp. 70–71.

trade contacts of many years' duration. Perhaps it is needless to emphasize that a functioning distributive organization is a valuable asset, and one with which any concern would be loath to part. Under the circumstances, the most feasible plan for the packing companies was to obtain supplies elsewhere and thus continue to serve European markets.

For the packers it was simply a question of securing livestock at the lowest possible cost, regardless of the country in which it originated. Argentina seemed likely to be the best source of supply, for it had the advantages both of low-cost production and of the ability to produce in large quantities. Topographical and climatic conditions were favorable, pasture land was abundant, and the soil was well adapted to alfalfa and other forage crops. Moreover, a substantial livestock and packing industry had developed prior to the turn of the century, and increasing contributions had been made to the British market. For this development two Irish families, the Nelsons and the Duggans, were mainly responsible. Two plants had been established in 1883, another in 1886, and four more shortly after 1902.[3] Part of the incentive for these later plants may have been furnished by the very profitable operation of the older plants during the Boer War. Being only ten days distant from South Africa by water, Argentina had been the chief source of meat supplies for the British army. But, after that war, profits were turned into losses because of an overcompetitive situation, and North American companies had little difficulty in purchasing existing plants. Only one was purchased immediately. In 1905, Swift and Company began negotiations which culminated in the purchase of the La Plata plant in 1907. Later, in 1911, a plant was built by the same company in Uruguay.

As might be expected, the World War increased the needs of the packing companies for additional livestock. Under the impetus of war demands, numerous plants were built,

[3] *Ibid.*, p. 72.

and others were acquired by purchase. Armour & Company constructed huge plants in Argentina and Brazil and a smaller one in Uruguay, and secured a one-third interest in Sociedad Anónima La Blanca, an Argentine packing concern. The other purchasers involved were Swift and Company and Wilson & Company, Inc. Ultimately, Armour & Company bought out the other two concerns and thereby assumed complete control. Wilson & Company likewise entered the South American market through the purchase of Sultzburger and Sons, another American packing concern. By that means Wilson & Company came into possession of a plant near São Paulo, where it started operations in 1913, and of an option to purchase the Frigorífico Argentino in Buenos Aires. This latter plant was operated under a rental agreement from 1914 to 1919, when it was acquired through exercising the option. So by the end of the war, the American packing companies were firmly entrenched in South America. Since that time a broadening-out process has been apparent. Old plants have been remodeled to make operations more efficient. Swift International Company has established two sheep-killing plants in Patagonia, a packing plant in Rosario, and new distribution facilities in Buenos Aires. The domestic market has become of greater importance in later years, and facilities have been needed by all companies to serve that market effectively.

A by-product of the packing industry—bones—likewise has caused the location of a branch plant in Argentina. Again the chief motivation was the need for raw materials to meet demands elsewhere. Consolidated Chemical Industries, Inc., of San Francisco, had purchased bones in Argentina for many years and had shipped them to the United States for further processing. But such a method was inadvisable for a number of reasons. Since the purchasers were not on the ground, it was quite likely that they were paying over-high prices for bone cargoes. Transportation costs were high, for the product in its original state is bulky and dirty and shipping companies would accept it only at high freight rates. Furthermore, bone cargoes were taken to processing plants on the Pacific coast of the United States and there processed, and finally the finished products, bone meal and bone coal, were shipped east to be used in sugar refineries and other industrial establishments. By the establishment of a branch plant in Buenos Aires, in which the product was cleaned thoroughly and perhaps ground into meal or otherwise prepared, shipment could be made directly to users in the eastern part of the United States. Total freight charges were thus reduced, and, since bones which had been through an extraction plant were no longer an undesirable cargo, ocean freight rates were lower. In addition, it is quite likely that the costs of handling and processing the product were less in Argentina than in the Pacific coast plants formerly used. The costs should be low, for the company claims that its Argentine plant is the largest bone-processing plant in the world.

One difference is observable between the situation pictured for this company interested in bones and the packing companies, but it is not a difference in kind, only one of degree. The packing companies were forced to build, or otherwise acquire, branch plants if they were to secure the needed supplies, for shipment of live animals to processing plants elsewhere was impracticable. In contrast, Consolidated Chemical Industries, Inc., was not compelled to locate a plant in Argentina in order to secure bones or bone products. Still, this proved to be the most desirable procedure.

The operations of the North American oil companies in Argentina furnish another example in which the presence of raw materials has been the central fact which accounts for the location of processing facilities. Here we are not particularly concerned with the international competition of the great oil companies. In the main, that competition has been for deposits which would furnish supply sources for importations to industrialized areas. If Argentine petroleum were produced and then shipped elsewhere in its crude state, such activity would not come within the scope of this study. Our interest springs from the fact that petroleum is refined within the country through what might be termed branch plants. The Standard Oil Company has established two refineries, and the Texas Company is financially interested in an Argentine concern which has recently built a refining plant. For these companies the presence of petroleum deposits was the necessary condition to, and therefore indirectly the motivation for, the establishment of plants. Reference will be made later to other influences which were also at work, particularly the pressure of competition and the need to hold an already established market.

No case provides a clearer illustration of the influence of raw materials than that of the International Cement Corporation in Brazil. Evidently the company had for some time been intending to produce in Brazil, but the necessary condition was lacking—that is, the presence of raw material deposits readily available without excessive transportation costs. The International Cement Corporation wished to produce near Rio de Janeiro, for another concern was already producing near São Paulo. Usually a cement plant is placed near the raw materials in order that transportation costs may be minimized, and also, if possible, near the market because of the heavy and bulky nature of the finished product. Obviously, production would be impracticable either in the northern part of Brazil or in the sparsely settled interior even though raw materials were found there. It was known that lime rock was present in the state of Rio de Janeiro, but it had previously been thought that the difficulties of obtaining the lime were insurmountable. However, after extensive and costly prospecting over a period of many years, the International Cement Corporation located a large deposit near Nictheroy, about twenty-five miles from the city of

Rio de Janeiro. This deposit has proven entirely suitable for cement purposes and has the additional advantage of being the only one ever discovered near the Rio market. The location of the plant is good for both inland transportation and coastwise shipping. Vessels can come directly to the delivery building, and railroad spurs and good highways on the other side provide for inland transportation. In addition, the plant is close to the largest potential markets. Even imagination could scarcely devise a more desirable location for a cement plant.

Other instances in which raw materials played a part will be dealt with summarily, for usually other factors played the more important role. For the pharmaceutical companies, the availability and low cost of alcohol, sugar, and glycerine have made local production more feasible. However, from the point of view of immediate motivation to migration, other forces—for instance, tariff charges— were more influential. Local production might have eventuated even if no needed materials had been obtainable locally. Still there is interconnection between raw material utilization and tariff rates, and the presence of raw materials may thus be more significant than initially thought. As will be pointed out in more detail later, the fact that there are native raw materials which could be used may be one reason for high tariff rates on finished products which embody like materials. Furthermore, the use of such materials may be a protection against tariff reductions after the branch plant is established, and thus a protection against a loss of business through competing importations. Industries which use native materials are more likely to be protected against competition from abroad, and are thought of as being more justifiable economically, less parasitical, than those which must rely on imported materials.

In summary, the presence of raw materials may be an inducement to industrial migration for three reasons: (1) the materials are needed elsewhere and must be processed before shipment; (2) the materials are needed if manufacture by a migrating concern is to be attempted and their presence and possibly lower cost may be an advantage; and (3) the utilization of local materials strengthens the position of the migrating company within the foreign country.

Production Incentives to Migration

Part of the inducement for industrial migration arises from the nature of the production process for certain goods. To illustrate, let us assume that the market demand for a certain product in one of these South American countries has been met entirely by importations, also that there has been a steadily increasing demand. Whenever the volume of imports reaches a total which would permit production locally at reasonable costs, there is an incentive to migration for those companies elsewhere which have had experience in manufacturing the product. Particularly does this apply to those concerns which furnish a portion of the imported goods. Perhaps the importation of 200,000 yards of rayon into Argentina would arouse no interest in local production, but an increase to 1,000,000 yards might lead to immediate consideration of the question and, ultimately, to the establishment of a branch plant. But whether such action will be taken depends in large measure upon the optimum size of the production unit for rayon, which in turn depends on the process used for manufacture of the product. For some products, fairly low unit costs can be attained in a small plant with a comparatively low output; for others, the cost per unit decreases rapidly as the output increases. In the first instance, small manuaturing plants designed to produce for a limited market demand can compete without too great disadvantage with large plants. Consequently, for some products it is feasible to build a branch plant, even though the present or potential demand is limited, because the disparity in costs will not too greatly favor the larger producers who are serving the market by direct importing. Carbon bisulphide, for instance, is a heavy chemical which can be produced economically in comparatively small quantities. For this reason, among others, it is produced in Argentina. On the other hand, the limited Argentine demand for products such as automobiles and shoe machinery, coupled with the fact that these products are so subject to decreasing cost with increasing output, practically prohibits their manufacture in Argentina.

Another illustration is furnished by the tire industry. Evidently, large plants have only a slight advantage over smaller ones because of lower unit costs. There is, however, some difference of opinion in regard to the extent of the advantage. It was stated by one factory manager that a production of 700 to 800 tires per day would achieve reasonable costs. Below that number, costs tended to increase rapidly. Another statement was to the effect that the optimum size for a tire factory is one designed to produce 3,000 to 5,000 tires daily. The reasons for these differences of opinion apparently are that different methods of production are being thought of, and that some plants use the Banbury mixer while others do not. There are two methods of manufacturing tires, the pit method and the watch-case or jacket-mold method. In the latter, tires are vulcanized individually whereas in the former they are vulcanized in groups of four to six. The opinion was expressed by people in the industry that the use of the pit method necessitates a larger output than does the watch-case method, in order to attain reasonable cost. In other words, the watch-case method was considered more flexible and thus likely to be the lowest-cost method with low-volume production. Also, slightly lower costs result from the use of the Banbury mixer. This machine will mix sufficient rubber in eight hours for 3,000 to 5,000 tires. If the production schedule calls for only 1,000 tires daily, the original investment in relation to output is too great to permit purchase. Thus, while there is divergence in costs according to the method and the equipment used, still reasonable costs can be achieved in relatively small factories.

When the original decision has been made and subsidiary plants have been established, unused capacity is often an incentive for what might be termed "additional migration." Perhaps it is needless to point out that a decision to transfer more operations to the branch plant, or to manufacture additional parts or complete products at the plant, is as truly industrial migration as the original decision. Only from the standpoint of the first break from traditional procedures of meeting foreign market demands, do the two cases differ. Perhaps plant capacity is available for new products or operations because of a temporary letdown in demand for the products usually manufactured or assembled. Such a condition has been quite the usual one among foreign subsidiaries during the past few years. Or unused capacity may be the result of error in the first decision in regard to the size of plant needed. In many instances North American concerns have been guilty of such overestimation, and they have thus created manufacturing facilities out of all proportion to the immediate demands of the market which they were designed to serve, even to the likely potential demands of a reasonable period in the future. As a result, there has often been an incentive to engage in the manufacture of additional items not contemplated at the time of the original decision to expand into South American countries. When a company has unused capacity, differential costs, instead of total costs, are the governing factor in reference to new activities. The additional cost is the essential question, and on such a basis it may be advisable to manufacture certain items which would be unprofitable if the decision necessitated added plant and equipment.

A variation of this condition appears from a consideration of public utility operations. Mention has been made previously of the extensive manufacturing operations of the Brazilian Traction, Light & Power Co., Ltd., in Rio de

Janeiro. In number of employees the shop of this concern is the largest foreign branch plant in Brazil. Some 1,300 men are employed. The subsidiaries of American & Foreign Power Company, Inc., also engage in some manufacturing activities. Of necessity, a public utility, especially one giving transportation service, must have adequate repair facilities. For example, streetcar trucks must be overhauled periodically, and many other repairs must be attended to if continuous and adequate service is to be given. While the organization and facilities brought into being for the purpose of repair service might conceivably be used for no other purpose, still their very existence is an invitation to manufacture needed items, since products can be manufactured at practically no additional cost other than the cost of direct labor and materials. Machinery and equipment must be installed for repair activities, but for that purpose alone, they are only partially utilized. We find the Brazilian Traction, Light & Power Co., Ltd., with a complete woodworking shop; foundries for the production of steel, brass, and aluminum castings; a steel galvanizing shop; facilities for electric, acetylene, and hand welding; and equipment for the reduction and insulation of wire. This list is far from complete, but it is sufficient to suggest the scope of this company's manufacturing facilities. With this equipment, the company takes care of its repair work and, in addition, manufactures a wide variety of products, not for sale, but for use in its extensive operations. Cost computations show that many products are manufactured at a cost lower than the landed cost of importations. Moreover, low cost is not the only incentive to such activity, for convenience and assurance of having the product when needed are additional advantages of local production.

Another production advantage gained by branch factories comes from the greater breadth of the supply sources for raw materials and assembly parts. Mention has been made of the inducement given toward migration by the presence of local raw materials. Here we are interested not in local but in outside sources. At times, certain needed products are procurable more cheaply in England or Germany than in the United States. One branch plant manufacturing radios in Buenos Aires was using parts from a number of European countries, as well as from the United States, and by so doing was able materially to reduce costs. If the same concern had been producing in the United States and later exporting to Argentina, it probably would not have been able to profit from using the cheaper European parts. Double transportation would have been involved, likewise double payment of duty charges. Another illustration is furnished by those concerns whose subsidiary manufacturing activities consist of shaping steel, tin, or other metal sheets. At times sheet metal can be imported more cheaply from the United States, at times from Germany, England, or Belgium. In 1932, because the United States was yet on the gold standard whereas part of Europe was not, delivered prices on our steel sheets in South American cities were appreciably more than on those from Europe. In one specific instance the price was $44 per ton from the United States, $22 from Europe. This price difference was partly explainable by a slight difference in quality. By manufacture within foreign markets, advantage can be taken of such lower prices. Without branch plants which could utilize semimanufactured products from Europe, it is doubtful whether some concerns could have stayed in the South American market.

Of course, this difference in prices may favor either the United States or Europe. There are both British and German branch plants using steel and other metal sheets in these countries, chiefly for the production of steel roofs. One German concern in São Paulo makes all types of steel containers for liquids. In the event that steel prices were less in the United States, these concerns which habitually purchase from Europe might find it to their advantage to shift supply sources, just as did the North American companies.

Often a competitive advantage is enjoyed by industrialized areas because of lower raw material costs, and additional costs for materials are a deterrent to the establishment of branch plants. In other instances, the chief raw materials must be imported, no matter whether production takes place in industrial countries or in Brazil or Argentina. Under such a condition, production in a branch plant is at a lesser disadvantage. In tire production, for instance, whether manufacture takes place in Akron or in Buenos Aires, the raw rubber comes from the Dutch East Indies. The cost of raw rubber in Buenos Aires would surely be no more than in Akron with comparable tariff charges, probably less since there is no inland transportation. For the fabric needed, the advantage admittedly rests with production at Akron, but in time tire fabric may be woven from Argentine cotton. Neither in regard to raw material nor in regard to the optimum size of production facilities are the branch plants of the tire companies at a great disadvantage in comparison to larger plants elsewhere.

The possible re-use of raw materials may have militated in favor of branch factories, in a limited number of cases. One case in point is the production of phonograph records. Three different North American companies produce records in temperate South America. When too many of a certain record are pressed and some of them fail to sell, those unsold can be melted and the material re-used. In contrast, let us assume that the records were pressed in the United States and exported to the market. Probably more errors would be made in estimating potential sales, and therefore more obsolete records would result. And it is doubtful whether the value of the record stock would be sufficiently great to permit reshipment to the United States for later re-use.

Whether executives held the belief that lower direct-labor costs would result from production within the ABC countries is open to question. Providing such a belief were entertained, it would furnish part of the motivation for migration. Statements of certain executives lead to the conclusion that the item of labor costs was considered a favorable factor in the investigation preceding migration. In other instances, no labor advantage was expected. Those of the first group probably were too greatly swayed by differences in wage rates and paid too little attention to the difference in effectiveness of labor. But whether their judgment was accurate or not, evidently some inducement was given by the belief that lower labor costs would eventuate. Later some attention will be given to the productivity of workers in the countries covered by this study, but at present our attention is centered on motivation.

The Effect of Competition

Whenever the question of migration arises, it is invariably connected in some manner or other with the competitive situation, either present or future. Competition may arise from one source or a number of sources. Perhaps the market demand is being met entirely by importations, or partly by importations and partly by local production. Furthermore, production within the market may be by native concerns or by foreign concerns, either European or North American. From this it is evident that competition may be offered by other importers, by foreign concerns operating branch factories, or by native concerns. Generally competition is international in character, but instances have been observed in which trade rivalry was confined to North American companies.

At the time that the companies now located in these countries made their original decisions to migrate, the most usual competitive situation was the one first mentioned—that is, a situation in which the entire demand was being met by importations from a number of concerns. When imports reached a volume which would permit local manufacture, or when there was evidence in the trend of events that such a volume soon would be reached, immediately the suggestion was given that here was a chance to eliminate competitors by the location of manufacturing facilities within the market. If it appeared that production costs would be less than the landed cost of imports, then competitors might be forced either to withdraw summarily or likewise to manufacture locally. But securing an early foothold as a manufacturer conceivably might forestall like action by competitors. Whether or not migration should be attempted depended largely on the present market demand for the product, the likelihood of additional demand in the future—both a natural increase and the increase which might result directly from local manufacture—and the possibilities of attaining a more favorable competitive position by capturing a greater share of the market by means of a branch factory. The belief that competitors would thus be eliminated has been a strong inducement for many companies to migrate.

Less was expected by other companies. The chance of entirely eliminating competitors was remote, but perhaps the number would be less and those remaining could operate profitably. At least, the first company to make a decision, build a plant, and get into production would have the preferred position. As the volume of imports indicated that conditions were becoming "ripe" for local manufacture, competing concerns often stampeded each other into hasty action. The situation in Argentina prior to the establishment of the Goodyear and Firestone tire factories is a case in point, although the evidence of hasty action is not so glaring as in some other instances. Demand for tires was increasing rapidly. Suppliers were Dunlop of England, Michelin of France, and all of the better-known United States companies. Goodyear was particularly strong and supplied about one-third of the total demand. From 1925 on, rumors, counter-rumors, and denials of probable action regarding migration were omnipresent. One rumor held that Michelin had purchased a plot of ground for a factory site, another that an investigating group from another concern was at work "on the quiet" in Buenos Aires, still another that immediate action was contemplated by a third company. Some of the rumors doubtless were based on fact, others were purely fiction. Evidently the Michelin rumor did have factual basis, for there is evidence that land was acquired in 1928. While it is very doubtful whether Michelin would have built a plant had others not done so, the action did constitute a threat, as did investigations by other concerns. The Goodyear company was a leader in the market and could not afford to lose its position; therefore, with the threat of action by other companies, action was taken by Goodyear and a factory was built in Hurlingham, a suburb of Buenos Aires. Soon after, the Firestone company reached a like decision and was ready to start production six months later than Goodyear. Michelin, some two years later, took like action, and now competition is among these three. Rumors persist that Dunlop will establish a factory, but to date no action has been taken. The Goodrich company, the Fisk company, and the United States Rubber Company have withdrawn from the market for tire sales, although the latter concern still sells other rubber goods.

It is doubtful whether any of the tire companies actually wished to establish a factory in Argentina. In all probability, their home plants were not completely utilized and production abroad would lessen production in the home plants to the extent of previous exports. Profit might conceivably be greater by branch operation, but the risk was immeasurably greater. There was more assurance of profit from exports, provided that all companies continued to serve the market by exporting. If all companies interested in the market could have been convinced, possibly through joint agreement, that the status quo would be maintained, that no concern would overturn the existing balance between them, there probably would be no tire factories in Argentina today. However, there was no possibility of agreement, in view of the differing nationalities of the interested parties. Therefore, because of competitive uncertainty, rumor, and "shadow boxing," definite action directed toward local production finally was taken, and the proverbial applecart was upset for all tire importers.

All importation does not cease with the establishment of branch plants. Some products continue to be imported; for instance, odd sizes of tires. The limited demand for odd sizes makes their local production impracticable, and therefore certain units are likely to be imported for some time in the future. But odd sizes constitute a meager part of total demand. No importing company could subsist on such business alone. Furthermore, in some products there is sufficient difference between various manufacturers' models, there is sufficient distinctiveness of line, so that a few of each will be sold, if offered for sale, with little regard to price differential. Automobiles are a case in point. Such cars as the Plymouth, the Terraplane of the Hudson company, and the Rockne of the Studebaker Corporation, sell in small numbers in Argentina and Brazil, even though they are in direct competition with the locally assembled Ford and Chevrolet, and at an appreciable price disadvantage. Their appearance is somewhat different, and a limited number of people will pay a higher price. One company which imported a light car into Argentina in a semi-knocked-down condition estimated that a list-price difference of 7 to 8 per cent in comparison to a Ford or Chevrolet in the United States increased to 22 per cent when the cars were sold in Argentina. Evidently the Ford and Chevrolet companies, by complete assembly in Argentina, obtained a 15 per cent price advantage over those companies which imported cars partly assembled, and even a greater advantage over concerns importing completely assembled units. The latter companies, suffering a price disadvantage of 15 per cent or more, find that sales are so limited that profitable operation by importing is extremely difficult where others are manufacturing or assembling locally. Such a disadvantage, if maintained, means virtual exclusion from the market. Thus, concerns which do not assemble locally find themselves in a veritable quandary as a result of the competitive situation. Volume of sales is needed if local assembly is to be accomplished at reasonable cost, but sales volume is dependent on the lower costs and prices achieved by local assembly. If complete assembly is undertaken, there should be a reasonable prospect of selling from 3,000 to 4,000 cars annually. But no cars other than Ford and Chevrolet sell in this volume. From this discussion two things appear evident, that if other companies are to secure a reasonable share of the business, they must assemble locally, also that during an indeterminate initial period they must be prepared to suffer losses or, otherwise stated, to assume developmental expenses while attaining a stronger competitive position.

If the competition is furnished by native concerns rather than by foreign-owned branch plants, importers are not so severely pressed. There are many instances in which importation has proceeded apace, despite local production. Native concerns usually are not so well financed, nor are they in possession of such effective production techniques. In addition, the goods which they produce often lack much to be desired from the quality point of view. Since importers may continue to thrive against such competition, there is less incentive for them to engage in local production. But at times competition from native concerns may be a positive factor rather than a negative one in its effect on decisions regarding migration. In certain cases, North American companies have regarded relatively weak native competition as offering an opportunity to undertake production with the likelihood of high profits, perhaps the opportunity to attain a dominant position in the market. Instances are numerous in which a foreign company is making acceptable profits, whereas a native concern manufacturing or processing the same product is operating at a loss. Only greater effectiveness in operations can account for the difference. In addition, native concerns have often directly aided their foreign competitors by acting as a buffer against untoward action by governmental entities. By protecting themselves they have also protected foreign interests. Whether or not this possible advantage was considered when the decisions to migrate were originally made is open to question. It is freely admitted that it has proved to be an advantage.

In certain instances, native competition has been of sufficient strength to induce migration. The experience of the petroleum companies, the Standard Oil Company in particular, is an example. North American oil companies had exported to Argentina for many years prior to the time that accumulated evidence indicated the possibility that Argentina might become self-sufficing in petroleum products. In the event that a state of self-sufficiency was in prospect, the North American companies with their well-developed distributive organizations were faced with three alternatives: (1) to withdraw from the market; (2) to obtain supplies from Argentine producing companies—in this case from Yacimientos Petrolíferous Fiscales,[4] the government-owned and subsidized organization; or (3) to obtain and drill petroleum deposits in order to secure supplies. Withdrawal would have been costly, for the distributive organization was a valuable consideration. Moreover, withdrawal would have entailed the sacrifice of potential future profits. Action based on the second alternative was inadvisable, because a foreign company would have been at the mercy of the YPF. In all probability, such action would have resulted in withdrawal, for the YPF had its own distributive organization, and the incentive to eliminate a competitor, particularly a foreign company, would have been strong. Because of this situation, the Standard Oil Company, with an eye to the future,

[4] Hereafter called the YPF.

initiated production in 1919 and now, with the exception of the YPF, is the most powerful company in the field. With production, came the establishment of refining plants. The motivation for production and processing consisted partly in the presence of raw materials, partly in the desire to hold an already established market and to continue to utilize already established facilities, and partly in the rapidly expanding native competition furnished by the YPF and smaller private companies.

The Tariff Incentive

Upward revision of tariffs has been more important than any other single cause in bringing the question of migration to the fore. Obviously a higher duty increases the landed cost of imports without simultaneously increasing the costs of local production unless the latter requires importation of raw materials on which tariffs have also been raised. But raw materials are usually on the free list. And even when they are dutiable and suffer an increased tariff charge, local production costs will be increased less than the landed costs of imports. Some raw materials are likely to be procurable locally, and on these prices will not rise, and, in addition, labor and overhead costs will not increase—at least, not immediately. Therefore, a higher duty on manufactured products results in a tangible advantage to local producers and constitutes a direct motivation to industrial migration. To produce locally is the one way in which a company can remove its goods from the dutiable merchandise classification. A partial circumvention of the tariff is achieved even if certain raw materials have to be imported.

Yet the increasing of tariffs to relatively high levels has not alone been sufficient incentive to induce foreign companies to establish plants. It is only when high tariffs are combined with energetic competition that there is a strong incentive. The experience of the Corn Products Refining Company is illustrative. Almost since the beginning of the century this company has been selling its various products in Argentina. Prior to 1928, it supplied the market by importing, but in that year it purchased a factory from a native concern. Some years before the decision was made to produce locally, native manufacturers had been successful in an attempt to have the tariff on corn products raised, and as these manufacturers became more efficient the volume of business secured by the Corn Products Refining Company declined. Higher tariffs coupled with developing competition made migration the only alternative to withdrawal. Imports of corn products are now practically banned by a duty which approximates the value of the merchandise.

It is not only the height of the tariff which has furnished a positive influence in decisions to migrate. The likelihood of tariff changes at a later date has also played a part. When a company has established a branch plant, it has an argument for higher tariffs should they be needed to eliminate competition from without. Instances are numerous in which upward revisions have followed the location of plants. In general, such action is more likely to eventuate where there also are native companies interested in manufacturing the product. Their influence is greater, and their pleas for protection are more likely to be favorably received since the taint of foreign capital interest is absent. Not even the most optimistic can deny that among the government officials of the ABC countries there is some ill will toward foreign capital in any form. Furthermore, until lately, foreign concerns have felt that they could rely with the utmost confidence on at least the maintenance of the status quo in relation to tariffs. In other words, the feeling was largely this: That now there is a certain protection given to local producers, and we can rely on at least that measure of protection if we decide to manufacture within the country. This feeling was a strong positive influence and was given full weight in numerous decisions. Surely there was precedent for such a feeling of assurance, for Argentina, prior to 1930, had not made one important tariff reduction prejudicial to the interest of manufacturers during the twentieth century. Unfortunately certain North American companies found that their faith was ill-founded. More will be said of this later. It is sufficient at this point to observe that the belief that tariffs would be maintained at the same level, or possibly that additional protection would be given if needed, was a factor which favored migration.

There are many different types of tariff changes, either in the rates or in classifications of merchandise, which have a bearing on the question of migration. In this connection four will be considered briefly. The first is illustrated by the situation of the Corn Products Refining Company. Since the chief raw material was procurable locally, any increase in the tariff on manufactured corn products damaged the competitive position of the company to the full extent of the increase. The second type of change is one which raises the rate on a manufactured product and may or may not simultaneously raise the rate on a raw material which must be imported if the product is to be manufactured locally. The question is whether the range between the two tariffs is increased or not. For instance, at one time the tariff on cabins for elevators was raised from 40 to 60 per cent, whereas the steel from which cabins were made continued on a duty charge of 5 per cent. Incentive for local production was given by a 20 per cent widening of the range in duty charge between the finished product and the raw material.

The third tariff change is a common one and analogous to the one just described. It is a change which places a higher tariff rate on a product imported in packaged form than on the same product imported in bulk. Because of such differences, pharmaceutical companies have often found it to their interest to import certain items in bulk and to package them within the market. A pharmaceutical company in Rio de Janeiro, for example, has an arrangement with the Rumford Chemical Company whereby Horsfords acid phosphates are imported in a concentrated form. Alcohol and other ingredients are added, and, after bottling, the product is ready for sale. As a result of this procedure, the duty on the product is reduced to about one-third of what it would be on the packaged article.

In Argentina the advantage of importing bulk goods rather than packaged merchandise is even greater, for the duty is assessed on the weight of the product plus that of the container whereas in Brazil it is assessed on the net weight of the product. When the container is relatively heavy, as in the case of bottles, the Argentine duty under similar tariff rates is actually appreciably higher. One concern started by importing gauze, bandages, and absorbent cotton in small consumer-size packages which in turn were packed in wooden boxes. Later it was found advisable to ship these products in bales with a cloth or burlap covering, and to package the product in Buenos Aires. Two savings were achieved. The bulk product took a slightly lower rate of duty, and, secondly, there was no excess weight in packages and boxes, on which the same rate of duty was charged as on the product itself.

Both the addition of liquids to imported concentrates and the packaging of goods are in a sense assembly. The fourth tariff change which has prompted migration involves what is more generally considered as assembly—that is, the fitting together of parts, as in the case of automobiles, trucks, farm machinery, and scales. In all temperate South American countries some tariff advantage has been given where such equipment has been imported C.K.D. (completely knocked down). These nations, by intent or otherwise, so constructed tariff schedules that a lower amount was collectible on an unassembled unit than on one which was imported as a complete unit. In some cases it was undoubtedly the intent of the importing country to arrange schedules in such a way that imports of semimanufactured goods would be encouraged. A bid was thus made for assembly plants through the medium of import duties, and foreign concerns were thereby encouraged to shift the location of a portion of their manufacturing operations. In October, 1931, Argentina changed the basis of assessment on trucks and passenger cars so that a 30 per cent reduction in duty would be given if the unit was imported C.K.D., and a 15 per cent reduction if it was imported in a semi-knocked-down condition. The tariff valuation was to be computed by taking the list price in dollars in the United States, deducting the normal dealers' discount (30 per cent for trucks and 20 per cent for passenger cars), and then adding 10 per cent to cover freight, insurance, and differences in exchange. The resultant figure would be reduced by 30 per cent or 15 per cent, as the case might be, to secure the valuation to which the duty rate of 57 per cent was to be applied. Brazilian tariff schedules (1933) gave a 20 per cent reduction in duties on automobiles, when they were imported C.K.D. Reductions in tariffs, such as these for automobiles, are undoubtedly an incentive for assembly within these foreign markets, but the error should not be made of considering them a net advantage, for assembly costs in the majority of cases are higher in South American than in North American factories. In fact the statement was frequently made by managers of assembly plants that tariff reductions barely compensated for increased assembly costs, and that the real advantage of local assembly consisted, not in reduced tariff charges, but in the marketing advantages which resulted.

When the transfer of assembly operations is under consideration, irrational tariff classifications frequently complicate the analysis. The question of migration must be considered, not only for each product, but for specific units or models within a line. Thus, one kind of equipment is classified according to weight, those units which weigh over thirty kilos being charged double duty, regardless of their relative values. For example, a unit of equipment weighing thirty kilos or less is given an aforo[5] of 25 pesos oro, plus 60 per cent, or 40 pesos oro. Other almost identical units of the same product weighing over thirty kilos are given an aforo of 50 pesos plus 60 per cent, or 80 pesos, on which the same duty rates are charged, regardless of the fact that the heavier units may be less valuable than the lighter ones. As a result, the lighter units are imported in assembled form, whereas the heavier units, which would be assessed the double duty, are imported as parts under an unnumbered classification and assembled within the country. Under this classification, the duty is paid on the declared valuation. If a product can be put through a customs house under either of two classifications, surely the classification which takes the lower duty will be chosen. For our purposes the point is that the overlapping of classifications, the possibility of putting a product through the customs as parts and thus paying a lower duty, may be an incentive to transfer assembly to the purchasing nation. Furthermore, the same incentive may not be given for the assembly of another model or size of the same product which differs only slightly in minor details. Evidently a decision in regard to the feasibility of transferring assembly operations frequently involves an analysis, not only of tariff restrictions on each product, but of differing restrictions on the various models and sizes of a product.

Higher tariffs, wider spreads in tariff charges between finished products and raw materials, and between assem-

---

[5] An aforo is an appraisement of value. Many years ago the Argentine government appraised the value of incoming goods, and from that time forward the values thus set were the amounts on which duties were paid. As values increased, instead of reappraising each specific product, the government added a flat increase of 60 per cent to each aforo. Needless to say, such an arbitrary system often creates wide discrepancies between the aforo and the true value of the imported goods. The term "oro" refers to the Argentine gold peso as distinguished from the paper peso which is commonly in use.

bled products and assembly parts, have served as a bait to attract industry and often have been effective in so doing. Another inducement has been the offer of a duty-free privilege on equipment and supplies for prospective industrial establishments. Some English concerns, both in Brazil and in Argentina, are still working under concessions granted many years ago which permit free entrance of products that now are assessed a heavy duty when imported by other companies. In other cases offers have been made to foreign concerns of free land, free water supply, and exemption from taxation over a certain period of years. In addition, verbal encouragement frequently is given by government officials and other prominent people. The migrating concerns usually do not accept such offers, as they fear that the givers will later demand compensatory favors. Nevertheless, free offers are an expression of the desire for industrial units and have given executives a more favorable attitude toward migration.

Undoubtedly the circumvention of tariff barriers, partial in the case of assembly operations, complete in the case of the manufacture of the entire product, is the most obvious reason for the location of branch plants in the ABC countries. But the obvious reasons are not always the most significant ones, and so it seems to be in many of the cases observed. It would not be contended that the tariff situation has been of little consequence as an incentive to migration, but merely that decisions to establish branch plants have been based on other factors also, some of which have been exceedingly influential. The decisions of those companies which went to South America to obtain needed raw materials were not affected by tariffs. Many of the companies which assemble their products locally would do so, even if no incentive were given through lower duties on parts than on completed units. Admittedly, to some concerns tariff changes have been the all-important inducement to migrate, but there

Marketing Inducements to Migration

Less Need for Forecasting Demand.—Because of their less tangible character, the marketing inducements to industrial migration frequently have been overlooked by commentators, even by business executives. There are many such inducements, and often they have played a major role in decisions to establish branch factories rather than to continue the usual foreign trade relationship. For instance, manufacture within the foreign country makes less necessary the forecasting of demand. If a North American company has a sales office in one of the ABC countries, the local manager must anticipate his wants by two or three months in order to be sure of having the product ready for sale when it is wanted. In addition, he must anticipate the demand for different models, sizes, and, perhaps, colors. If the concern were importing only one product and there were no variations in the product which permitted choice on the part of the potential purchaser, then predetermination of demand would be less difficult, and errors in estimating demand would be less costly. But many products do allow choice on a number of bases. Some, such as automobiles, contain a style element; others may be varied to suit particular uses, as, for example, elevators and other such equipment.

For some products there is little possibility of forecasting probable demand. A case in point is phonograph records.[6] Whether a record will "take" the public fancy or not, is beyond accurate prediction. Anywhere from one thousand to twenty-five thousand units of a given record may conceivably be sold. In a branch plant the records are pressed a day or so before sale, and the need of demand

---

[6] By reference to Table 2, p. 15, it will be observed that there are five branch plants in the radio and phonograph field. In four of these plants phonograph records are pressed.

prediction weeks in advance is eliminated. However, in the case of some products the demand for which is difficult to predict, it is not feasible to transfer production entirely to the foreign market. Then there is need of an intermediary manufacturing unit in which variations in the semimanufactured product can be made quickly, in accordance with demand. The assembly plant serves this purpose. For those products which have fewer variations and for those in which assembly cannot be divorced from other manufacturing operations, there is less inducement to establish branch plants.

Availability of Product.—When the need for predetermination of demand is at least partially eliminated, certain advantages appear. Greater flexibility is given to the buying and selling, inventory, and delivery procedures. Lower inventories need be carried, for replenishment from production units can be accomplished quickly. Turnover of merchandise is more rapid. One firm stated that, when it was importing for sale in Buenos Aires, turnover was two times annually. Now, through local production, its turnover is six times each year. Moreover, a heavy inventory with a low turnover causes obsolescence of product. For instance, it was estimated by an importer of paints that 3 to 5 per cent of his stock becomes obsolete and has to be sold at whatever it will bring. Inventory costs for space, interest, and insurance, plus obsolescence costs, may make deep inroads into profits or, if fully allowed for, may raise the price of a product to such an extent that demand is lessened.

Despite the heavier inventories carried by importers, it is difficult for them to keep on hand stocks sufficiently complete to fill buyers' demands. As a result, a company may be out of certain items when they are called for by dealers or consumers. Perhaps stocks have failed to last because of unusually heavy sales. Replenishments may have failed to arrive as expected because of delays in transit or difficulties in clearance through the customs. Inaccuracy in marking the packages or in listing the contents is among the things that often cause delays in clearance. But dealers and consumers often will not await the arrival of supplies and consequently may purchase elsewhere. Availability of product when it is called for, quick delivery, lower inventories, higher turnover, and the lesser need for predetermination of demand, all serve as incentives to manufacture within the market as an alternative to importation.

Transportation Costs.—Lower packing and transportation costs figure prominently as a means whereby retail prices can be reduced. When raw materials are procurable within a country, over-sea transportation obviously is eliminated. And even when the raw materials used in branch plants must be imported, some saving is achieved through migration, because transportation charges often are less on raw materials than on manufactured products. The latter are likely to be more bulky and thus to occupy greater space. Also, slower, less costly transportation is frequently used for raw materials.

For semimanufactured products instances are numerous in which savings in packing and shipping costs have resulted from the establishment of branch factories. There is no better illustration than that furnished by automobile assembly plants. An automobile is a bulky object when ready for use, and comparatively few can be placed in an ordinary boxcar for shipment to the coast. Completely assembled cars are not economical of space. Even when the completed car is partially knocked down at the factory and crated, there is still a wastage of space. In the case of foreign assembly, the parts are packed to the best advantage and shipped in bulk. The space used in shipment is thereby materially reduced. For example, one make of passenger car, when exported C.K.D., occupies 176 cubic feet in ocean transit. The same car exported S.K.D. (semi-knocked-down) occupies 401 cubic feet. Since ocean freight rates are based entirely on the space used by the shipment, or, more exactly, on the cubical content of the crate, the saving achieved in this instance was well over 50 per cent—an amount of approximately $50. Likewise, handling and port charges are lower on less bulky shipments. Therefore, it is quite evident that appreciable savings are effected by the shipment to South American markets of parts rather than of either completely or partly assembled units.

The activities of Armco International Corporation, the foreign sales subsidiary of the American Rolling Mill Company, provide a clear-cut example of savings made in shipping costs. The products manufactured by this company are culverts for road building, and it has small production units in various parts of South America for the sole purpose of cutting, shaping, and riveting steel sheets. Completed culverts are so bulky that shipping costs would be excessive. At times they are shipped in what is known as "nestable" form—that is, in halves which fit together nicely. While this method of shipping conserves space, the product is not so acceptable in quality, for two rivetings are required instead of one. Consequently, the Armco corporation imports steel sheets and shapes them into culverts in the local plants. In this instance, a saving in shipping costs is largely responsible for the small manufacturing units.

Adaptation of Products to Consumer Demand.—Another basis for comparing local manufacture with importing is the degree to which the product can be adapted to the needs of the market in which it is to be offered for sale. Better adaptation may be secured by changes in the product itself, the package in which it is placed, or the price at which it is sold. In regard to the first of these, there is no better illustration than that afforded by elevators. Practically all elevators are made-to-order jobs. No two are exactly alike. The elevator is planned in accordance with the structure of the building in which it is to be used, and there are always variations from standard models. Furthermore, there are differences, not only of size and shape, but likewise of materials and workmanship, which create variations in the appearance of the finished elevator. For industrial structures an elevator is purchased with utility in mind, whereas for a high-class apartment building the utility buying motive may be equaled in strength by considerations of style or appearance. Therefore, because of the need to adapt the product to varying demand conditions, it is almost imperative that cabins, doors, and certain control devices be manufactured locally. Otherwise, the plans of the elevators would have to be drawn and sent to the United States, the elevators there constructed and shipped to South America. This would be a time-consuming process. Many months would elapse, and when the elevator arrived it might not be exactly right or the purchaser might have changed his mind about certain details. In either case, adjustment would be difficult if there were no local production unit. In addition, service must be given by the maker of the product. Frequently a complete overhaul and rebuilding of the elevator is required. Such work can be done only in a well-equipped shop. But if service work demands production facilities, then it is only a short additional step to manufacture of the product itself. Surely production within the market and effective after-service dovetail nicely, and if the latter is necessary, the former may be undertaken with greater assurance.

The assembly of automobiles furnishes another example in which marketing inducements for industrial migration were uppermost in the minds of business executives. As in the case of elevators, a prime requisite for the effective cultivation of South American markets was that the product be so constructed as to meet the needs and desires of buyers in those markets. While significant changes in the chassis cannot be made by a mere shifting of assembly operations to São Paulo or Buenos Aires, it is possible by such action to cater to local preferences as to type of body, color, upholstery, and minor variations. In 1933 one assembly plant was able to furnish twenty different combinations on a 131-inch truck chassis, and another plant fourteen different passenger car models, each of which was available in a number of different color combinations. In addition, minor options were given the purchaser; for instance, the spare tire could be placed in the rear or in a well on the fender. Without local assembly, it would be entirely impracticable to cater to the desires of consumers in respect to these various combinations. Predetermination of consumer preferences, when such a width of choice is offered, is extremely difficult. But, without accurate forecasting, the stocks of cars carried would have to be unduly high in relation to sales. When completed cars are shipped to far-distant markets, there is little possibility of making subsequent changes, although another color may be desired, or demand may have veered to one model rather than another. Yet, the ability to furnish buyers exactly what they want may shift the demand from the product of one manufacturer to that of another. Surely the company which imports automobiles as parts and assembles locally in accordance with consumer preferences has the preferred position.

Better adaptation of a product to market needs may result from differences in packaging or wrapping, or in the size of packages. In the ABC countries, purchasing power is lower than in the United States, and therefore many consumers wish to buy in smaller quantities. Pharmaceutical companies have found it advisable to offer products in small package units. Otherwise consumers withheld purchase, and the sales volume suffered. Certain products which in this country are habitually sold in bulk to physicians and druggists are there packaged and sold directly to consumers through drug stores. Either people have less confidence in doctors, or they are unable to afford their services. Whatever the cause, people in South America are confirmed users of proprietary drug products, and the packaging problem is not easily solved. Moreover, the reading matter on the wrapper must be in Portuguese if the products are to be sold in Brazil, and in Spanish for other countries. When exporting to these countries, it is not an impossible task to package a product so that it is adapted for sale in South America. However, the quantity requiring special packaging constitutes only a small part of the total output, and the special handling complicates production procedures. It is easier to cater to consumer desires from the package standpoint, when the product is prepared in a branch plant within the market. Also, in view of the differences noted, there is little economy in preparing the product for sale in South America as a part of that to be sold in the United States.

Finally, local manufacture may adapt a product to market needs from the price standpoint. This is an important consideration, for few other inducements for the establishment of branch plants have been so cogent as the need to bring products within the purchasing power of foreign consumers. A reduced price is achieved through saving on transportation charges, inventory costs, import duties, and other costs. In general, the savings which can be made are not great enough to reduce prices to the level of those paid in industrial nations, but frequently the savings are sufficient to lower prices to a point appreciably below prevailing prices on imported merchandise. For automobiles the competitive advantage of those concerns which assemble locally over importers of completed units makes possible a price lower by 10 to 15 per cent. Tire prices in Argentina were reduced 15 to 20 per cent after the Goodyear and Firestone factories started operations. Under conditions in which demand is flexible in its relation to price, such price reductions appreciably increase total demand. Briefly stated, the motivation for migration springs from the lower price which may be charged through manufacture in branch factories and the increased demand which it is believed will result from price reductions.

Not only may production in branch factories make possible price reductions as contrasted with importation, but in other circumstances it may make unnecessary price increases. This point is illustrated by the experience of branch sales organizations of North American companies after 1929—in particular of companies selling small-value convenience goods. As exchange depreciated in South American countries, it was necessary to charge higher and higher prices in pesos or milreis for the imported commodities, in order to secure the same dollar return. In most of these products there was competition from native manufacturers—quite ineffective under normal conditions—and from European concerns. In neither instance was the competing product likely to be of as good quality. Even after price increases on the North American product, it is questionable whether the purchaser actually received as much for his expenditure, quality considered, if he bought the competing products, particularly those manufactured by native concerns. But despite this fact, the North American concerns lost business rapidly to other suppliers. For example, a concern which had been selling in Argentina for many years found its sales volume reduced to 10 per cent of its former volume in a period of less than three years. People were simply buying lower quality merchandise—most of which was produced locally, although some was imported from European countries.

The reason for this shift to other suppliers was the unusual degree to which people in South America are influenced by customary price. If at all possible, consumers continue to pay the same price and let the quality vary. If they are in the habit of paying, let us say, 2 pesos for a given product and the price is advanced to 2½ pesos, they hesitate to purchase and are unlikely to do so if an inferior product of like type can still be bought for the customary price of 2 pesos. Just why these people are so influenced by customary price is difficult to determine, but it must be remembered that their income level is low and inflexible in relation to the prices of imported commodities. For many, income is barely enough to cover necessities. Therefore, if an additional amount is paid for some product, others thought equally necessary will have to be foregone. Moreover, as yet, there is less appreciation of quality than in this country, no doubt partly because of the lack of education among the poorer classes.

Whether the quality of a product should be changed to conform to changed buying habits induced by the lack of purchasing power and the force of customary price is open to question. Companies selling within the ABC countries were loath to make such changes. Local representatives attempted to influence home-office executives to manufacture a lower quality product specifically for the South American market, but their suggestions were usually rejected. There was an inherent prejudice against lowering quality, or, conversely stated, a strong belief in quality merchandise. Then, also, some of the advantages of mass production would be relinquished if different qualities were produced for the foreign and the domestic markets. In certain instances, markets were practically lost before home-office executives could be convinced of the seriousness of the situation. These markets might have been retained through the operation of branch plants. Since such plants produce for the one market only, changes in the product can be made rapidly, as the market dictates, without interfering with production for the larger home markets. The greater flexibility secured favors branch plants, particularly under a condition of disordered exchange.

Perishability (Deterioration, Breakage, Obsolescence).—Perishability of product constitutes a further inducement to manufacture within foreign markets. Although in no case among the branch factory operations studied was perishability the controlling motive for migration, still in a few instances it was a strong contributing motive. Three types of perishability were observed: the tendency of the physical product to deteriorate, fragility or the likelihood of breakage in transit, and the tendency to style obsolescence. Each of these will be considered briefly.

There are products which must be produced a few days, perhaps a few hours, before they are consumed, and which otherwise are of no value. Impairment of quality takes place rapidly. Therefore, production facilities must be located close to the consuming market. Obviously such products do not appear in foreign trade. Other commodities require special storage conditions to prevent deterioration, but under such conditions last for some time. Still others deteriorate slowly, but nevertheless do deteriorate, and are less acceptable to consumers if consumption is deferred, as it must be if they are shipped from other countries. Consider cement, for instance. This product has been imported into South America in vast quantities and still is imported into some countries. However, dampness hardens it, and imported cargoes frequently arrive in other than perfect condition. At the present time, cement is being produced in Brazil, Uruguay, and Argentina by the International Cement Corporation. While savings in transportation costs, the competitive advantages to be gained, the presence of raw materials, and the tariff situation played the major roles in this company's decision to migrate, there was a further incentive in the fact that local manufacture enabled the company to furnish a fresher, more pulverized cement to purchasers.

While yeast will keep in excellent condition for many months if properly refrigerated, still the ability to furnish a fresher, more uniform product was in all probability a factor favorable to the establishment of a plant near Rio de Janeiro by Standard Brands, Inc. Spoilage results from improper refrigeration, and at times refrigeration on ocean carriers cannot be relied upon. Handling in unloading and delays in clearing through the customs may likewise cause deterioration. Even when products themselves are not subject to deterioration, their salability may be lessened if containers become soiled and shopworn. In importing, overestimation of demand may create a time interval of many months between production in the United States and final sale to consumers in South America.

The likelihood of breakage in transit has in some cases been another reason for transferring manufacturing operations. One company found that the base of a certain piece of equipment, when imported in assembled form and ready for use, was frequently broken before arrival. The product defied packing to prevent breakage, yet, when it was imported unassembled, no breakage resulted. Largely because of this condition, minor assembly operations are now performed abroad. One firm assembling automobiles has suggested that, if cars were imported completely assembled, a paint shop would be needed in the foreign market because of impairment of the finish on cars while in transit.

Frequently a product loses value quickly because of changes in consumer demand; in other words, it has style perishability. Referring again to the case of phonograph records, we find an excellent example. Suppose that a thousand units of a certain record were made in New York and exported to Argentina; furthermore, that the record encountered a brisk demand. The supply on hand might be sold quickly, and new supplies would need to be ordered from New York. But in the interim, before the supplies arrived, something else might have captured the public fancy. Heavy sales of a record rarely last over three months. Therefore, it is necessary to meet demands as they appear, and this can be accomplished only by pressing the records within the market where they are to be sold.

Other examples are less striking. One concern selling a combination of the less technical equipment for road construction and engineering service stated that the three months' importation period was too long for a product which was perishable from the point of view of frequent changes in design. This concern is having various parts of its equipment manufactured by other concerns in Buenos

Aires and later assembled prior to the beginning of a project. In this way the waiting period involved in importation is partly overcome. In any instance, when new designs are forthcoming rapidly, that concern which is most prompt in placing new models on the market is in the favored position. Local production rather than importation may make possible the necessary prompt action.

Control over Distribution.—Another advantage of foreign manufacturing subsidiaries, as important as the ability to change the form of the product to satisfy the needs of the market, is the control secured over the distribution of the product. In general, those companies which have established branch plants in South America have also taken over the wholesale distribution of their products, instead of leaving selling activities to independent middlemen. This is true of the automobile concerns, of the General Electric Company in Brazil, and others. It would not be argued that the operation of branch establishments which distribute the product to retail dealers would be impossible without local manufacturing operations, nor that local manufacture is unprofitable unless combined with branch merchandising. But the two activities, direct sale to retailers and local manufacture or assembly, do complement each other.

The problems of manufacture are simplified if further control is maintained over distribution, because demand variations, both as to time and as to type of unit wanted, can be predicted with greater accuracy when a more direct contact is maintained with the market. Conversely, direct distribution through a branch organization is greatly facilitated by local manufacture of the product; in fact, it is somewhat questionable whether direct merchandising would be advisable in South American markets unless manufacturing operations were performed there as well. The branch plant becomes the center of all company operations within the country—manufacturing, selling, and servicing. The same executives can supervise all activities. The product in process at the branch plant constitutes the inventories necessary for the branch sales organization. Thus, through the association of these various activities, the fixed investment in buildings, equipment, and inventory is probably little greater than it would be if only manufacturing were undertaken and the sales task delegated to independent distributors. Then the mere fact that the company is operating a manufacturing plant within the country improves its competitive position and enables it to increase sales to such volume that direct distribution is advisable. More direct distribution can be considered an outgrowth of foreign manufacture or assembly, likewise the reason for shifting from importation to local production.

For a rapid and sustained growth of the export market, more controlled distribution is a primary requisite. South American distributive agencies are far from efficient merchandising units when measured by our standards. One export executive, after spending some time in visiting foreign markets—South American among them—said that the inertia of wholesalers and retail dealers hampers foreign sales more than any other single factor. Their unwillingness to use new ideas and methods suggested to them by factory representatives, their procrastination in making changes, and their generally non-cooperative attitude are not conducive to an enlarged sales volume. Perhaps there is some basis for their skeptical attitude toward the merchandising methods used in the United States. Market conditions in South America are not identical with ours, and they call for a different approach to the selling problem. Yet, in general, American merchandising methods have been eminently successful when used in other countries. If at all possible, the wholesale function should be assumed, and this should be followed by careful control and supervision of the activities of retail dealers. In 1931 the General Electric Company of Brazil, because of poor sales resulting from a lack of dealer initiative, established a chain of retail outlets. Later, dealers followed the same merchandising methods used in these stores and sales increased appreciably.

An educational program in merchandising methods is required, and the retail dealer is the focal point toward which educational efforts should be directed. He needs to know more about the use of various methods of demand creation, especially about the possibilities of advertising. He needs instruction regarding price policies, accounting records, and service work. Training of this sort, as well as a better control of inventories, is likely to follow a change from the use of independent distributors to the use of a branch selling organization connected with a branch plant. Service training is achieved by bringing service men to the factory for actual demonstrations. Even in our domestic market, independent distributors have been found inadequate for the general supervision of retail outlets, for the carrying out of training programs, and for the control of dealer inventories. They are even less adequate in South American markets. Distributors cannot be relied upon to develop the dealer organization. This is a task which cannot be delegated to others if the market is to be thoroughly cultivated and the greatest sales volume thereby secured. It requires high-grade executive talent. Probably the greatest justification for assembly in South America is that it has made possible a more direct control of distribution.

The "Buy at Home" Attitude.—One further influence of a marketing nature is that exerted by national sentiment which favors those products originating within the country. When manufacturing operations are transferred, the company making the change becomes a part of the industrial life of the country in which the plant is located. When manufacture is completely transferred, obviously the products are national rather than foreign in origin. Even after local assembly, the product is partly national. Inhabitants are given work, and domestic materials are used in the construction of the plant and in its later operation. The local purchase of supplies and materials used in branch plants augments the business of many other industries, gives employment to many people, and thereby increases both the ability and willingness to purchase the output of branch plants in preference to importations.

In periods of prosperity there is little "buy at home" propaganda. In fact, the imported product may possess a certain glamour which aids its sale, providing there is no great disparity between its price and that of local manufactures. At times also, particularly in Brazil and Argentina, there has been a distrust of goods locally produced either by native or by foreign concerns because of a fear that the quality was poorer. For instance, there was a discernible attitude of skepticism in regard to the tires locally produced by the Goodyear and Firestone companies. People had more confidence in the imported products, evidently inferring that quality standards would be relaxed in branch plants. But in times of depression, when protectionist sentiment is particularly strong, there is a real stigma attaching to imported products which are directly competing with home manufactures. Under conditions such as those of the past few years, when imports were being discouraged in various ways and as a result industry was expanding, national sentiment distinctly favored products from home industry. "Industria Argentina" and other like inscriptions of origin came to possess a real significance. The government ordered that this inscription be placed on all Argentine manufactures. Undoubtedly it has had some effect on purchasing habits, particularly on governmental purchases. Goods produced within the country have been bought by governmental units in preference to imported goods, even when the price of the latter was considerably less.

A variation of this preference for products of local manufacture appears when, as a condition of branch plant establishment, certain arrangements for sale are made with a government. Take as an illustration Fabrica Chilena de Aviones Curtiss-Wright. This is a branch factory established in Santiago in October of 1930 by the Curtiss-Wright Corporation. Its activities consist largely of assembly, but it also manufactures some parts. The exact arrangements between this corporation and the Chilean government prior to the establishment of the factory are unknown, but it is said that the company had a contract to produce twenty aeroplanes in each of the first two years after location was effected. It is likely that the contract was arranged before the factory was built, the assurance of business given by the contract thus serving as the immediate motivation for migration. It likewise is conceivable that the giving of the contract was conditional upon the establishment of the factory. From the standpoint of the Chilean government the incentive for so dealing with the Curtiss-Wright Corporation may have been the desire to strengthen the national defense. Therefore, this may be a case not only of preference for products of local origin but the creation of a local manufacturing unit by means of such preference.

Preference for some products obviously suggests prejudice against others, or at least the absence of a neutral attitude in which questions of quality, price, and service are the determining factors. Local production in branch plants tends to remove some of this prejudice but, unfortunately, not all. Ill will toward foreign capital does exist. There probably is a more friendly attitude toward foreign capital invested in branch plants than toward that invested in raw materials, public utilities, or in government securities. But companies operating branch plants are forced to give better values or better service than locally financed companies, in order to compete successfully.

Summary

From the foregoing discussion it is evident that the inducements for industrial migration have proceeded from a multiplicity of conditions. Some of these conditions had to do with the characteristics of the product: whether it was bulky in relation to value, whether it was perishable, either physically or in relation to style, whether it needed ready adaptation to conform to consumer desires or needs, and whether it was a product for which manufacturing cost was small in relation to price charged. Moreover, product characteristics have induced migration under two wholly different sets of conditions, both of which have been present in South America. Because of the nature of the product, it may be desirable to engage in manufacturing operations near the market. On the other hand, production near the source of raw material supplies may be advisable. Of the former there are many illustrations and for entirely dissimilar products. Pharmaceuticals and food products frequently must be produced near the foreign consumer in order to prevent deterioration. Automobiles and construction equipment need an intermediary production unit near the consumer because of their bulkiness and the heavy transportation charges to which they are subject, and because there must be ready adaptation of the product to shifting consumer demands which cannot be predetermined. Of production near the source of raw materials, there is no better illustration than the processing of livestock. Perishability and cost of transportation dictated the establishment of packing plants in Argentina, Brazil, and Uruguay if meat was to be secured for European markets. Obviously the essential condition was the presence of raw materials and the likelihood that additional supplies would be forthcoming as needed. For other products, likewise, the presence of raw materials has been the chief motivating factor for migration. Among these are cement, certain heavy chemicals, explosives, and refined petroleum products. While other factors have also been pertinent and therefore have warranted consideration, yet without the essential condition of available raw material, branch plants would not have been established.

Other conditions which induced migration have been the method by which certain products were manufactured, the competitive situation, tariff barriers, and the need for effective distribution. From a manufacturing standpoint the incentive was greater, or, conversely stated, the disadvantages of transferring production were less, if the optimum size of the production unit was relatively small, if the manufacturing process was not complex and did not depend upon local conditions, and if part of the production process could be shifted to another location.

In the majority of cases the competitive situation, either present or potential, furnished a strong incentive to migrate. Competition may have appeared from a number of sources: from other importers, from native manufacturers, or from branch plants operated by other foreign concerns, either European or North American. One or a combination of these often made the competitive situation of a certain company such as to induce migration. Perhaps the motive for migrating was to forestall like action by other companies, or perhaps, under other circumstances, the establishment of a branch plant was the only possible means of continuing to serve a market.

Tariff changes of various kinds have raised the question of migration more frequently than any other single factor. Increased tariffs raised the landed cost of imports and thus created an advantage for competitors producing within the country. If raw materials were procurable locally, the advantage to local production was commensurate with the tariff increase, but if some materials were necessarily imported the extent of the advantage depended upon the increase, if any, in duties on the needed raw materials and upon the importance of raw material cost in the total manufacturing cost. Differences in the rates charged on bulk and on packaged merchandise, and on parts as contrasted with assembled units, likewise irrational tariff classifications, have led to the establishment of manufacturing facilities within South American markets. Through migration at least a partial circumvention of tariff barriers has been attained.

Manufacturing in branch plants simplifies marketing procedures. Predetermination of demand is less necessary. As a result, inventories of merchandise are less burdensome; turnover is higher; obsolescence of product and inventory costs are reduced. In addition, stocks of merchandise are not so likely to be depleted when demand appears. The product can be changed more readily to meet market demands. Adaptation, likewise, may be secured by different packaging, by lowering the price to conform to the purchasing power of potential consumers, or by changing the quality of product to meet customary price. Above all, a greater control over distribution is a complement of branch factory operation.

Among these reasons for industrial migration some are of a tangible nature, their influence is quantitatively measurable. Others are intangible, and the weight which they should be given in decisions regarding migration is problematical. For example, the advantage which a branch plant might enjoy over importers because of the tariff is a definite and easily ascertainable amount. An analysis of tariff schedules in force will show just what saving can be made on import duties if equipment is assembled within the importing country instead of being entered as complete units. But no analytical work will yield information to the effect that so many dollars can be saved, or, perhaps, so many additional dollars earned, because a product can be better adapted to the needs of potential buyers if produced completely or assembled within a country, because better control can be exercised over distribution, because prejudice against foreign products can be overcome, or because competition can be bested. These factors are of a different character from tariffs, packing costs, and transportation charges. They have to do with less definite, less measurable things: supervision, control, adaptation, prejudice. Because the effect which they may have is so indeterminate, they are likely to be overlooked or at least accorded less significance than they actually merit. It is not inconceivable that companies have established branch plants with the thought in mind that the change was justified by such factors as lower import duties and lower shipping costs, and that later such reasons have become of less importance relatively, and these other less definite reasons, which either were not considered at the time of the original decision or were then thought to be of little importance, have actually proved to be the real justification for the change. Or it may be that business executives have recognized the relative importance of these various inducements to establish branch plants, but commentators have given altogether too much weight to the motivation furnished by tariffs. Frequently the possibility of circumventing tariff barriers has been advanced as the all-pervasive inducement to migrate. In some cases it was the chief consideration, but in others it was of little or no importance. Tariffs did not enter into the decisions of the packing companies. Nor was the tariff incentive of much significance for those companies which produce phonograph records, heavy chemicals, and food products, or for those which assemble automobiles and construction equipment and materials. At least, the advantages actually gained by local production or assembly have appeared from other sources.

CHAPTER 4

DIFFICULTIES ENCOUNTERED BY MIGRATING COMPANIES

The difficulties which have arisen in the establishment and operation of branch plants are many in number and diverse in character. No company has been immune, and therefore each has had something to contribute on this subject. Perhaps production was delayed by the inability to secure a small repair part for an essential machine; perhaps revolutionary activities or some illogical governmental decree hindered continuity of operation; or perhaps labor disturbances were particularly subversive to company interests. Apparently trouble can arise from many sources, and frequently when it is least expected.

In the next few chapters an attempt will be made to interpret the experience of those companies which have migrated to the ABC countries and Uruguay. This chapter will center attention on certain factors which make business decisions and operations in those countries essentially more difficult than they are in this country. These factors are the lack of information on which to base decisions, distance from the home office, prejudice against foreign capital, differences in race and nationality, a lack of stability in government, currency depreciation, and the inadequacy of commercial law. In later chapters attention will be given to difficulties which emanate directly from governmental decisions, such as tariff changes, taxation, and social legislation, and to production difficulties, such as the ineptitude of labor, labor disturbances, and the lack of auxiliary industry.

In a consideration of the source of business difficulties, one thing should be kept clearly in mind: They may arise from errors in judgment on many and diverse questions, or they may be the outgrowth of the general environment—political, racial, or economic—in which the business enterprise is located. Frequently, in the case of branch plants, it is hard to determine whether the difficulties have been due to erroneous decisions or whether circumstances have been chiefly responsible. At times, shrewd analysis, well-reasoned decisions, would have mitigated the effect of seemingly uncontrollable factors; in fact, the exercise of good judgment, over a period of years, might even have prevented the occurrence of unfortunate incidents which disrupted plans and activities. In other cases, apparently nothing could have been done to prevent the appearance of unfavorable circumstances. Whenever decisions appear to have been unwise, and even to have had disastrous effects, extenuating circumstances can be observed in the situation. It might have taken unusual vision to decide otherwise. Therefore, in the following discussion no attempt will be made to draw a sharp dividing line between difficulties which were the result of poor judgment and those which arose from general environmental conditions.

LACK OF INFORMATION ON WHICH TO BASE DECISIONS

The majority of those concerns which migrated to South America had little, if any, previous experience with manufacturing subsidiaries abroad, particularly in nonindustrial countries, and thus they lacked what is usually the most fruitful source of information. Furthermore, there was practically no published material on the subject giving the experience of others. Had there been available the necessary data regarding the countries to which migration was contemplated, correct decisions would have been made more easily, but the facts obtainable were inadequate and sometimes unreliable.

In this country, when a company considers the advisability of building a new plant or of manufacturing a new product, a careful market analysis study is likely to precede decisions. Those intrusted with the making of decisions have recourse to a large amount of statistical data on the size and characteristics of the population and the degree of industrial or agricultural activity. Thus decisions can be made with some measure of accuracy. Let us contrast this situation with that in South American countries. Of the limited amount of data available for market studies, even population statistics are none too illuminating. Brazil, for instance, claims about fifty million inhabitants, but such a figure, even if approximately correct, has little significance. What a concern wishes to know is the number of people in Brazil who have sufficient purchasing power to buy the product which it expects to manufacture. Such a qualification in the case of Brazil eliminates 80 to 90 per cent of the population. For example, an insurance company estimated that there were only 309,000 people in Brazil financially capable of purchasing insurance. Again, a branch office of one of our largest advertising agencies was called upon to determine the number of families in Brazil that were potential purchasers of a low-value convenience product. After as thorough a study as the available data permitted, it arrived at the figure of 193,244 families. Argentine statistics are somewhat more complete, and population data are thought to be more reliable, but there is not sufficient information on which to base judgments. For example, the last industrial census in Argentina was taken in 1914.[1] When data on wealth, income, literacy, industrial activity, previous sales of certain commodities, and a host of other factors are limited, or entirely non-existent, there is little possibility of estimating correctly the present or potential demand for products.

The result of this lack of information is that unwise decisions have been made regarding branch plants, and

[1] A decree issued by the national government on May 18, 1935, appointed a commission to organize a national industrial census. Both manufacturing and extractive industries are to be included in the census.

these decisions have caused difficulties. The most usual mistake was an overestimation of the potentiality of markets. Because of this misconception, factories were built which, in view of the demand that actually has appeared, were unnecessarily large. Few branch factories, with the exception of packing and cement plants, have been operated at a reasonable per cent of capacity. Forty per cent of estimated capacity is the maximum attainment of a number of plants producing quite dissimilar products. In 1932–1933, many were operating at 20 per cent and less. While it is true that this was a depression period, industry in South America was not at the low ebb that it reached in industrial nations. As a matter of fact, branch executives freely admit that too much business was expected from South American markets and that building for the future was overdone.

Both in the purchase and in the construction of production facilities, a lack of information proved to be a stumbling-block. The majority of migrating firms had to build their own plants, but a few found local production facilities available for purchase. Small public utility enterprises were acquired in Brazil and Argentina, and some factories for the manufacture of miscellaneous products were also bought. In every purchase, it was difficult to ascertain the value of the physical properties, and doubly so to determine the goodwill value of going concerns. The North American companies were largely in the dark, for few would-be sellers had adequate records of past performance, and, as previously stated, market data were lacking. Therefore, to determine whether the price asked was reasonable or not was largely a matter of conjecture.

While lack of information made it difficult to come to accurate decisions in regard to either the size of the facilities which should be constructed or the price that should be paid for those purchased, yet it does appear that the North American companies made too little careful investigation before building or buying branch plants. Too much optimism was exhibited in regard to both the size of the plants which were built and the prices which were paid for existing ones. Careful observation, a more skeptical attitude, and the use of that information which was available would have led to more reasonable decisions. That the plants built were too large is reasonably clear. Admittedly, it is more difficult to prove with any degree of certainty that the prices paid were too high, or that the North American companies acted unwisely and without sufficient information. The situations which existed at the time of the purchases cannot be reconstructed in their entirety, and evidence is meager. Then, also, present judgment of past action is likely to be influenced by hindsight. Nevertheless, the opinion is ventured that the prices paid for fixed assets in South America were too high and that a less insistent, more deliberate buyer could have bought the same assets at appreciably lower figures. What evidence there is, including the opinions of informed individuals who were stationed in South America during the 1920–1930 decade, indicates that European companies and native concerns "unloaded" on the too-willing North American purchaser. In one instance, a public utility property had been offered to another company at a certain price. The property was not bought because the price asked was considered to be unduly high. A year later, the same property was bought by a North American company at approximately double the price asked previously. In another case, a factory was bought practically "unsight, unseen." Because of our lack of basic knowledge of these countries, and because of our excessive haste to do business there, we paid more than was necessary for the privilege of operating in South America. Whether through construction or purchase, in many branch plants more capital was invested than was necessary. The result has been unduly high overhead costs, which constitute a severe handicap to profitable operation.

Distance from the Home-office Organization

Migration to Canada is one thing, migration to South America is quite another. In the former there is the advantage of proximity, but in the latter five to seven thousand miles separate the parent organization from the branch executives. This mere fact of distance gives rise to many problems.

The position of a branch manager in a foreign country is essentially a difficult one. His work covers many subjects with which a branch plant executive in the United States does not have to concern himself. For example, there are the problems of foreign exchange and tariffs and dealings with the government. One branch manager in Argentina stated that two-thirds of his time was taken up by dealings with government officials. One day he might be visiting government executives in an attempt to persuade them to grant him more exchange, the next day he might be arranging to have goods cleared through the customs. In addition, advertising work and arrangements for installment credit are frequently among the duties of the branch manager in South America, whereas in this country they are more often handled at the central office or by an independent agency.

In performing this greater variety of duties, the branch manager must, because of his dissociation from the home office, assume a greater measure of responsibility and be able to make decisions on a wider variety of questions. Despite the existence of telephone interconnections and regular air mail service with the United States, it is impossible for the branch manager to enjoy the full benefit of the legal, technical, and sales advice which surrounds executives in this country. There is less specialization of activity. Nor can the branch manager secure the advantage of thorough discussion of branch problems with the home-office executives. Consequently, the latter sometimes fail to appreciate the problems which arise in branch plants, and their attempts at control without knowledge frequently result in the issuance of orders which they would recognize as absurd if they understood all the facts of the situation and the probable consequences of their instructions. For example, one branch manager received persistent demands from his home office for an explanation of lower per capita sales in Paraguay than in Argentina. Even a rudimentary knowledge of these two countries and their economic status would be sufficient to indicate that as high per capita sales could not be expected in Paraguay. Fortunately, this incident is not a typical indication of the extent of knowledge possessed by the average home-office staff which deals with branch records. Nevertheless, there are too many evidences of a lack of knowledge to permit us to dispose of this indication of ignorance lightly.

There is a constant struggle on the part of branch plant executives to satisfy the absurd demands of uninformed, perhaps misinformed, home-office executives. Furthermore, decisions which should be made quickly are frequently delayed because the branch manager lacks complete authority and home-office executives cannot see the need of immediate action. When exchange was very difficult to secure from the Exchange Control Commission in Argentina, one branch manager suggested to his superiors in the United States that Uruguayan quebracho extract which was held in bond in Argentina be purchased and shipped to the United States. The extract could be bought with the Argentine pesos which the company wished to convert into dollars, and, since the extract was of Uruguayan origin and was held in bond, the exchange secured through the transaction would not have to pass through the Exchange Control Commission. When the suggestion was made, the extract was worth $56 per ton. Although the extract was salable in this country and although the risk involved in such an investment was not great, the home office refused to follow the suggestion of the branch manager. Later, the home office decided to reconsider its decision, but by that time the price had advanced to $72 per ton. Others had taken advantage of the opportunity.

For the lack of understanding at the home office, the branch managers are partly responsible in that they fail to keep their superiors fully informed. On the other hand, the home-office staff is at fault in that they fail to realize that conditions in foreign countries are appreciably different from conditions in this country. The same yardsticks cannot be used in the solution of problems, for the legal, social, and economic conditions surrounding the problems are dissimilar. Both through visits of home-office executives to branch plants and through periodic visits of branch executives to the United States, immense strides have been made in a more complete dissemination of knowledge about the administration of branch plants. But difficulties will continue to arise in so far as the lack of harmony is largely due to a lack of proximity.

PREJUDICE AGAINST FOREIGN CAPITAL

Unfortunately, many individuals in South America do bear some ill will toward foreign capital, regardless of the form of its investment. While there appears to be less ill will toward capital invested in branch plants than toward that invested in either raw material deposits or government obligations, yet all capital invested by North Americans comes under the often-repeated stigma of economic domination and inspires the fear that North American capitalists are trying to control the economic destinies of both Americas. Perhaps it is needless to say that all individuals do not share in such beliefs, but the number of those who do is large enough to constitute an important adverse influence. The advantage of branch plants to the countries in which they are located should be sufficiently apparent to dispose of unreasoning judgments against them, but the very fact that the attitude taken is emotional instead of rational nullifies the effect of what might well be considered irrefutable proof of benefit. Still it must be admitted that the action of some representatives of North American concerns, particularly during and soon after the war, was not such as to inspire confidence. The upshot of the whole situation, of interest in this connection, is that branch plants do labor under a real handicap. By certain groups they are considered an extraneous part of the national economy which should be hampered whenever the opportunity presents itself. Native firms often take advantage of this attitude, to the detriment of the foreign concerns with which they compete.

These conditions place an additional burden upon branch managers and home-office executives, who must select individuals of the right caliber for executive positions in the ABC countries. Many of those selected, in earlier years particularly, were choices none too wise. Both their attitude and their actions were such as to strengthen, rather than to overcome, existing prejudices. Anyone familiar with the type of the majority of North Americans now in executive positions in these countries hesitates to question the effectiveness of branch factory personnel. Some individuals have been in their present positions for many years, are doing excellent work for their respective companies, and are highly respected by the nationals of the country in which they are located. But it must be remembered that a weeding-out process has occurred and that the less effective individuals have been replaced. Some of the present executives are now striving to overcome prejudices resulting from the mistakes of their predecessors.

Race and Nationality Factors

Hindrances to successful operation frequently are an outgrowth of racial differences. The people of South America are partially of Latin origin, and they speak either Spanish or Portuguese. Problems of adjustment continually arise, for the representatives of North American companies must not only learn the language but also acquire a knowledge of the racial characteristics—that is, the habits, the mode of living, and the desires—of those individuals who comprise the market. Often the comment is made that there is no real understanding between people in South America and the representatives of foreign concerns. Such a broad generalization cannot be made with accuracy, for there are too many friendly relationships between them, both business and social, to permit one to believe that sympathy and understanding are always lacking. The more accurate statement is that misunderstandings which prevent or jeopardize business relationships often arise because of differences in motives, habits of thought, and accepted procedures, and that these differences in turn are an outgrowth of the difference in racial backgrounds. North Americans entering the ABC countries face a troublesome problem of adjustment. Some of them adapt themselves to the new conditions readily, others never do make an effective adjustment. When authority is given to individuals of the latter type, difficulties are sure to arise, for such persons do not possess the requisite knowledge of the market nor the proper attitude toward the people who comprise it.

Another assertion commonly made is that North American companies do not adapt themselves readily to the business customs and practices of the country to which they migrate. In this there is the implication that different racial conditions, among other factors, dictate different business procedures. It is, of course, true that executives hesitate to discontinue methods which their experience has proved to be successful elsewhere, although at times it is necessary for them to do so, lest they create ill will by not adhering to the practices which are firmly established in the foreign business community. Several informed individuals have observed that certain North American companies made things exceedingly difficult for themselves by demanding the same credit terms as those demanded at home. In the United States, in the sale of certain types of construction equipment, it is customary to require a 20 per cent down payment when the order is signed. Further payment is made at the time of installation, and the final payment, six months later. In the ABC countries, more lenient credit terms are generally expected and given. One branch manager stated that payment in advance of delivery simply could not be secured, and that demand for such payment would be considered a reflection on the buyer's integrity.

Another contrast in business practices relates to the extent of bargaining, special favors, and so on. The approach to business relationships in South America is more devious, more indirect, than it is in this country. An indication of this is given by the query of a native salesman who compared the Argentine market to a jungle and asked a branch factory manager whether he did not think that a rubber cord could be extended through the jungle more successfully than a steel rod. In other words, he doubted the efficacy of such practices as quoting the same terms to all buyers and maintaining a uniform price. In South America haggling over price is still a usual practice. The policy of offering the same terms to all buyers who purchase in like quantities, although violated often, still is firmly embedded in the minds of business executives trained in this country. This policy is usually adhered to when selling in the ABC countries, and perhaps rightly so, but difficulties do arise in its application.

Yet the significance of these differences in business practices becomes questionable when one considers the notable success with which branch plants have used some methods which were copied from North American practice. One branch plant executive who has been in South America for nearly two decades stated in conversation that few, if any, generalizations can be made with safety on the differences in methods of doing business between Latin and Anglo-Saxon countries. It was his opinion, moreover, that the safest generalization is that the differences are few in number and greatly overstressed. Other observations lead to the same conclusion. For instance, one assertion which is frequently made is that sales in South America depend largely on social contacts, the implication being that, if the sales representative applies himself assiduously to making such contacts, orders will appear thereafter in abundance. It is quite true that friendly relations are an aid to sales, but such relations are more often than not a result, rather than a cause, of mutually beneficial business relationships. Selling in South America or anywhere else is largely a matter of diligent effort on the selling job itself, of many calls on prospects, of demonstrating the product to potential users, and of convincing the potential buyer that it is to his own interest to acquire the product. Other assertions regarding differences in method likewise prove to be untenable when they are subjected to the test of actual results. In regard to such day-to-day matters as sales methods, advertising, credit terms, and service, there is probably little basis for the belief that differences in race and nationality are of great significance. In general, methods developed and used successfully in the United States are likewise acceptable for South America.

Racial characteristics affect also the problems of labor productivity and control. The attitudes and reactions of labor groups tend to vary somewhat with the racial backgrounds of the workers. For instance, it is not safe to assume that workers in South America will respond to wage incentive schemes as they do in this country, nor that they will be physically able to do as much work even though they may possess the ability to do a task satisfactorily. Furthermore, in the event that there are not available enough workers trained in industrial pursuits, there is the question of whether untrained individuals of the racial or nationality groups there represented can acquire facility at industrial tasks. Racial and national characteristics have had a profound influence on labor disturbances, as more than one branch executive will freely testify. There is more violence, also greater property destruction. In a subsequent chapter the various problems regarding labor will be dealt with in some detail. Here the purpose in mind is simply to indicate that unusual labor problems do arise in branch plants, and that their source often lies in the racial composition of the individuals who must be employed.

Affiliations between business concerns or individuals of like nationality may decrease the likelihood that other concerns can operate profitably. Competition is likely to be international in character, and trade relationships tend to follow nationality lines. National sentiment and prejudices have full sway. For instance, there may be three or four concerns able to furnish a certain product. One may be Brazilian or Argentine, others may be branch plants of English, French, and North American companies. British buyers in the market are likely to buy from the British company unless either the quality or the price offered by one of the other companies provides a substantial inducement to shift purchase elsewhere. Similarly, the North Americans, the French, and others will follow much the same course, and it is only natural that all should do so. People of like nationality have many contacts with each other through clubs and chambers of commerce. Frequently, there is a connection between two companies of like nationality because the same individuals may be stockholders or directors of each. Such affiliations are productive of trade. North American companies are at a disadvantage in this particular, for the North American communities, both in business and population, are smaller than those of some European nations. There are large groups of English, Spanish, and Germans in each of the ABC countries. In Argentina there are probably six persons who are British subjects to one claiming United States citizenship. Likewise the capital invested and the business done by British companies are much greater. As a result, such companies do enjoy some advantage over the North American concerns with which they are in direct competition.

In one further respect, the differing nationalities of competing companies affect the operation of branch plants. Competitors, for their common benefit, need at times to associate. Joint action may be necessary to regulate competition or to ward off some prejudicial action by the government or by some competing industry. Another reason for joining forces is to advertise cooperatively. In this country we have trade associations for such purposes, but where there are firms of different nationalities, it is difficult to secure joint action. The English and North American packing concerns have cooperated effectively in resisting adverse action by the Argentine government, but certain other attempts at understandings between concerns have been futile. In one instance particularly, two North American companies were in difficulties because of tariff changes made after their factories were established. A third company, French in origin, was also affected. This company not only refused to cooperate but acted in such a manner as to thwart the attempts of the North American companies to have the situation remedied. In addition, the French concern acted in bad faith. There was no understanding, no "meeting of minds," thus no possibility of effective joint action.

Lack of Stability in Government

One of the requisites for successful business operation is a continuity of law and order, and this South American countries frequently do not possess. One need only review the past five years to confirm this statement. Since 1929, Brazil has had two revolutionary disorders— one in 1930, another in 1932. The former overthrew the constitutional government but was not very serious from the standpoint of disrupting business activities. The latter, in 1932, was probably the most serious revolt which has occurred in

South America in recent years. Business activity of the normal type was completely paralyzed in the state of São Paulo for over a three-month period. Argentina had its so-called "bloodless revolution" in 1930. This, however, was a boon to business rather than a deterrent, for the government in power was hopelessly corrupt, and a change of administration was sorely needed. During the past five years, Uruguay, also, has had a change of government amid scenes of bloodshed and disorder, and as this is being written, further disorders are taking place. The recent history of Chile has been troubled in the extreme. In the period of one year there were four major revolutionary upheavals, and as many new administrations came into control. Only Argentina appears to be reasonably stable politically, and even its stability is questioned by many people on account of the strength of the Radical party. Admittedly, the governmental difficulties of the past five years have been mostly an outgrowth of unfortunate economic conditions, but revolutions are not confined to depression periods; in fact, the 1930 revolution in Brazil had other bases than the economic situation.

Governmental instability may be incidental or chronic in nature. When chronic, it is likely to be the outgrowth of racial admixtures. From this point of view, Argentina and Brazil form an excellent contrast. In Brazil, we find a heterogeneous admixture of many races and nationalities. The basic stock was Indian. Between 1820 and 1930, the country received a total of 3,491,846 immigrants from Latin countries; these constituted 78 per cent of the total immigration.[2] In addition, limited numbers came from northern Europe, particularly from Germany; large numbers of Negroes were brought in from Africa; and recently about 150,000 Orientals have entered. Brazil is thus found to be a racial melting pot. It was estimated that in 1890 the percentages were as follows: white, 44.0 per

[2] C. R. Cameron, "Colonization of Immigrants in Brazil," *Monthly Labor Review* (U. S. Department of Labor), October, 1931, p. 41.

cent; black, 14.6 per cent; Indian, 9.0 per cent; and mixed, 32.4 per cent.³ "It is impossible to calculate the proportion of the various elements making up the present Brazilian population, owing to the fact that only about one-half of the foreign immigrants remained, to the different rates of increase of the various races, to a considerable mixing of the new arrivals with the other ethnic elements already in Brazil, and to the fact that the immigration during the Republican period has been spread irregularly over a period of 41 years."⁴ If the various elements of the Brazilian population were spread evenly over the inhabited sections of the country, political instability might not result; but such is not the case. In the southern part of the country, including the states of São Paulo and Rio Grande do Sul, the inhabitants are mostly white. Farther north, in Minaes Geraes and around Rio de Janeiro, a large part of the population is Negro and mixed. In the interior and the North, practically all of the population is Indian or mixed. The people in various parts of the country are different, not only in color and racial composition, but also in wealth, in abilities, and in the extent to which they have progressed generally. When it is recalled that Brazil is larger territorially than the United States proper and that there is little transportation other than along the coast, the difficulties in achieving political unity and stability are apparent.

Argentina, in contrast, has achieved a measure of racial uniformity. The first colonizers were the Spanish, who intermingled freely with the native groups. Later, between three and four million Italians entered. They came largely from the northern provinces of Italy and were industrious, thrifty individuals. Racial admixture took place readily between the Argentines and the Latin peoples, and a new racial uniformity is gradually being achieved. Furthermore, Argentina from a physiographical standpoint lends itself to political unity. If the sparsely settled South is

³,⁴ *Ibid.*, p. 42.

left out, the country is, roughly, fan-shaped, with Buenos Aires at the lower end of the main rib. Transportation inland along the ribs of the fan is reasonably adequate, and, in addition, waterways form an important transportation link. Racial uniformity and territorial unity thus give at least greater likelihood of political stability.

The effect of governmental instability and of changes of administration which occur in other ways than by orderly constitutional procedure can easily be overstated. Because newspapers in this country habitually overstate the happenings in Latin America, people are led to believe that conditions are much more serious than they actually are. At times, business goes on much as if nothing were happening in the political arena. The victors take over the reins of the government without greatly disturbing arrangements with business concerns or making other changes which affect business indirectly. On the other hand, there have been occasions when the revolutionary period or its aftermath paralyzed business for some time, as in São Paulo in 1932. The effect of these political disturbances can easily be observed in such indexes as those of electric power consumption. When overhead charges are heavy, even a partial cessation of business is a costly experience. Moreover, it has happened, although rarely, that property damage to the holdings of foreign concerns has been a part of revolutionary activities. In such cases restitution seldom compensates for actual losses.

It is not so much the events of the revolutionary period as the events of the aftermath which are subversive to business interests. Business executives are in a constant state of apprehension over the possibility that the new government will rescind agreements of the former government, or that it will make changes in tariffs and taxation. A revolutionary government is likely to be hasty in its actions, and for months after the cessation of hostilities there is a state of uncertainty. Executives of branch plants in their dealings with the government must negotiate with a different group of individuals. Any goodwill or friendship previously developed is entirely lost; in fact, to the extent that there were friendly relationships with the old regime and such relationships were known, to that extent is there distrust on the part of new officials.

There are a number of things which a new administration may do to harm branch plants. It may withdraw certain concessions which the old government gave, such as exemptions from taxation or a duty-free privilege on imported equipment. Such withdrawal of privileges may be the expression of a greater measure of anti-foreign-capital sentiment. Or the new government may renew litigation over taxation. In one instance a North American company had been involved in legal difficulties over the payment of a stamp tax. The Minister of Finance of the pre-revolutionary administration had given a written opinion that the company was not subject to the tax, and the matter was thus considered to be closed. Someone in the new administration discovered that the stamp tax was not being paid, and the case was again taken to court. At the time this instance came to the writer's attention, the matter was not settled, but it was considered likely that the stamp tax would have to be paid. A further way in which business may be harmed is through tampering with the currency. This will be considered in some detail shortly. New governments always are in financial straits and may attempt to better their immediate situation by devaluation.

There are numerous other ways in which a new administration may act to injure foreign business concerns, but enough has been said to show the type of difficulties which may emerge. Little can be done to avert such difficulties. They simply are a part of the general environmental situation. Where it appears that the situation is one in which a large measure of governmental instability is likely, foreign concerns should be skeptical about placing a heavy capital commitment in land, buildings, and equipment.

One thing which should be kept in mind when placing branch plants in South America is that later events may necessitate withdrawal. This can be accomplished without too great losses if the investment has been kept at the minimum figure.

Currency Depreciation

When administrations change often, and particularly when they change by other than orderly procedures, there is not sufficient continuity of policy in regard to monetary matters. Experience in South America has indicated that instability of government and disorders of the currency are intimately connected. Of the four countries included in this study, Brazil has had the most turbulent political history and there the currency has depreciated to the greatest extent in relation to foreign currencies. Argentina, in contrast, has been relatively stable politically and also stable from a monetary standpoint. These facts are illustrated by Chart 1, which shows the average annual exchange rates between the currencies of these four countries and the dollar since the turn of the century.

It will be observed that the Argentine peso has held remarkably steady except during the few years after the 1920 depression and during the past few years; also, that it has often been above par ($.4245). The record of the Uruguayan peso is almost identical. Both the Chilean peso and the Brazilian milreis have had a more checkered career. The former has depreciated almost steadily in relation to the dollar since 1900. At times in 1933 it was worth only between 2 and 3 cents. The history of Brazil's currency likewise shows a constant depreciation in relation to the dollar, with infrequent periods of temporary recovery. The tendency has been downward for an even longer period than that shown by the chart. In 1834, par was set at 27 pence or between 54 and 55 cents in our currency. From that time forward, the milreis gravitated around par until the Republic was established in 1889.

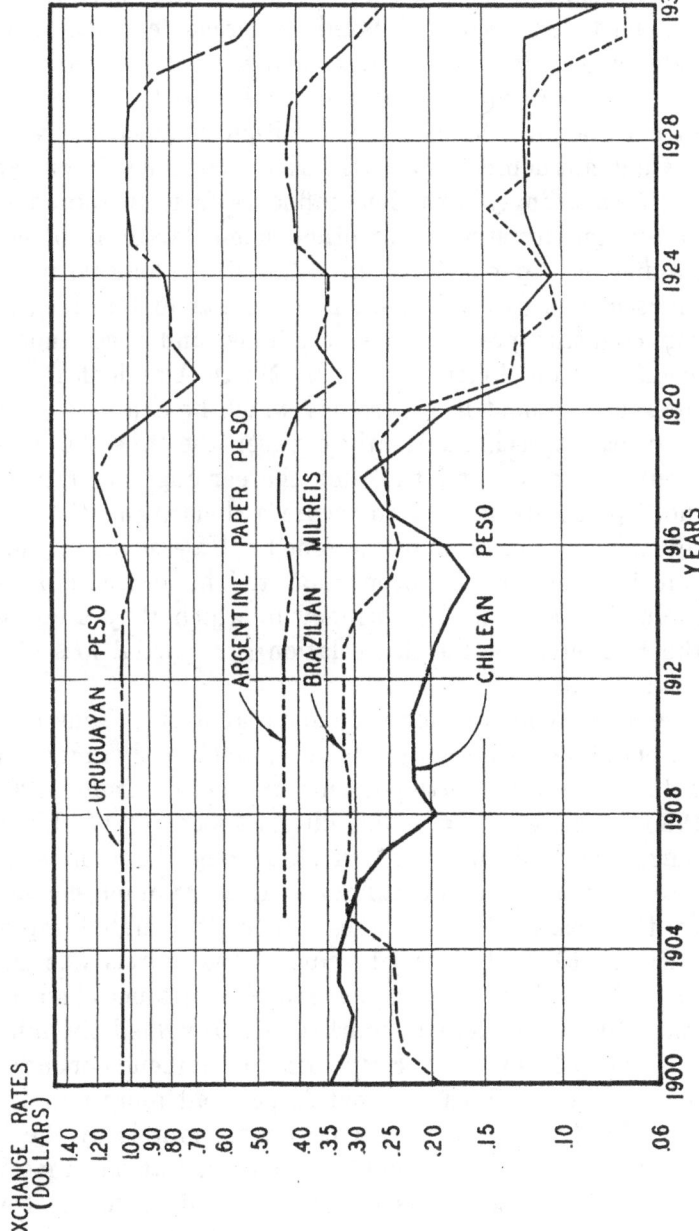

Chart 1.—Average Annual Exchange Rates between Various South American Monetary Units and the Dollar, 1900–1932*

*For the data supporting this chart, see Appendix III.

Since then it has gradually but persistently declined. In the past few years all South American currencies have depreciated markedly in the exchange markets. Argentina has been the most successful, Chile the least successful, in maintaining the exchange position of its currency.

Constant depreciation of the exchange value of a currency is an exceedingly pernicious influence from the standpoint of foreign investors. No other single factor is of equal significance, particularly in relation to long-term fixed investments. Earnings on investments in South American countries are in pesos or milreis, and these must be exchanged for dollars before the North American investor receives payment in a currency which he can use. If the peso has depreciated greatly between the time the investment was made and the time the earnings are returned, more pesos are needed to secure a dollar, and the dollar returns are accordingly lessened. Unless net earnings can be increased in proportion to the decrease in the exchange value of the currency in which they are made, the real effect of the depreciation is a partial loss of the original capital.

A concrete illustration will aid our analysis. American & Foreign Power Company, Inc., invested heavily in Brazilian public utility properties during the period from 1926 to 1930. This was during the administration of Washington Luiz, who had succeeded in stabilizing the milreis at a level equivalent to approximately 12 cents in our currency. In the years following, the milreis depreciated rapidly. Early in 1933, the official value of the milreis was equal to 7.5 cents, but the greater share of remittances had to be made by use of the free market, which valued the milreis at about 5.4 cents. The remitting of dividends or interest to the United States required 60 per cent more milreis by the official rate and 122 per cent more milreis by the free market rate than it would have required at the time the original investment was made. Even if exchange could have been secured at the official rate, net earnings on investment would have had to increase 60 per cent between the time of the original investment and 1933 in order that the same dollar return might be remitted to security-holders in this country.

In order to protect their future earnings from the effect of a lowered milreis exchange value, the public utility companies attempted to secure the insertion of gold clauses in their contracts with various government entities. They were successful in the majority of cases. These clauses gave authority for an increase in rates to compensate for a decrease in the value of the milreis in relation to currencies backed by gold. Thus, if the milreis decreased in value in relation to the dollar, the rates charged by the utilities could be increased sufficiently to make up the difference. A proportional increase in rates was not needed, for all expenditures did not vary with the exchange position of the milreis. Among those which did vary with the value of the milreis were expenditures for the use of capital and salaries which were paid in dollars. The relative amounts of these items differ widely among utility companies. In the case of electric power for large users, particularly when furnished from hydro-electric plants, about 90 per cent of the total cost of servicing is capital cost. In the case of street railways, the capital cost is a much smaller proportion of the total, for much day-to-day labor is needed. The Brazilian subsidiary of American & Foreign Power Company, Inc., evidently figured that approximately 50 per cent of its expenditure was capital cost or, at least, that dollars were needed instead of milreis to the extent of 50 per cent of its expenditures, for it proposed that the rates charged should be subject to adjustment to the extent of 50 per cent according to changes in the exchange value of the milreis. Its contract with the municipality of Curityba in Brazil contained the following provision: "All prices established in the present contract are on the basis of 8$300 for one dollar, United States currency. One half of each bill will be subject to adjustment in accordance with the variations of the rate. . . . "[5] This provision, or one of like type, has been inserted in most of the contracts secured by the public utility companies during the past decade, not only in Brazil, but in other South American countries likewise.

These gold clauses were found to be of little use, however, when exchange depreciation threatened the position of the utility companies. The right to increase rates was exercised reluctantly and with a premonition of the unfortunate after-effects which appeared promptly in the form of active ill will, hostile demonstrations, and, in some cases, property damage. Protest campaigns were started, which were encouraged by political groups and newspapers. Consumer strikes were organized and blacklists were circulated. In Bahia it is said that forty street-cars were burned by a mob. Although high government officials freely admitted that the companies were justified in raising their rates, still they were either unable or unwilling to control the actions of the protesting consumers. There is a powerful appeal in the statement that a huge foreign concern is oppressing the poor by charging exorbitant rates on services, whether there be any truth in the statement or not.

Ill will was partially responsible for lessened consumption, but in all probability the most important factor in reducing demand was the higher rate charged for services. Purchasing power levels were simply too low to permit of the same degree of use at the new rates. The great majority of the people in South America are barely above the subsistence level. Since their earnings did not increase as the milreis decreased in value in relation to foreign currencies, no additional margin was forthcoming to meet increased tramway fares or other service charges. In view of this situation, the exercise of the rights given in the gold clauses served as a protection against exchange depreciation to only a limited extent.

[5] State Decree, Number 1045, *Diario Official*, State of Paraná, Brazil, Aug. 7, 1928. The expression 8$300 stands for 8 milreis 300 reis, or 8.3 milreis.

The position of branch plants has not been jeopardized to a like degree by exchange depreciation, because return on capital investment is a much smaller proportion of total costs. A firm such as Refinerías de Maíz, S. A., the subsidiary of Corn Products Refining Company in Argentina, has little to remit to the home office other than interest and earnings, and, since these capital costs constitute but a small part of total costs, a small increase in the prices charged for the products manufactured will compensate for a decrease in the exchange value of the peso. Other companies with higher overhead costs, likewise those which secure assembly parts and raw materials from abroad, may be injured to a greater extent. Moreover, the increased price in pesos or milreis, which they must necessarily charge, may decrease total sales. On the other hand, exchange depreciation may be beneficial if it curbs the entrance of competing imports. However, it can hardly be gainsaid that the net effect of currency depreciation is an adverse one. While funds are accumulating for remittance, they decrease in value. During the past few years it has at times been impossible to secure exchange quickly enough to prevent losses on peso or milreis balances. For instance, the operation of one branch plant, by dint of much hard work on the part of the manager and his assistants, yielded a profit of 300,000 pesos over a two-months period. This was a part of a much larger sum which was awaiting remittance to the home office. Before exchange cover was secured, this profit was completely wiped out by a pronounced decline in the exchange market.

Experiences such as these, and they have been common during the past few years, are not conducive to successful operations nor to particular optimism about the possibilities of profits accruing from branch plants in South America. Operating in Brazil or Chile is particularly hazardous, in view of their long history of persistent currency depreciation. Some of the risk involved may be avoided if as few dollars as possible are invested in the first place and if accumulated funds whose value may decline are remitted regularly. It has been suggested that the best way to secure capital for industrial enterprises in South America is to borrow the money in those countries on the strength of security elsewhere. Then interest payments could be made without securing exchange, and, in the event of withdrawal after further depreciation of the currency, exchange losses on the original investment would not be incurred. While this method is admittedly of limited applicability, it does further emphasize the exchange difficulties under which a branch plant is forced to labor.

Inadequacy of Commercial Law

South American countries have not as yet developed an adequate body of commercial law to facilitate the conduct of business and to protect the interests of buyers and sellers. Laws in relation to trade-mark rights and privileges, bankruptcy, conditional sales, and rights in raw material deposits are frequently inadequate and obscure, and the procedures suggested and allowable under the law are clumsy and ineffective. Thus, when North American companies wish to engage in installment selling, they find that there is no conditional sales contract authorized which fully meets their needs. Progress toward a more complete and adequate body of law is, however, being made. Chile adopted a new and improved bankruptcy law in 1929, and Argentina followed in 1933. Moreover, many court decisions in recent years have clarified the rights of business concerns under existing laws. With an improvement in laws and legal interpretations, the difficulties encountered by branch plants as a result of inadequate laws can be expected to diminish. Still, they are sufficiently common at the present time to merit attention in any study which seeks to interpret the experience of branch organizations.

In this connection it should be mentioned that, in all the countries considered in this study, legal structures are based on Roman rather than on English common law.

This fact in itself imposes a handicap upon executives trained in this country and now holding executive positions in South America. The law, although it may be adequate, is different. The trade-mark law, for example, appears to North Americans to furnish undue opportunity for commercial piracy.

The confines of this study will not permit a thorough discussion of the commercial law of the countries under consideration, nor is such a procedure necessary. Much of the law is adequate and in no way adds to the difficulties of branch plant management. Furthermore, changes are constantly being made which obviate conclusions of the moment. On the other hand, the inadequacy of certain laws and the absence of certain safeguards in the conduct of business have been and still are keenly felt. Therefore, some attention will be given to the difficulties of effective operation under the existing laws of conditional sales, bankruptcy, and trade-marks.

Conditional Sales.—Conditional sales transactions, such as are recognized and used so widely in the United States, are not valid in these countries; neither are hire-purchase agreements nor others which attempt to overcome legal obstacles in connection with retention of title.[6] In Argentina an agrarian pledge, known as the Prenda Agraria, is used extensively by the automobile, business equipment, and farm equipment companies, and with some success, for the benefits of retention of title can be achieved by use of the instrument. However, since it was not designed for the conditional sale of automobiles, cash registers, and like products, and since the procedures outlined for its use are clumsy and costly, it is being used only in the absence of something better. The law states that the instrument may be used "on machines in general, implements and farming appliances."[7] While a mass of judicial opinion has

[6] See *Trading under the Laws of Argentina*, U. S. Department of Commerce, Trade Promotion Series, No. 74, pp. 20–22.

[7] For a translation of this law, see *Laws of Argentina*, compiled and translated by J. A. and E. De Marval (Buenos Aires, 1933), p. 906.

accumulated which favors the inclusion of non-agricultural equipment under the law, some difficulty is still being experienced in country districts regarding the inclusion of automobiles. Repossession is possible under the Prenda Agraria, but it is a long-drawn-out process. The following steps are required: the purchaser must be proved before the court to be in default; the court then issues an order for repossession; with the court order, and in the presence of a court officer, the property may be repossessed; the property is placed in the hands of a third party; the purchaser and the selling company representative then appear before the court, and, if the court decision is favorable to the selling company, the property is ordered to be sold at public auction; the property is sold, and, if a sufficient amount is realized, the company receives its claim. In the majority of instances the original seller bids in the property at the auction.[8]

Obviously there is too much "red tape" connected with repossession under the Prenda Agraria. The cost is too heavy, and in some cases companies abandon the equipment rather than assume the cost of repossession. For automobiles the legal cost averages around 300 pesos (at the present rate of exchange about $100) for each repossession. Both cost and bother result from the fact that the order and the contract must be made on stamped paper. Other expenses amount to about 10 per cent of the amount realized at public auction. A further expense, not easily calculated, is the time of executives which is taken by these procedures.

In view of the difficulties involved in repossession, companies operating in Argentina must take greater care in investigating the applicants for credit. Finance costs in general are much higher than they otherwise would be, and as a result sales volume is reduced. Furthermore,

[8] An automobile concern states that 70 per cent of cars are bid in at the sales by the original seller, whereas an office equipment concern states that 95 per cent are bid in.

although the law provides for penalties in the event that property purchased under the Prenda Agraria is sold before payments are completed, still the courts are apparently undecided as to the rights of the unsuspecting third party, and there is, consequently, legal uncertainty in regard to the recovery rights of the original seller. There is general agreement that the Prenda Agraria is an ineffective instrument for conditional sales. However, it can be used, and its use has a good moral effect on the purchaser. Since repossession is legally possible, property is frequently relinquished upon request.

In the other countries as well, business firms have been forced to work with "dull" commercial instruments designed for quite different purposes and ill adapted to conditional sales. In Chile, sales have been made under an industrial pledge law, which was designed as a means for encouraging the development of industry through the granting of credit secured by pledges of machinery, tools, and other equipment. Automobiles, however, according to a court decision in 1931, cannot be sold under this industrial pledge law. In all probability, conditional sales laws such as we have in this country will eventually be enacted by South American countries, and then this particular source of difficulty and expense will be eliminated.

Bankruptcy Laws.—A revision in bankruptcy laws has been needed in South American countries for many years. This has been particularly true of Chile and Argentina. In the former, the bankruptcy laws enacted in 1929 superseded legislation which dated back to 1867. The Argentine law which was revised in 1933 dated back to 1890. Prior to these revisions, there had been numerous denunciations of the laws and of the manner in which they were being administered. Certainly the changes made in the Chilean law were beneficial. The new Argentine law has been in force for less than two years, and, since it postdates the collection of the information on which this study is largely based, the attitude of businessmen toward it is unknown.

First, let us observe some of the conditions which the new legislation was supposed to correct—in other words, the basis of the denunciations made. It was stated, among other things, that many of the "bankrupts" were not actually insolvent, that the bankruptcy courts were used simply as a means of swindling creditors, that many of the creditors in bankruptcy action were entirely fictitious, that such creditors frequently overshadowed legitimate creditors, that good merchandise was often replaced by old before sale at auction took place, and that assets were frequently hidden by the debtor. Businessmen had little confidence of fair treatment under the law. The statement was a common one that little was expected from bankruptcy claims, and, in fact, some concerns wrote off any assets that found their way into bankruptcy courts. Not only businessmen, but those of the legal profession as well, testified to the need of change. One judge noted the "continuous irregularities" which were committed in bankruptcy actions.[9] Perhaps the most severe and continuous criticism of the bankruptcy laws came from judges who realized that little could be done under the existing law to remedy abuses.

In the preparation of the new Argentine and Chilean laws, conscientious attempts were made more fully to safeguard the rights of creditors. Under the old laws, the debtor was the individual whose interests were most carefully protected, the implication being that the creditor could look after himself. The new legislation, in contrast, is based on the recognition that creditors' rights had been overridden because of the inadequacy of the law and because of questionable procedures under the law. The

[9] "Judge Amuchastegui Denounces Artifices in Bankruptcy Case," *Comments on Argentine Trade*, published by the Chamber of Commerce of the United States of America in the Argentine Republic, March, 1929.

following quotation, although referring to the Chilean law, applies equally well to that of Argentina:

> The previous bankruptcy system differs from the new one in that the latter is intended to make more expeditious the administration and the liquidation of the properties involved in a bankruptcy by leaving such matters almost entirely in the hands of the syndic [receiver] and the creditors, whereas, according to the former, the fuller intervention which was given to the court in this connection, it is said, only resulted in delays and inconveniences. Furthermore, the new system imposes penalties in fraudulent bankruptcies of merchants and provides a new procedure through which the syndic from the very beginning may prevent a bankrupt from concealing or disposing of his property in defraud of his creditors.[10]

Article Number 20 of the Argentine law provides for removal of the debtor from the management of his business if he acts in such manner that the interests of the creditors are likely to be jeopardized.[11] Part XIX outlines fully the various acts which constitute fraudulent practice on the part of debtors, acts for which punishment is provided under the Penal Code. The list includes many fraudulent practices that were not uncommon under the former law, and it is likely that henceforward bankrupts will be forced to watch their steps more closely. These new laws, if properly administered, will make it much more difficult for persons to defraud through bankruptcy and will, therefore, constitute additional protection to the legitimate creditor.

Trade-marks.—The protection of trade-marks has been a continual source of trouble for North American companies, partly because they were not sufficiently foresighted to observe the need for protection at an earlier date. The basis of property rights in a trade-mark in South American

---

[10] "Chilean Code of Commerce under Reform," *Commerce Reports*, Apr. 22, 1929, pp. 197–199. Included in this article is a partial translation of the new bankruptcy law.

[11] *Laws of Argentina*, compiled and translated by J. A. and E. De Marval, pp. 1162–1218.

countries is priority of registration, *not* priority of use as in the United States. Neither priority of use in the country or outside, nor even registration abroad is taken into consideration. This legal difference has opened the way for what appears to be, from the viewpoint of the United States company, a large measure of commercial piracy. It has often happened that an individual has come to the United States, become familiar with well-known trade-marks, and subsequently registered these trade-marks in some South American country under his own name. After a period of thirty to sixty days reserved for protests, the trade-marks become legally his property and can be defended as such. Since the presumption of ownership is undoubtedly in favor of the registrant, the legitimate owner is not likely to attempt to change matters by costly litigation.

If, later, the North American concern wishes to sell, or produce and sell, within the country in which its trade-mark has been registered by another, it must either do so under a different mark or make some arrangement with the legal owner. When the owner is amenable to monetary inducements, the transaction is often referred to as "buying back your own property." From the standpoint of the company, the individual who registered the trade-mark has usurped property rights, and in a sense with legal sanction. If, however, the law is strictly interpreted, the individual has not engaged in commercial piracy, for he has acted legally. But in such an interpretation, intent is not taken into consideration. If, as one strongly suspects in many cases, the purpose was to establish legal ownership solely for the purpose of compelling the originator of the mark to purchase the trade-mark rights at an exorbitant price, or to take other advantage, then it is commercial piracy in intent, even if not declared so legally.

The development of a situation such as this, in which unscrupulous persons have usurped commercial rights, cannot be ascribed entirely to a lack of foresight on the part of the original owner. Of course, if the owner had anticipated action by others by registering his trade-mark in all countries to which migration or selling activities might ultimately have been extended, no difficulty would have resulted. But such a step would hardly have been practicable in view of the heavy expenditures necessary to effectuate registration and particularly in the absence of actual or immediately potential business. Then, also, it is doubtful whether, before the World War, many of our concerns visualized expansion of activities into South America. Some companies, it is true, have sold in South America for fifty years or longer, but they are few in number. The majority entered these markets in the past two decades, and they were ill prepared to cope with the problems presented. In all probability, the executives of many companies did not know that the basis of trademark rights was priority of registration, rather than priority of use—the difference which has been the source of the difficulties encountered. Unless a company had definite plans to enter South American markets, there was little incentive to obtain the legal information required for such action. Moreover, there was no active dissemination of information relative to legal requirements in foreign markets until after much of the damage was done. Later, the Department of Commerce issued several warnings.[12]

Such an apology cannot be made for all North American concerns, however. Even after repeated warnings, many failed to register their trade-marks, and the difficulties which followed were of their own making. One company, a producer of abrasives under a well-known trade-mark, sold its product through a representative who appointed agents in South America. The company under this representation was successful and developed a good volume

[12] *Trade-mark Protection in Latin America*, U. S. Department of Commerce, Trade Information Bulletin, Number 219. This bulletin contains the essentials of all Latin American trade-mark laws. *Commerce Reports* of May 7, June 4, and Nov. 19, 1928, also carried articles of an admonitory nature on trade-marks.

of business. Later, it became dissatisfied with its representative and discharged him. Unfortunately, the company had neglected to register its trade-mark. Its former representative did so and thus secured full legal rights. He then interested capital in the production of abrasives and started manufacture under the mark of his former employers. Since this individual likewise had control of the market, the goodwill of the original owner of the mark was entirely lost. Finally the company withdrew from the market. Failure to protect itself from encroachment by its own agent was a costly mistake.

A variation of this situation appears when a foreign agent registers a trade-mark in his own name while still working for his principal. This may be done either with or without the knowledge of the latter, but the agent, in law, then is the owner of the mark, and the principal may later discover that the express consent of the agent is needed if goods are to be sold within the country. Perhaps the registration is made with no intent to defraud, but simply as a matter of protection against third parties. Whether there is intent to defraud or not, the agent has assumed control of the product, and, if the principal wishes to shift from one agent to another or to sell through a branch sales organization, he may have difficulty in doing so. If he can prove that the agent, contrary to instructions, has registered the mark in his own name, the court may decide that fraud has been perpetrated and restore rights in the mark to the principal. But even if this is the case, the fact is difficult to prove and the cost of litigation is likely to outweigh the benefit obtained by the action. For its own protection, a company should do one of two things: either have the trade-mark registered in its own name in the first place, or arrange for an assignment of the mark to the company at the time it is registered in the name of the agent.

In recent years, conditions have improved, and there is less opportunity for piracy of trade-marks. Some protection has been given by a clause in the Brazilian law which states that unless the registrant actually uses the mark within three years after registration he forfeits his right of ownership. Therefore, the individual who may have usurped trade-mark rights cannot hold a mark indefinitely without use, in the meanwhile attempting to force the rightful owner to pay an exorbitant price. In 1931 a decision of the Argentine Supreme Court, although reaffirming the general principle that rights are established by registration and that only, did lay down the dictum that "no one is entitled to a mark of manufacture, commerce, or agriculture unless he is a manufacturer, a trader, or an agriculturist. Further, such manufacturer, trader, or agriculturist is entitled to registration in respect only of the particular class of goods or products manufactured, sold, or grown by him."[13] The article quoted points out that two new grounds for refusing trade-mark applications are given; namely, (1) that the applicant is not a manufacturer, trader, or agriculturist, and (2) that, even if he is one of the three, he is seeking to register a mark relating to goods outside his normal interests. This court decision was roundly applauded by foreign concerns, for the operations of some offenders—those who had no intention of using the mark in commerce—were strictly curbed.

Additional facilities for registering trade-marks in South American countries were afforded North American companies through a trade-mark convention, an outgrowth of the fifth Pan-American Conference of 1923.[14] This convention provided for Inter-American Bureaus or registration offices, one at Havana and the other at Rio de Janeiro. Under the plan outlined, a concern which desires

[13] J. A. and E. De Marval, "Argentine Supreme Court Renders Decision Restraining Trade-mark Piracy," *Comments on Argentine Trade*, March, 1932, p. 32.

[14] *Convention between the United States and Other American Republics for the Protection of Commercial, Industrial, and Agricultural Trade-marks and Commercial Names*, Treaty Series, Number 751, U.S. Department of State, 1927.

to protect its trade-mark in any of the countries adhering to the convention may do so by registering the mark with the United States Commissioner of Patents. By payment of the necessary fees for registration in the countries desired, the concern may have all details of registration taken care of through arrangements between the Commissioner of Patents and the Inter-American Bureaus. This convention went into effect on September 30, 1926. Brazil, among others, ratified the convention, but the other countries under consideration here (Argentina, Uruguay, and Chile) failed to do so. Hence the effect of the convention in creating a more acceptable situation was limited.

Even though registration procedures have been improved, difficulties continue to arise through activities which constitute infringement of trade-mark rights by other concerns. In this country, as the result of a long series of legal decisions, those situations which are likely to give rise to cases on trade-mark rights are commonly known. Such situations arise, for example, when there is question as to which company actually had prior use, when territorial limitations are involved, when it is desired to extend the rights in the mark to merchandise other than that for which it was originally used, and when the modernization of trade-marks causes a company to encroach upon the rights of others. The first of these questions is not productive of litigation in South America, for registration date can be easily ascertained. Neither do the others cause dispute to a like extent. What does cause litigation is the deliberate attempt on the part of small business concerns to create a mark very similar to that owned and used by branch plants, and, moreover, to use the mark on similar merchandise, thereby creating confusion in the minds of consumers as to the origin of the product. Instances of this sort are numerous, and they are very difficult to control. For example, one of our large soap producers with a trade name known in many parts of the world has its product manufactured in South America. Likewise a large British company has a plant. Both of these concerns are continually bothered by imitations of trade-marks, packages, and product name. One of these companies in one day discovered five new imitations. Since these companies have their trade-marks duly registered, it is not difficult for them to secure judgments against infringers. A judgment, however, means little from the standpoint of stamping out the practice. The offending concerns are small, fly-by-night companies, and, even though a judgment against them may mean their dissolution, they soon start again under a different name and continue their nefarious practices. Such activities will probably continue to be a source of constant irritation to branch plant executives. Moreover, through litigation over infringement, expense is incurred. Those companies which sell small-value convenience goods, such as grocery products, will be particularly affected, likewise those companies which sell machines and equipment for which small repair parts are needed. In both instances, the product can be copied roughly and manufactured in small quantities without unduly high costs. Under these conditions, small producers are likely to appropriate the goodwill attached to the product of another concern, even though such action constitutes infringement.

Not only in relation to trade-marks but in relation to commercial law as a whole, branch plant organizations will continue to experience difficulties. The underlying reason is that South American countries present a relatively new industrial situation. Commercial rights as yet are not so clearly defined as they are in this country or in Europe. Also, the administration of commercial law is not so effective. For some legitimate business practices, such as those involving conditional sales, there is no adequate legal provision. Although there are laws under which such sales can be effectuated, still they were designed for something quite different and fail fully to protect the seller.

In other cases, the inadequacy of laws and their administration have permitted abuses which have prejudiced the interests of business enterprises. Such was the case in bankruptcy actions. Finally, certain fundamental differences in laws, such as those which establish the basis for granting trade-mark rights, have been a source of difficulty to foreign concerns.

Nevertheless, the whole situation is improving, and fewer difficulties will be experienced in the future. Antiquated laws are being replaced by improved ones. Recent legal interpretations have been helpful in curbing illegitimate practices. With more adequate laws, the courts will have greater opportunity to prevent abuses, and the interests of legitimate business will be more fully protected. Furthermore, as North American companies adapt themselves to the laws of the countries in which they are operating, their situation should improve. With a more thorough knowledge of the law, many of those happenings which have caused difficulty and expense could have been foreseen and avoided.

CHAPTER 5

TARIFFS AND TAXATION

Many of the actions affecting business which have been taken by the governments of the ABC countries appear to have been wholly unpredictable. Decisions on the part of goverment officials frequently are made without thoughtful consideration of their probable effect upon business enterprises. Furthermore, decisions are often put into effect so quickly that adjustment to them is difficult. Businessmen, especially those who represent foreign concerns, are constantly in doubt as to what will happen next, for there is little assurance of continuity in any existing situation. Uncertainty is the very essence of business existence, and most of this uncertainty is attributable to the government. There is no better example of this than abrupt changes in tariffs, which have seriously jeopardized the interests of business concerns. The discussion of this chapter will be concerned with changes in tariffs and port charges, tariff classifications, customs administration, and the nature and extent of taxation.

CHANGES IN TARIFFS AND PORT CHARGES

No other action taken by South American governments has been so destructive of confidence as the changing of tariffs soon after branch plants have been established. Unfortunately, such action has been taken in a number of instances. The companies affected feel that the tariff protection accorded when the decision to migrate was made constituted an invitation to enter and produce within the market, rather than to continue importing. The tariff in force prior to migration thus was a condition of entrance.

Capital commitment was made in land, buildings, and equipment, and there was little possibility of withdrawal from that commitment without serious losses. Then, when it was too late for the migrating concerns to reconsider the question, the government in a sense "withdrew the invitation" by materially changing the conditions which were the basis of entrance. The companies felt that such action was evidence of bad faith, although no guarantee of the maintenance of tariff rates had been given.

No one would deny the fact that governments have the right to change tariff schedules. It is a right vested in every government. Nor could a branch plant organization expect that from the time its factory was established no tariff changes would ever be made on the products in which it was interested. But it might well expect that protection would be maintained for a reasonable time in the future, or until the whole situation had changed so markedly that revision was called for.

The case which aroused the most ill feeling, and which made foreign business executives exceedingly skeptical about placing additional branch factories in South America, was the reduction in the tariff on automobile tires soon after the Goodyear and Firestone companies started operations in Argentina. The facts of the situation were substantially as follows: In 1930 the Goodyear company constructed a factory in Hurlingham, a suburb of Buenos Aires, and in January, 1931, manufacture was begun. Six months later, in June, 1931, the Firestone company started operations in a factory which it had built in Llavallol, another suburb of Buenos Aires. The capital invested in these two enterprises was roughly 18,000,000 pesos or, at the average rate of exchange during 1930, $6,600,000.[1] Both factories were completely modern in every detail, and each was capable of producing from 800 to 1,000 tires daily.

The average rate of exchange for 1930, as given by the *Commerce Yearbook*, Vol. II (1931), was $0.3674.

The building of the tire plants attracted wide interest throughout the Republic. Argentina definitely wanted new industries, and the establishment of tire factories was considered an epochal event in the industrial advancement of the country. The inauguration ceremonies for both plants were attended by the President of the provisional government and other high officials. Leaders in industry also attended and took part in the festivities. From the accounts of these events it would appear that the tire companies were enthusiastically welcomed as a part of the industrial life of the Republic.

For the tire companies the greatest incentive to produce locally had been the differential in duties between finished casings and crude rubber. Numerous other materials are used in the manufacture of tires, the most important being fabric which is made from long-staple cotton, but, from the standpoint of cost, rubber is the principal item. For many years prior to the Goodyear and Firestone companies' decision to migrate, the duty on finished tire casings had been 32 per cent on a tariff valuation of $3.20 $^o/_s$ per kilo, or $1.024 $^o/_s$ per kilo, and the duty on crude rubber, the principal raw material, had been 5 per cent on a tariff valuation of $1.60 $^o/_s$ per kilo, or $0.08 $^o/_s$ per kilo.[2] There had thus been a spread between the two of $0.944 $^o/_s$ per kilo. Although it was anticipated that the costs of tire manufacture would be higher than in the United States, still this spread in duties appeared to be sufficiently large to permit local manufacture on a profitable basis and even to permit the charging of lower prices on tires than those current on imported merchandise. In fact, during 1931 the tire companies reduced their prices by about 15 per cent.

In view of the duty on tires and the reduced prices being quoted by the Goodyear and Firestone companies,

[2] Throughout this discussion, the symbol $ represents pesos and not United States dollars. The symbol $^o/_s$ is that of the Argentine gold peso, which is worth 96.48 cents at par, whereas the paper peso (par value, 42.45 cents) is represented by the symbol $^m/_n$. Thus, $0.08 $^o/_s$ means 0.08 pesos oro (gold).

importers were unable to compete. Their position was jeopardized, and therefore they exerted every effort through their organization, Asociación Importadores de Neumaticós, to have tariff charges on tires reduced. They were successful, and on January 19, 1932, the tariff valuation on tires was cut to $1.60 °/$_s$ per kilo. This amounted to a decrease in duties of 50 per cent. At the same time an internal revenue tax of $0.66 °/$_s$ per kilo was imposed on all tire casings, whether locally manufactured or imported, including those which were imported as a part of new cars. It is true that the same decree provided for a reduction of the tariff valuation on crude rubber from $1.60 °/$_s$ per kilo to $0.20 °/$_s$ per kilo with a duty rate of 10 per cent instead of the former 5 per cent, but this reduction in the duty on crude rubber was not to go into effect until the additional 10 per cent which had been imposed on all tariffs in March of 1931 as an emergency measure was removed. In fact, this was an indefinite postponement, for the emergency tariff has not yet been withdrawn (1935).[3]

As a result of these tariff changes, the protection given to the tire companies was materially reduced. The duty paid on tires after February 1, 1932, was 42 per cent (32 per cent plus the additional 10 per cent) on a valuation of $1.60 °/$_s$ per kilo, or $0.672 per kilo, while the duty on crude rubber was increased to 15 per cent of $1.60 °/$_s$ per kilo, or $0.24 °/$_s$ per kilo. The spread between the two was thus only $0.432 °/$_s$ per kilo, whereas at the time the factories were built it had been $0.944 °/$_s$ per kilo. The loss of protection amounted to $0.512 °/$_s$, or 54 per cent. Moreover, increased duties on other raw materials placed the tire companies at a further disadvantage in relation to importers. The tire manufacturers' association, Asociación De Industriales Del Caucho, estimated that changes in

[3] There have been no changes in the duties on tires or crude rubber between 1932 and 1935. However, the internal revenue tax on tire casings was raised from $1.50 $^m/_n$ ($0.66 °/$_s$) per kilo to $2.00 $^m/_n$ per kilo, effective Jan. 1, 1935. At the same time this tax of $2.00 $^m/_n$ per kilo was made applicable to solid tires as well as to casings.

tariffs had lessened their protection to the extent of 62 per cent, and this is in all probability a reasonable estimate.

The tire plants are not the only example of North American companies which were harmed by the withdrawal of tariff protection. Because the duty on wooden parts for radio cabinets was much less than the duty on completed cabinets, one concern built an annex to its factory in 1931 for the assembly of cabinets from imported parts. Soon after the annex was completed, a decree was issued by the government which equalized the duty on parts and finished cabinets. Fortunately, in this case no great loss was incurred, for the company was able to secure cabinet parts from local manufacturers and thus continued its assembly operations.

Watt meters were another product for which tariff rates made local assembly desirable. Prior to February, 1932, these meters were being assembled from imported parts by one North American company and by a number of European companies in Buenos Aires. There was an appreciable advantage in local assembly, for the parts as entered took a lower rate than the completed product. In February, 1932, the government issued a decree which raised the duty on parts to an absurdly high point, well above the duty on finished meters. As a result, assembly ceased. Here again, the loss suffered was not great, for no new buildings had been required and the equipment needed for assembly was neither large in amount nor costly.

Another example of the harmful effects of tariff changes is to be found in the case of hog cholera serum. Prior to 1931, this serum had been imported free, but in that year a duty of approximately 30 per cent was placed on the product. This duty and the unfavorable exchange situation provided the incentive for two companies which had previously been importers of the product to establish laboratories to produce serum. One of the concerns, although an Argentine company, was owned and managed by North Americans. Experts were brought from the

United States to establish the laboratory, and the finest and latest equipment was imported. During the two years that production facilities were being created, the duty remained in force. Then, about the time that this thoroughly modern laboratory was opened, the duty protection was removed. While the laboratory has continued to operate, there is some question whether, in the event of an improvement in exchange, the company can without protection compete successfully with importers.

In 1932 there was a serious threat of tariff action that would have been unfavorable to European branch factories producing corrugated steel roofs for the Argentine market. However, the manufacturers succeeded in preventing the passage of the measure through the Argentine Senate. Most building materials must be imported into Argentina, for the country lacks iron deposits, likewise readily available wood. In the farming districts steel roofs are habitually used. Because of the lower duty on black steel sheets, five companies had been established for galvanizing and corrugating sheets for building purposes. Some of these companies had been a part of the industrial life of the country for many years and had been protected by a difference of about 20 per cent between the duty on black steel sheets and the duty on steel roofing. One morning it was announced in the papers that the lower house of Congress had voted to abolish the duty on steel roofing. The duty on steel sheets was evidently to be retained, for it was not mentioned. Until this time, the roofing companies had had no intimation that such action was contemplated. Since they were convinced that their entire 21,000,000 peso investment was jeopardized, they were up in arms as a group. The struggle lasted for two months, but in the end no action was taken to change the status quo, for the Senate refused to approve the tariff reduction and the proponents of the measure could not muster the necessary two-thirds majority in the lower chamber to send the measure to the President. This is not a case in which tariff reductions were made soon after factories were established. Neither should the inference be taken that the protection given was necessarily justified. But the illustration does show the attitude of South American legislators toward protection and the rapidity with which unexpected situations may arise.

Branch organizations are not always so fortunate as were the roofing manufacturers in warding off unfavorable tariff action. At times changes which work havoc with company plans are made with great rapidity. Later, enough influence may be brought to bear to have the action revoked, but frequently the companies affected simply have to make the best of a bad situation. In October of 1931, the tariff on lubricating oils was raised, the increase to take effect immediately. One concern, anticipating that changes might be made in the duty, had a shipment in transit which it hoped to import under existing rates. But the period usually allowed before putting new schedules into effect was not granted, and therefore the shipment was caught in transit. Then the question arose whether the shipment ought to be allowed to enter or should be sent back. Finally, cost considerations dictated entrance, and the oils were sold on a non-profit basis.

A final example of governmental action which aroused the ire of interested concerns is drawn from the experience of companies located in Brazil. The Brazilian 1932 budget law promulgated in December, 1931, provided that, effective ninety days after date—that is, on March 28, 1932—the 2 per cent gold port improvement tax, which had previously been levied at nearly all major Brazilian ports with the exception of Santos, would henceforth be collected at all Brazilian ports without exception. Santos being the port of entry for the whole São Paulo region, this change affected the imports of all the branch plants there located. Accordingly, these branch plants, particularly those assembling automobiles, ordered heavy shipments which were due to arrive before the new port charge went into effect. This was a legitimate business move and was not subject to censure on any reasonable basis. However, there was concurrently under consideration a change in the tariff on automobiles. A government commission had studied the matter and in so doing had secured the cooperation of the automobile companies, which apparently were satisfied with the rates suggested by the commission and understood that those rates were to be adopted. Quite to the surprise of the companies, and probably to the surprise of the commission as well, a *Diario Official* in early March carried a decree which not only raised the duties on automobiles far above the suggested figures, but also put the new duties into effect retroactively as of March first. Thus, the large shipments which had been induced by the announced change in port charges were caught in transit. Usually a period of ninety days had been given after announcement before tariff changes were put into effect.

Furthermore, the automobile companies were particularly concerned because hasty preparation had left the new schedules faulty and ambiguous and therefore subject to arbitrary interpretation by customs officials. In this connection it was said that customs officials at Santos were changing their minds every few hours in regard to what the automobile companies should be asked to pay under the new schedules. It was stated that on one shipment then in transit different possible interpretations of the new schedules would make a difference of nearly $2,000 in duties.

In two other particulars the new duties were unsatisfactory to the assembly plants. A 30 per cent reduction previously given from the regular duty if cars were imported C.K.D. (completely knocked down) was changed to only 5 per cent. Also, the new schedules appeared to favor the importers of very light European cars, such as Morris and Fiat. Because of the hurried and arbitrary nature of the whole proceeding, organized protests were made. Naturally the companies wished the usual period of grace, or, at least, waivers on the shipments then in transit. The pressure brought to bear was sufficiently strong, and the decree as originally announced was never put into effect. There were numerous suspensions of fifteen to thirty days, and a modification of the original decree finally went into effect on July 1. So extensive were the revisions of the first decree that the schedules appeared to be entirely new. The duties were much lower, and the reduction given for C.K.D. imports was fixed at 20 per cent.

The 2 per cent gold port charge levied upon all imports into Santos after 1932 was not only of significance in relation to the tariff controversy over automobiles.[4] Of itself, it constituted a change of condition which appreciably altered the status of branch plants. When decisions were being made in regard to where to locate branch plants within Brazil, São Paulo was usually chosen, partly, at least, because of the absence of this port charge, which was assessed against imports arriving at all important Brazilian ports other than Santos. The charge was originally assessed elsewhere to finance port improvements, and it had been in force many years—probably sufficiently long to pay a number of times for the improvements actually made. Santos, and therefore indirectly São Paulo, had been exempt from the charge because port improvements were made under a contractual arrangement with the Santos Dock Company rather than directly by the Brazilian government. The services and the improvements secured from this private concern were paid for by a special set of charges on imported merchandise, which in total were appreciably less than 2 per cent of either tariff valuations or declared values at the time of importation. After the change, however, imports into Santos were assessed not

[4] This charge was originally supposed to become effective on Mar. 28, 1932. However, because of the protests made by business interests, its collection was deferred. Subsequently, uprisings broke out in the state of São Paulo, and the port of Santos was closed by the federal government. The port was reopened on Oct. 6, 1932, and on Oct. 10 the actual assessment of the 2 per cent charge at this port was begun.

only the old charges but 2 per cent gold in addition. Therefore, Santos was placed at a marked disadvantage as compared with Rio de Janeiro and other ports.[5]

The city of São Paulo has always had one disadvantage as a location for branch plants because of its inland position. Since it is about forty miles distant from Santos, haulage costs are assumed on all imports, and these costs are high because of the monopolistic position of the São Paulo railway, which is the only means of transportation. But, despite this fact, São Paulo was selected for branch factories because it was the largest single market and because of the benefit of lower port charges. If the incentive furnished by the latter factor had not been present, it is quite conceivable that plants would have been placed in Rio de Janeiro rather than in São Paulo. Those new plants which have been established since the port charge was imposed on Santos have been located in Rio de Janeiro. Under the present situation it would be advisable to have a plant in each city if the total demand was sufficient.

Undoubtedly, the companies which placed factories in São Paulo expected that the advantage of lower port charges would be permanent. The condition was one of so many years' duration that it seemed safe to assume that no change would be made. But business executives did not reckon with the possibility that by revolutionary means a new government might come into power which was antagonistic to São Paulo, and that such a government, believing that São Paulo through its lower port charges was reaping an undue benefit in relation to other Brazilian coast cities, might place a port charge on Santos imports. From the experience of branch plants it may be argued that it is unwise to assume that any condition in regard to tariffs or

---

[5] The new Brazilian tariff which became effective on Sept. 1, 1934, abolished the port charge and numerous other surtaxes for all Brazilian ports and substituted therefor a flat surtax of 10 per cent of the import duty rate charged on any class of merchandise.

port charges is permanent in South American countries. Precedent or long-continued stability is of little value in predicting future happenings.

Reasons for Tariff Changes

In the foregoing paragraphs a number of cases have been cited in which the action of governments in regard to tariffs and port charges has been prejudicial to the interests of concerns operating branch plants. These changes were of four general types: a lowering of the tariff on finished products of the kind produced in branch plants, a change in the relationship between duties on raw materials or assembly parts and duties on finished products, a change in tariff rates which was put into effect so quickly that companies were unable to make adjustments with sufficient rapidity to avoid undue loss, and a change in an existing condition, such as that described in respect to port charges, which, because of its long standing, was considered to be permanent. In each instance the tariff or port charge in force before the change was made was a condition of the foreign company's entrance into the market as a manufacturer. Now we turn to a consideration of the motivation behind these changes.

First, it should be pointed out that tariff changes were detrimental only to foreign concerns. In none of the cases mentioned were locally financed business enterprises unfavorably affected. This fact suggests that the motivation for tariff changes has root in an anti-foreign-capital sentiment. Admittedly, there is such sentiment in all South American countries. It is particularly evident in the actions of certain political parties and of certain individuals who temporarily may occupy important positions which enable them to hamper the operations of foreign companies. There are instances in which prejudicial action appears to have arisen almost entirely from antipathy toward foreign interests. In other cases, the action was prompted by other factors as well, such as personal interests, the need for government revenue, or, perhaps, a feeling that a tariff never should have been imposed in the first place. When action might have proceeded from a number of conditions, it is difficult to say with any degree of sureness which one exerted the major influence.

Prejudicial action of the first type is taken when certain individuals, known to be antagonistic to foreign enterprises and apparently prompted solely by such antagonism, deliberately scheme to molest foreign concerns. The ill-conceived attempts at tariff changes on automobiles in Brazil appear to have been of this type. The changes announced in early March of 1932 were detrimental in a number of ways: Protection for assembly was decreased from 30 per cent to 5 per cent, the ambiguity of the schedules paves the way for unjust interpretations by customs officials, and no period of grace was given before the new rates were put into effect. Many people familiar with the circumstances believe that three or four individuals were wholly responsible for these tariff modifications and that other people in the government who were supposed to be connected with tariff activities knew nothing of the changes until they were announced. This incident does not furnish convincing proof, however, that all the influential people of Brazil or all political groups are strongly antagonistic to foreign capital. It cannot safely be assumed, as too frequently it is, from the actions or the expressed ideas of particular individuals or political groups, that there is antipathy on the part of all individuals or groups toward foreign capital invested in manufacturing plants and that consequently the operations of branch plants will be hampered to an increasing extent. Instances such as the one just noted evidence, above all else, a weakness of government. Otherwise, measures detrimental to business could not be hurried through governmental channels without the needed deliberation and scrutiny by trained people, nor could government officials be so easily influenced by people who are actuated by unreasoning prejudices or personal interests.

The reduction in tariff protection for tire manufacture in Argentina can also be attributed in part to a weakness in government, for it appears that government officials were unduly swayed by individuals antagonistic to the tire companies. The tire situation was a complex one, however, and the influences behind the decrease in protection were numerous. Therefore, in order to appreciate fully the influences which were brought to bear upon those government officials who were empowered to make tariff changes, more details about the whole incident must be given.

Evidently the tire companies had stated that they would reduce prices when production was under way. Whether such statements obligated them to do so is open to question. Still, it was the natural thing for them to do, for they needed to exclude imports and thereby secure the entire market for themselves in order to achieve reasonably low production costs. Accordingly, over a period of months, prices were reduced about 15 per cent. Apparently the tire companies thought they had nothing to gain by rapid price reduction; therefore, prices were reduced slowly in order to cause importers as little loss as possible while they were in the process of withdrawal. Lower prices gave importers no alternative to withdrawal. Their only possible method of retaliation was to get the tariff reduced. Hence they exerted every possible effort through their organization, Asociación Importadores de Neumaticós, to accomplish the desired result.

Prior to the change in rates, hearings were held by a government investigating commission. Arguments and counter-arguments were advanced by all interested parties. On both sides many of those advanced were of little real significance, and some were entirely unsound. The importers' association was particularly guilty in this respect. It was stated that the rubber imported was not crude but semiprepared rubber, and thus was subject to a higher rate on the basis of existing schedules. As a matter of fact, the rubber is exactly the same as that imported into the United States and Europe, where it is designated as crude rubber. Another argument was that the manufacture of tires constituted an uneconomic activity for Argentina, that it was parasitical in nature because it depended upon tariff protection. Admittedly it does, but so does the greater share of Argentine industry, the protection for which has been increased rather than diminished. An impartial analysis will yield the conclusion that the manufacture of tires is much more economic than the majority of manufacturing activities in the Republic, for the optimum size of the plant is small and, wherever production now takes place, the chief raw material must be imported. Moreover, the need for protection was known by those government officials who offered definite encouragement to the tire companies to enter and produce within the country. At the hearings other statements were made which placed the tire companies in an unfavorable light. For example, it was stated that tires had been offered to the automobile assembly plants for less than half the price charged dealers. From this the commission thought that the companies were making exorbitant profits and could easily reduce prices to Argentine consumers still further. Then the fact was stressed that the government was to lose some fifteen to twenty million pesos annually in duties previously collected on tire imports. The chief contention of the tire companies centered about the fact that they had been induced to establish plants in Argentina by the presence of certain conditions, among which the most important was a tariff on tires; that they would not have come if such conditions had not been present; and that it was, therefore, an act of bad faith to change those conditions immediately after factories were established.

The decision, as outlined previously, was adverse to the interests of the tire companies, the reduction in their protection being estimated as 62 per cent. They were loath to accept the decision as final, particularly that part which continued the high duty on crude rubber until the emergency tariff of 10 per cent should be discontinued. Until that time they would be forced to pay $0.24 °/$_s$ per kilo instead of $0.02 °/$_s$ per kilo. With the removal of the 10 per cent emergency charge, the reduction in their protection, instead of being 62 per cent, would be about 48 per cent. Industrial countries have no tariff on crude rubber, and the tire companies contended that if the tariff on the finished product was cut so drastically, the least which the government could have been expected to do was to remove the tariff on crude rubber, and to do so immediately. Had the government done this, in all probability the tire companies would not have continued to negotiate for a reconsideration of the whole question. But they maintained their opposition to the decision, and might have achieved some result had it not been for a statement by the Michelin Tire Company, which was likewise placing a tire factory in Argentina, to the effect that it was entirely satisfied with the tariff schedules on tires as they then stood. This statement was made in a petition presented to the government, the purpose of which was to secure free entrance of equipment for the Michelin factory. The petition also denied any desire to cooperate with the North American companies and stated that the presence of the Michelin company would prevent a monopolistic situation from developing through possible understandings between the other two producers. This statement, coming during the time that the North American companies were raising serious objections to the tariff changes, strengthened the case of the opposition and made a change in the new schedules very unlikely. The position of the tire companies was considerably weakened, for the Michelin company did build a factory in Argentina after the tariff changes were made. Since its only commitment previous to the change had been the purchase of a site for the factory, the company could have abandoned its plans for manufacturing in Argentina without sustaining serious loss. From this action by Michelin the assumption was made that the North American companies would have come despite the tariff change and that consequently they had no legitimate objection to the new conditions.

While this discussion of the tire incident is doubtless somewhat sketchy and, perhaps, inexact in certain small details, it will serve as a background for a consideration of the forces which worked together to produce the changes in duties. The first motivation for the change came largely from the association of importers; in fact, it is questionable whether any action would have been taken by the government if the case for a change had not been presented so skillfully by the association representatives. But if this statement is true, and many people familiar with the situation think that it is, then in all fairness we must admit that the motivation for a reduced tariff came in part from other North American companies, for the importers' association was composed of both North American and European companies. At least, the interest of the North American business community in Buenos Aires, and, therefore, the interest of the United States as a political entity, was not entirely on one side of the controversy. Any critical judgment on the whole incident must be tempered by the fact that our own business concerns were contributing both their funds and their influence to attain directly opposed objectives.

Some exception would probably be taken to this assertion —that certain North American companies contributed to the difficulties of others—on the ground that the action taken by the importers can be attributed in large part to the secretary of the association and that much of the incentive for action came from him. However, it is only reasonable to conclude that the members of the association were in sympathy with the action taken, that they gave tacit approval to the tactics used by their representatives, and that hence they were jointly responsible for the association's activities.

The secretary of the association was an able individual of Argentine nationality, who formerly had been assistant manager of one of the producing companies. When that connection was severed, he became local representative for another North American tire company and thus was still directly interested in the tire business when the tariff question arose. This individual was exceedingly active in obtaining the information needed and in directing the campaign for lower tariffs. His incentive for action apparently proceeded from antipathy toward foreign capital, especially North American, and from a hearty dislike of the tire companies, either one or both. Undoubtedly he had some political influence, and, in addition, something which those who represented the tire companies lacked; that is, a real skill in appealing to the emotions and the prejudices—if there were such—of those who possessed the power of decision. There was a bond of sympathy and understanding which probably affected the outcome of the controversy.

When it is possible for one or a few individuals thus to influence government officials toward action which is prejudicial to foreign business interests, the major difficulty lies in the weakness of government. There will always be some individuals who are antagonistic to foreign interests. Under a strong, well-organized government they are impotent, but in South America they frequently have considerable influence—perhaps not directly with the highest government officials but rather with people in the customs, on tariff commissions, and on special investigating groups. Political maneuvering is their stock in trade, and by such action they attain their objectives despite the remonstrance of the business concerns affected.

In contrast to the stratagem of the opposition, the tire companies were inept in their handling of the entire affair, and thus to some extent they brought disaster on their own heads. There were rumors—too many to be entirely discounted—that too much was said about the huge profits which were to be realized through local production, and that a tire manufacturing company might expect to regain its original investment from profits in a three-year period. Such statements smack of exploitation. If they were made and later came to the ears of government officials, some antagonism must inevitably have been aroused and prejudicial action against the companies induced. Moreover, at least one of the tire companies, when it was first established, completely ignored the Union Industrial Argentina, the strong organization of practically all industrial interests, which could have been a powerful ally. Later both concerns became members. There also is a feeling that insufficient reliance was placed on the experience and, in some cases, the advice of companies which had been producing in Argentina for many years. The tire companies had been in the market before, but not in a producing capacity, and hence the problems which arose were essentially different from those which they had confronted previously. Something could surely have been gained from the experience of others. It is also asserted that they antagonized the investigating commission by their unwillingness to give the exact information called for. Later, further ill will was created by their failure to accept the findings of the commission and the change in duties with better grace. Admittedly their position was materially weakened by the changes and they had sufficient grounds for objection, but further agitation at that time was probably ill-advised.

Yet another cause of the change in tariffs on tires and crude rubber was the government's need of revenue. Usually this need supplies the incentive for higher protection, but in this instance it had the opposite effect. If all tires were to be produced locally, the government would lose from fifteen to twenty million pesos annually, the amount previously collected on tire imports. Revenue was sorely needed, and therefore the tariff was lowered in an attempt to stimulate imports, and an internal tax was placed on tires. Of course, it was not reasonable to suppose that any volume of tires would be imported unless the duty was so low that the producers were actually driven out of the market, for they had to supply the total demand in order to use their facilities and achieve reasonably low production costs. But the tax on tires and the duty on crude rubber did aid in maintaining revenue. Hence we may asssume that the need for revenue served as one reason for the change.

A reduction in duties may be made simply because government officials feel that the protection given is more than is needed and that its effect may be to increase prices to consumers. In the event of free competition between two or more producers, the degree of protection given will have little effect on prices even though landed cost is somewhat more than the cost of production. In the event of monopoly or price understandings between producers, however, the price could be fixed at a point just below the level at which imports would enter, and thus the effect of protection would be to increase the profits of the manufacturing concerns. Although there was little evidence of a monopolistic situation in the case of tires, for prices during the first year had been reduced materially below the level previously in force, still the action of the government may be explained in part by the fear that a truly competitive condition might not prevail. On one occasion, the government stated that the new tariff was set at a level which would equalize the competitive situation between importers and local manufacturers. This, in a sense, implies that no real competition was expected between the two local manufacturing concerns, for competition between them would be just as effective in reducing prices as would the permitting of imports through lower duties.

Reasoned judgment may dictate tariff changes. Perhaps a duty never should have been imposed on a certain product in the first place, and, after the duty has been in force for some time, this fact becomes apparent. A duty on hog cholera serum, for instance, should not have been imposed. The product was a minor item on the list of imports and could be purchased more cheaply if produced in large quantities elsewhere and imported into Argentina. It had not been subject to any duty until 1930, when a rate of 30 per cent was established. Two years later, this duty was removed, with unfortunate effects to those who had started to produce the serum locally. It is very doubtful whether any ill will toward the companies affected was involved in the decision. And, since there was complete removal of the duty, except for the 10 per cent emergency charge, it does not appear that the government was actuated by any incentive to lower the duty in order to increase imports and thus attain some revenue. Rather, it is probable that those who made the change thought that it was the best thing to do, even though it did injure some parties; or, more likely still, they may not even have realized that local business concerns would be injured if the change was made.

At times, changes in tariffs arise from carelessness in legislation. The proposed reduction in the tariff on steel roofing, without any accompanying reduction in the tariff on steel sheets, is a case in point. It is possible that the action taken in the lower house of the legislature was malicious in intent, but more likely it happened in some such manner as this: The Argentine legislative bodies are addicted to numerous practically all-night sessions, particularly when they are considering some important matter, such as the budget. Usually a budget measure also involves some shifts in tariffs. The night before the change in the roofing tariff was announced in the morning papers, the Argentine lower house had been engaged in one of these long, sleepy sessions. Tariff changes were being considered, and probably someone suggested that there should not be a tariff on steel roofing, which was used extensively by poor people in farming areas, or the "camp," as it is called. The suggestion seemed reasonable to those who were awake, and consequently a reduction in the tariff on roofing crept into a group of suggested tariff changes and was passed by the house in the early morning hours. It may well be that, when the measure was read before a vote was taken, many people were asleep and those who were awake did not realize the difference which the tariff change on roofing would make to various business enterprises. Perhaps certain individuals were antagonistic to the British iron companies, which largely control the roofing business, and they accepted this late session of the lower house of the legislature as an opportune time to rush through tariff changes in accordance with their own desires. But it is unlikely that there was any general antagonism toward the roofing concerns.

From the discussion of this section it appears that prejudicial changes in tariffs and port charges may be the result of a number of influencing factors, working either alone or jointly. They may be motivated by antagonism toward foreign capital interests. Large capitalistic concerns with investments in many nations are frequently the subject of suspicion, unjust or otherwise, and are considered legitimate prey by those who have the power to create obstacles for them. They are always at some disadvantage when controversies arise in which South American governmental bodies are the arbitrators. But, more often than not, there is neither a general antipathy toward foreign concerns operating branch plants nor a desire to see them so treated by the government that profitable operation is impossible. There are, of course, certain individuals and small groups who are actively antagonistic to foreign capital, or, perhaps, to certain companies, and they are able, because of the disorganization and weakness of the government, to put through their malevolent schemes to hamper foreign interests. At times it is difficult to ascertain whether the action taken was prompted by malicious intent, because carelessness in legislation may itself bring unfavorable action.

Motivation for the reduction of tariff protection may be given by those companies, either European or North American, which are displaced as suppliers of the market when branch plants are established. The sales volume of these concerns is inevitably reduced, and their only means of retaliation is to obtain a reduction in the protection of the local producer. The withdrawal of protection may make it possible for them to import once more. The ineptitude of the branch plant-executives, their unwillingness to take advice and to profit by the experience of others, and their lack of observance of the amenities of the situation may also be contributory factors. Again, unwillingness to rely on the producing companies to maintain competition has prompted tariff action when the government has realized that price understandings, if there were such, would create a monopoly element in price in view of the tariff protection given.

Whatever the reasons for the reduction of tariff protection, once branch plants have been established, the act itself is entirely destructive of confidence. If a reduction is made soon after the factory begins operation, it is likely to be construed as an act of bad faith. This is particularly true when the government has been active in inducing the foreign company to produce in the local market, giving it every encouragement to become a part of the industrial life of the nation. The tariff is a condition of entrance, and the foreign concern has an equity in the maintenance of that condition for a reasonable time in the future. Unless some reliance can be placed on the maintenance of existing conditions, foreign companies will be loath to place branch plants in South America.[6]

The general significance of these instances of reduced tariff protection is not easily determined. Admittedly they are few in number compared with the opportunities

---

[6] A number of companies have withheld action on branch plants because of the action that was taken against the interests of the tire companies. In at least one instance, the site had been purchased.

for such action, and many branch plants were given additional protection. Moreover, they appeared during a time of unusual economic stress and strain. It is not likely that the ABC countries have repudiated their protectionist attitude toward industry, or that they are less desirous than they formerly were of increasing their industrial activity. In general, industry will be protected, but there always will be uncertainty for any particular industry and, therefore, for any particular company. Until there is more evidence to the contrary, it is advisable for North American companies to assume that all conditions relating to tariffs, port charges, concessions, or other matters directly under the control of the government, even though they are of long standing, are subject to change, and probably to change without much notice. There is a major business risk involved, for little dependence can be placed on the maintenance of tariff levels or other conditions initially present, and therefore branch plants should not be established unless profitable operation is possible with much less favorable conditions than those in force when the initial decision to migrate is made.

Illogical Tariff Classifications

Although branch plants are partially within tariff walls, still all but a very few import assembly parts, supplies, or raw materials, or bulk products for packaging locally. On these, tariff classifications frequently are woefully illogical and inexact, much more so, for instance, than on finished products. Two products which are to be used for the same purpose and which have similar properties may appear in different classifications and may be subject to widely divergent tariff charges. The manager of one North American branch factory stated in conversation that there simply was no "rhyme nor reason" to tariff classifications in Argentina. Undoubtedly this is an overstatement of the situation. Perhaps it was made soon after an attempt to straighten out some difficulty and therefore was partly the outgrowth of a recent unfortunate experience. But this attitude is so common among branch plant executives that we cannot ascribe its appearance to isolated incidents. In Brazil, likewise, difficulties have been encountered on this score, but some improvement may have resulted from the recent revision of the tariff structure.

At one time or another, the great majority of companies have had trouble because of illogical tariff classifications and because of changes in classifications that have apparently been made for no good reason. One concern had for seventeen years been importing a supply under a certain classification. Someone in the customs house conceived the idea that a chemical analysis of this product was in order. The analysis was made, and it was discovered that the percentage of one ingredient in the product was slightly more than that allowed in the description. As a result the product, although its manufacture had been unchanged for many years, was subjected to a much higher duty rate.

Another incident involved rubber tile. With differences in the color of tile, there are also slight differences in the chemical analysis. This fact was discovered by someone in the customs house, and on the basis of the analysis, different rates were assessed against tile in different colors. One company, unaware of the change, quoted prices on the tile to be used on a large construction job. When the tile arrived, the company was forced to pay some fifteen thousand pesos in duties above the expected charge. In this case there appeared to be no logical reason for changing the classification on the basis of color. The product was but slightly different and was to be used for exactly the same purpose.

One further incident involved a slightly different situation. A branch plant imported carbon black for use in the manufacture of commercial inks. This product was classified under two headings, Numbers 2934 and 2935.

The descriptions for the two were the same, with one exception: Number 2934 read, "packed in kegs, barrels, or bags (sacks)"; whereas Number 2935 covered that product which arrived in packages, evidently meaning smaller packages inclosed in a wooden box. On product classified under Number 2934 a duty of $0.0672 per kilo was assessed, in contrast to a duty of $0.1344 per kilo under Number 2935. The problem of the company was to ship the product so that it would not be damaged in transit and yet would be assessed the lower rate. First it was shipped in paper bags inclosed in a wooden box, but on this shipment the higher duty was imposed. Later, shipment was made in jute bags inclosed in a wooden container. The first shipment packed in this manner was entered under Number 2934 without difficulty, but a later shipment was evidently cleared under the supervision of a different individual in the customs house and was placed under Number 2935. Protests were of no avail, and the higher rate was paid. Still later, shipment was made in bags inclosed in a larger bag, and the product was classified under Number 2934. The seriousness of such difficulties will be realized when it is pointed out that, at the time of the incident, carbon black was worth only $0.0689 per kilo C.I.F. Buenos Aires. Under one classification the duty was approximately equal to the delivered cost, under the other it was almost double the cost.

Such incidents as these are not conducive to profitable business operations. They are irritating to business executives and take attention from other, more important matters. If a company attempts to have tariff classifications changed to conform more closely to significant differences in product, it engages in time-consuming and perhaps futile negotiations. Yet, when classifications are ambiguous and inexact, uncertainty is created and estimates of landed cost cannot be made with confidence. In view of the widely divergent tariffs on products which may conceivably be put in more than one classification, changes in the way in which schedules are interpreted inject an unpredictable element into many computations. Moreover, because of faulty classifications, companies in numerous instances have been forced to pay duties under protest. The goods were needed and would not be released unless payment was made. To wait until the matter was finally adjudicated would have reduced the value of the shipment appreciably and, in addition, would have hindered operations. Therefore, duties were paid in accordance with the decision of the customs house official. Many times the cases are allowed to drag along and are never finally settled; again, the case may be decided in favor of the protesting company, but the amounts that have been paid under protest are not returned. A packing company in Uruguay, an oil company in Brazil, an automobile company in Argentina, and others in all three countries have amounts on their books which they believe are rightfully their due from the various governments. Some of these amounts are of long standing, others are comparatively new; but in all cases there is little hope of collection. In one particular instance, a government promised that the duty collected on the raw material for containers would be refunded later, when the filled containers were exported. The company did not press the government for repayment, and later the government was in such dire financial straits that there was no hope of collection. Now the amount has been written off as a loss, for a new government is in power and collection is extremely doubtful.

It should, of course, be recognized that inexact classifications at times give branch plants the opportunity of importing merchandise under lower rates than were contemplated by those who framed the schedules. In other words, inexactitude may be penalized if it allows importers to take advantage of the lowest of varying rates. That they frequently have taken advantage of the loopholes in tariff structures is beyond question. Such action smacks of sharp practice, but actually the government permits it by failing to make clear-cut distinctions in classifications. And whatever gains firms have been able to achieve have probably been more than counterbalanced by losses. Branch plants undoubtedly would be in a better position if tariff classifications were more nearly logical and exact.

Administration of the Customs

Investigation of customs house procedure is a not infrequent activity of South American governments. There is always objection to the manner in which incoming shipments are handled, and when the clamor becomes too insistent, an investigation is ordered. There have been investigations in all of the ABC countries in the past five years. Particularly after the overthrow of a government by revolutionary means, there is likely to be an entire reorganization and, for a time at least, an improvement in administration. Before the overthrow of the Irigoyen regime in Argentina in 1930, the administration of the customs had reached a particularly low level. Nothing could be cleared expeditiously unless people in the customs were paid to hurry matters. When the government was overthrown, there was a pronounced feeling of relief on the part of all business concerns which had anything to do with the customs. Conditions improved under the provisional government, but there still was objection. In 1932 President Justo, moved by the charges of irregularity and inefficiency which had come to his attention, appointed a commission to investigate the customs.

Matters pertaining to customs house procedure, documentation, storage, appraisal, and clearance are important to the management of all branch plants. When there are frequent changes in administration, incompetence, and graft, the operations of a branch plant are thereby hindered, and in some cases appreciably so. Furthermore, incompetence appears to be the usual situation, instead of the exception. On no other point is there such great unanimity

of opinion among branch plant executives. They object to
a number of things, among which are the delays and uncertainty involved in ascertaining where the merchandise will
enter the customs warehouse and when its discharge from
the boat will be completed; the time required to get merchandise through the customs and to have it delivered to
their own premises; the difficulty of obtaining prompt and
proper customs appraisal for the payment of duties; the
practice of allowing merchandise to be kept for an abnormal
length of time in unprotected storage places where it is
likely to deteriorate; and the time and effort needed to
settle matters when difficulties arise. For example, when
there is a question about the classification under which a
shipment should enter, when containers are mismarked, or
when the actual shipment fails to conform in all respects to
the descriptions on the documents, it is difficult to get the
matter straightened out quickly. The question may
appear to be one requiring only a few minutes' negotiation,
but in all probability it will be hanging fire for some time.
No one seems to have the required authority to settle such
matters finally. There is endless "red tape," and only
after much time has passed and there has been much irritation and possibly expenditure of funds, are adjustments
finally made.

In one instance, through the mistake of an employee in
the United States, a shipment containing two products,
much alike except that they differed in color, was mismarked. The documents said that containers numbered 1
to 5 carried one of the two products, whereas these containers should have been numbered 6 to 10. The employee
had simply reversed the numbers. This error was discovered in the customs house. If it had not been discovered, the government would have lost about five
hundred pesos in duties. The inference taken from this
incident was that the company was attempting to defraud
the government, and, on this supposition, the government
threatened to confiscate the shipment. After detailed

explanations, coupled with a certain amount of subterfuge, the shipment was finally cleared, but not without the expenditure of considerable time and effort over a period of days.

Other objections which branch plant executives commonly raise against customs house procedure have to do with the lack of knowledge and cooperation on the part of customs house brokers and the fact that illogical and inexact tariff classifications place too much power in the hands of officials in regard to the amount which will be collected on a shipment. A customs official occupies such a strategic position that he can make things exceedingly unpleasant for an importer; also, he may make unreasonable demands which the importers cannot afford to refuse.

Irregularities in the Argentine customs house are more prevalent than they otherwise would be, for the reason that when attempts to defraud the government are discovered, the inspector and the customs house broker are considered the guilty parties. As a result, the receiver of the goods may permit chicanery which he would not allow if, in the event of discovery, he were to be considered the guilty party and thus made subject to fines and perhaps even more drastic punishment. Recently there has been more inclination on the part of the courts to attempt to collect from the receiver, if the broker is unable to pay the fine assessed, and therefore the receiver may have to be more careful in the future. As the customs have been administered in the past, there has been an element of protection for the receiver. However, any advantage which he may have derived from this has been more than counterbalanced by the irregularities which the system has induced in customs house procedure.

Another ruling by the government further contributes to the unhealthiness of the situation. Any person who discovers irregularities in the dealings of a company with the government through the customs house is awarded one-half of the fine which is assessed against the guilty parties. Since the fines are usually heavy, this potential reward for information has created a group of individuals who do little but attempt to ferret out situations in which the government has been defrauded. Perhaps this practice constitutes a protection for the government, but it undoubtedly constitutes a threat to business, even when legitimately operated. The incentive offered to these individuals prompts them to start action if there is the slightest basis for the belief that the government may have been defrauded, and thus business firms become involved in the refutation of charges which have little basis in fact, or in cases in which there was no intent to defraud. The whole scheme of paying informers so generously results in unfounded charges and uncalled-for action and thus creates distrust and a state of apprehension on the part of business concerns.

Interstate and International Tariffs

Interstate tariffs were declared illegal in Brazil by the provisional government which came into power in 1930, but vestiges of them still remain and they cause some difficulty. Such tariffs appear in the guise of consumption taxes or inspection charges, but these are simply subterfuges. Meat, for instance, is largely processed in São Paulo and other states to the south and shipped to Rio de Janeiro. On the meat shipped by one packing company from São Paulo in 1933, the consumption tax averaged 12 per cent of the value. This is a big hurdle to overcome, in view of the competition from some products which are not similarly assessed, and in view of the fact that the tax cannot be entirely shifted to consumers. In time, interstate tariffs and charges of various types will probably cause less difficulty than they do at the present time, for now all governmental units are attempting to bolster a greatly reduced annual income.

Perhaps it is unnecessary to mention that branch plants would have a much greater chance for successful operation if it were not for the high tariffs between South American countries. If a branch factory in Buenos Aires could serve Uruguay, Paraguay, and Bolivia, in addition to Argentina, its total volume would be appreciably increased and its production costs would be lower. But high tariffs make this impracticable, and therefore a plant is restricted to the volume afforded by the demand of only one nation. For some products there is little doubt that the elimination of tariff barriers and reliance on a branch plant in a neighboring country would be economically advantageous to both countries involved. It would, however, reduce governmental revenue, and therefore it is not to be expected.

Taxation

The right of taxation may be so exercised that it is prejudicial to the interests of all business enterprises, whether they are of local or of foreign origin, or it may be exercised in such a manner that it is prejudicial only to the latter, and thus discriminatory. Taxes may be of such nature that they impose undue burdens on business from an administrative, or compliance, standpoint. Furthermore, the level of taxation may jeopardize the interests of branch plants. If taxes on business enterprises are unduly high, the prices charged for the commodities produced are necessarily higher, total demand is consequently lessened, and the opportunities for profitable operation are decreased. A high general level of taxation will have much the same effect, through the reduction of purchasing power. When it is recalled that the demand even in the largest and most advanced South American countries is often barely sufficient to permit manufacture at reasonable costs, the importance of any factor which tends to reduce demand is recognized. Although the nature and the extent of taxation are thus seen to be of considerable significance to migrating concerns, major interest has centered about discrimination and evasion, since foreign concerns are always fearful of taxation which will injure their competitive position. First, however, a brief statement will be made in regard to the former topics.

In all South American countries taxation is predominantly of the indirect type. Chief reliance is placed on the revenue secured from tariffs, consumption taxes, the so-called nuisance taxes, and monopolies in such products as salt and matches. Federal district taxation in Brazil in the years from 1926 to 1931, inclusive, averaged 83.6 per cent indirect and 16.4 per cent direct.[7] The taxation of the Brazilian states is indirect to an even greater extent. Argentina relies somewhat more on direct taxation than does any other South American country, but even there the customs duties averaged 42 per cent of the total federal government revenues during the 1920–1930 decade.[8] Newer countries with a lesser economic development are forced to rely on indirect methods of taxation largely because the administration of such taxes is much less difficult. The collection of property or income taxes depends on a well-developed administrative technique; otherwise, evasion is not difficult. The inability of South American governments to collect such levies with any effectiveness has been demonstrated time after time. Then, also, another reason why property, particularly land, has not been taxed has been the political influence of the rich land-owning classes.

The so-called nuisance taxes, which are a direct heritage from the Spanish and Portuguese colonizers, tend to persist. Among them, stamp taxes are the most common, being widely used in all South American countries. Stamps must be placed on all important business documents,

[7] Sir Otto Niemeyer, G.B.E., K.C.B., *Reorganization of Brazilian National Finance* (Rio de Janeiro: The British Chamber of Commerce in Brazil), p. 13.

[8] *Direccion General de Estadistica de la Nacion*, Boletin No. 209, pp. 19, 36.

including promissory notes, contracts, invoices, and, in some countries, even checks; otherwise, the instrument has no legal standing. Then there are numerous other taxes which, although not oppressive, are bothersome to business executives. Compliance is costly, both from the clerical standpoint and because of the executive attention demanded. While some of these are of long standing, many are of recent origin, having been enacted to bolster up the revenue from tariff charges, which diminished rapidly after 1929. At each legislative session new levies were devised, most of them hastily and without sufficient analysis and forethought. Brazil has an annual tax on business establishments which is based on two considerations—the type of business and the number of men employed; a license tax of city or state origin on a like basis; a tax imposed on buildings according to their rental value; a profits tax on manufacturing concerns; and excise taxes on a wide variety of articles, including cement, textiles, tobacco, beverages, and many others. In Argentina there are taxes of every conceivable sort. Some of those which affect branch plants to the greatest extent are taxes on gasoline, tires, foreign remittances, business profits, and insurance; also, charges for governmental analyses of various products and charges for the authorization and inspection of corporations. In addition, there is an income tax and a tax on transactions. It is not our purpose to list here all the taxes that are in use, but only to show that there is a multiplicity of them and that many are of the nuisance variety. Furthermore, many of them were hastily conceived and are ineffectively and arbitrarily administered. Frequently it is difficult to determine just what payment the government demands and therefore just what full compliance entails. In the case of excise taxes, there is little question of the amount demanded per unit manufactured, but it is sometimes hard to determine the number of units to which the tax applies. The government places in the plant inspectors who are expected to check the output figures. Since the companies are frequently forced to pay the salaries of these individuals, the cost of inspection really constitutes additional taxation.

There is one further type of taxation which has become increasingly important in the past few years and which in time may be subversive to the interests of branch plants. It is taxation designed to finance social legislation. An example will aid our analysis. In Uruguay, for the purpose of financing retirement pensions, business concerns are assessed 9 per cent of their payroll. In addition, 5 per cent is deducted from the amount due the worker, and a three-mill tax is imposed on net sales for the same purpose. For each of two branch plants, the payments to the government on this account were actually 25 per cent of the total payroll. Socialistic activities are more advanced in Uruguay than in any other South American country; hence, it may not be safe to generalize from the situation there. But if questionable, costly, and poorly administered social experiments are to be financed through levies on business, particularly on business financed from abroad, then there is little hope of profitable operation for branch plants. More will be said later about socialistic tendencies. Here it is sufficient to observe that such tendencies may lead to higher taxation in the future than has been imposed in the past.

Despite the number of taxes, the total taxation of business enterprises in the ABC countries is not unduly high. In fact, before the unfortunate economic changes of the past few years, which necessitated more internal taxation, it was almost negligible. In a situation such as that in South America, where the chief reliance is placed on revenue from tariffs, business concerns are not likely to be excessively burdened. Branch plant executives, with but few exceptions, do not feel that the degree of taxation is a deterrent to successful business operations. Objection centers on the type of taxation which makes compliance unnecessarily costly, and on the administration of taxes which at times results in discrimination.

There is much talk of taxation which is discriminatory in character, and such taxation is greatly feared by foreign concerns. Perhaps it is somewhat of a bugbear, for there appear to have been but few instances in which taxation was so conceived and applied that foreign interests undoubtedly were discriminated against. But when there is so much talk of a tendency to tax foreign concerns "out of existence," there probably have been instances in which they were unfairly dealt with. Still, in conversations on the subject few actual examples come to light. The fear of adverse action is not an unnatural one, however, for foreign concerns are vulnerable because of their dominant position in particular branches of industry—for instance, the packing and the tire industries in Argentina, and public utilities in each of the ABC countries. There is an opportunity for governments to force foreign interests to contribute heavily to tax revenues, and there has undoubtedly been the desire to do so on the part of certain legislators; nevertheless, there is little evidence to indicate that discrimination was contemplated by those who have actually framed tax legislation.

Indirectly, however, taxation has at times resulted in some measure of discrimination. When a product manufactured exclusively by foreign companies is taxed and competing substitutes manufactured by locally financed companies are not, a competitive advantage is given to the latter. This has happened in two instances, to the knowledge of the writer, and perhaps in many more. There is likewise some measure of discrimination against public utility enterprises in Brazil. These companies must have manufacturing and repair facilities for their servicing work, and it would be profitable for them to use these facilities in part for commercial work. However, taxation prevents public utility companies from so doing. When the shops are used only for company purposes, they are free of taxation, but when any commercial work is done, no matter how little, they become subject to all business taxes. In other words, both the utility and the commercial facilities are then taxed as business property. Under such circumstances the extent of taxation is out of all proportion to the potential profits from commercial work. Therefore, in effect, the tax structure denies a public utility the right to do work for others, in connection with its own manufacturing and repair activities, and thus discriminates against the public utility in favor of smaller producers.

Furthermore, evasion of taxation may have the same result as open discrimination. If there is evasion on the part of one company, and another directly competing company is forced by the exigencies of the situation to pay in full, faulty administration has brought about discrimination. As noted previously, the technique and the organization for the collection of internal taxes have not been developed to any great extent in South American countries. Therefore, evasion of taxes is not unusual. The native companies are smaller and less noticeable than are their competitors of foreign origin. They are not so likely to have adequate records. Moreover, if they are caught in evasion, disciplinary measures are not likely to be so severe. Foreign concerns, on the other hand, are watched closely. They must comply fully with the demands of the government in all respects, in order to protect their position, and if any evasion of taxes is discovered, whether it was premeditated or otherwise, the fines imposed may be out of all proportion to the seriousness of the offense. In Brazil, for instance, the government demands $1\frac{1}{2}$ per cent of all gross revenues from public transportation agencies, for the maintenance of a pension fund. In addition, employees must be given a fifteen-day vacation period with pay. A firm such as the Brazilian Traction, Light & Power Co., Ltd., which is of Canadian origin, and which operates both street railways and busses, must meet these demands punctiliously. Whether it would wish to evade either the tax or the vacation provisions is beside the point. A foreign company cannot afford to do so. The risk is too great. On the other hand, it is quite likely that small bus companies, in direct competition with the Brazilian Traction, Light & Power Co., Ltd., do evade the tax on gross revenue either partially or wholly, and that they pay little attention to the vacation provision. As long as there is a lack of effective administration of internal taxation, this condition, which in effect is discriminatory against foreign concerns, will persist.

Foreign concerns frequently have some protection against either unduly high or discriminatory taxation in the concessions given them by the government at the time of their entrance. Some companies have not thought it advisable to accept such a favor as the waiving of taxation for a period of years, even though tendered, but others have obtained agreements to the effect that no taxes would be imposed for a determined future period. This type of provision appears to have been much more common in Brazil than elsewhere. Whether it is advisable to negotiate for tax exemption is open to doubt, for the granting of such a favor may pave the way for demands of other types upon the company at a later date. But considered only from the standpoint of taxation, concessions probably constitute an effective protection, if not against all taxation, at least against excessive taxation. Firms do not actually expect to evade all taxation for the stipulated period, but the provision will probably hold until such time as a firm is less noticeable and more able to protect itself by other means.

Although there is some limited evidence to the contrary, it does not appear that the taxation power of South American governments has been used in such a manner that it has seriously prejudiced the interests of branch plants. This does not necessarily indicate, however, that the tax power will not be so used in the future. In the past few years there has been an increase in the taxation of business enterprises, and taxes when once levied tend to persist.

Furthermore, there has been a tendency to place taxes on business to finance social experiments, and such action does not augur well for the future. When we recall the rapidity with which tariffs have been changed, it does not appear wise to expect that favorable conditions in regard to taxation will last indefinitely.

Chapter 6

GOVERNMENTAL CONTROL OF BUSINESS ACTIVITIES

Until recently, business in South America has been relatively free from governmental interference and attempted control. Only in isolated instances have governments prescribed rigid conditions under which business concerns were supposed to operate. But the unfortunate economic position into which these countries were thrown by the depression intensified control efforts, and these, at times, have been detrimental to concerns operating branch plants. The ABC countries, and Uruguay in particular, have followed the general tendency away from a policy dictated by laissez-faire doctrine and have adopted many rules and regulations which affect business materially. In the past decade each country has instituted a large body of social legislation. This will be discussed in the latter part of the chapter. First, however, we will consider attempted regulation of longer standing which has been subversive to the interests of those North American companies which process raw materials and agricultural products.

The meat-packing companies, the oil companies, and those interested in nitrates for many years have been subject to some measure of control. They are particularly vulnerable because the products in which they deal are very important to the national economy. When it is recalled that foreign companies practically dominate the processing and exportation of Uruguayan and Argentine meats, the extraction of Chilean copper and nitrates, and, to a lesser degree, the extraction and refining of Argentine petroleum, the motivation behind government regulation and control is not difficult to comprehend. It proceeds in part from a distrust and fear of the motives, the power, and the actions of all large, capitalistic foreign organizations. Rumors of the misuse of power by the oil companies in other countries, particularly in Mexico, although in most cases unfounded, have had a disquieting effect and have prompted regulatory action. In addition, socialistic elements have been active in denouncing foreign concerns. They have used as ammunition such phrases as "foreign economic domination," "dollar diplomacy," and others of like implication. Furthermore, the activities of the packers and the oil companies have not been without regulation in the United States, and this may have suggested like action to other countries. Finally, regulation really may have been needed to protect the public interest. Under the circumstances, it would have been noteworthy indeed if there had not been some attempt at control.

It is not the fact of regulation, but the singular ineptness of the attempts to regulate, which has been subversive to the interests of foreign concerns. Intelligent regulation is not difficult to cope with, nor is it likely to arouse undue antagonism on the part of the business concerns affected. But regulation which can serve no good purpose and under which there is no possibility of profitable operation, perhaps no possibility of operation at all, has been the lot of certain North American companies. First we will consider the attempted regulation of the packing companies, and later that of the oil companies.

Regulation of the Packing Industry

Before specific regulatory measures are considered, some further information is needed to acquaint the reader with the interrelationships between livestock producers, the packing companies, and the government. The packing industry in Argentina and Uruguay is in truth affected with a public interest, and for that reason difficulties have arisen for the packing companies. Of total Argentine exports, 35 to 40 per cent are of livestock products. The producers of livestock are the aristocracy of the country and are politically coherent, being banded together in the time-honored and politically powerful organization, *Sociedad Rural Argentina*. Between this group and the European market we find the packing companies. They are, with two or three relatively unimportant exceptions, foreign-owned and controlled. Included are Swift International Corporation, Armour & Company, Wilson & Company, Inc., and the huge Anglo concern, of British origin. Only one company in the export trade, Sansinena, appears to be entirely Argentine-owned, and it has never been successful. Here we have a large measure of foreign domination, and domination of a portion of the Argentine economy which is of utmost significance to the welfare of the nation, particularly to the influential and politically active group.

Under such conditions, it is not at all surprising that Argentines have at times been irritated by the degree of foreign participation in the meat trade and that they have envied the control exercised and the profits achieved by the packing companies. Some native control has been secured in both Argentina and Uruguay, but, because of ineffective management it has resulted in losses rather than profits. In 1928, the Uruguayan government acquired a packing plant which has since been operated as a national project. While Argentina as a nation has not engaged in the packing industry, the city of Buenos Aires owns and operates a municipal packing plant. Neither of these projects has achieved even a modicum of success, and, in view of this fact, there should be a large measure of doubt in regard to government participation in the packing industry. Still, the Argentine government has been flirting with the idea for some time, and eventually the packing companies will, in all likelihood, be competing with a nationalized unit. Each legislature spends a part of its time in considering bills for the nationalization of the packing industry or for additional control of the independent companies now operating.

Regulation and control are the outgrowth of depressed conditions in the meat trade. When things are going smoothly and prices are high, there is little agitation against the packers, but when prices are on the down grade and producers are not making adequate returns, there is always the inclination to blame the packing interests and to accuse them of taking too high margins, of combining to drive down the prices paid to producers, and of using unfair methods. The first major attempts at control appeared after the 1920 depression. During the period between 1921 and 1924, three laws were passed for regulation of the industry. They were known as the Minimum Price Law, the Live Weight Law, and the Packers Control Act. Of these, the Minimum Price Law, Number 11,227, was by far the most difficult to cope with. This law, briefly summarized and freely translated, was in part as follows:

Article 1. This law empowered the Chief Executive to fix periodically minimum buying prices for cattle intended for export. Such prices should not be below the average calculated cost price. Power was also given to establish maximum prices for the sale of meat intended for local consumption in the Capital of the Republic and the national territories.

Article 2. This article prescribed the appointment of an advisory committee of six members to cooperate with the Chief Executive in giving effect to the law. One of these members was to be nominated by the packing companies.

Article 4. This article proposed that the committee should suggest to the Chief Executive the minimum and maximum prices referred to in Article 1.

Article 6. This article provided a penalty of 100,000 pesos for infraction of the law. It also contained a provision whereby an establishment could be closed down by the Chief Executive in the event of repetition of an infraction.[1]

These provisions indicate the severity and the uneconomic character of the law. It was an extraordinary piece of legislation, and it had highly unusual results. Five

---

[1] This information was taken from p. 677 of the Sept. 21, 1923, issue of the *Review of the River Plate*. It is not a direct quotation.

members of the committee were appointed, the sixth place remaining vacant, since the packing companies refused to cooperate.

About thirty days after the promulgation of the law, the first prices were established by presidential decree. Three prices were set, one each for cattle purchased for export in the form of chilled, frozen, and continental beef. The prices were 27, 24, and 19 centavos per kilo for cattle on the hoof suitable for these three types of beef. The packing companies were compelled to pay these prices at the *estancias*,[2] despite the fact that there were a number of recognized grades within each type and that the cattle would come from different parts of the country. Moreover, the prices set were somewhat above those generally prevailing in the weeks prior to the decree. They were too high to permit profitable operation by the packing companies, in view of the market situation in the European countries to which shipments were habitually made. Therefore, the packers simply refused to buy cattle, and for a number of days operations were virtually at a standstill. Although cattle were offered, the companies could not take the risk of buying below the prices established in the decree, for by so doing they would become subject to the heavy fine provided in Article 6 of the law.

In explaining their position, executives of the packing companies stated that compliance with the decree was commercially impossible, that the effect of the law would be to ruin cattle producers as well as the packing companies, and that prices were not, as a matter of fact, set by the packers, but by the consuming markets in Europe. They also stated that their failure to purchase was not merely a demonstration in opposition to all regulatory measures but that they had no alternative other than heavy losses if the provisions of the law were adhered to. Furthermore, they declared it to be their belief that the law was unconstitu-

[2] The word *estancia* refers to the extensive land holdings of an Argentine livestock producer.

tional. However, since the situation could not await judicial interpretation of the constitutionality of the law, they suspended purchase until some satisfactory understanding could be reached with the government.

It soon became apparent that the packers were in a stronger position than the government, or, at least, than those individuals or groups who sponsored the measure. Obviously the stalemate could not be allowed to continue. Memorials poured in upon the committee and the Chief Executive, protesting against the action of the government and demanding that something be done. More often than otherwise, criticism was directed, not at the action of the packing companies in their refusal to purchase, but at the legislation which had created the difficulty. The following excerpt from one of the memorials presented to the government is illustrative of the general attitude taken by the cattle producers:

> It is evident that the men and the institutions who promoted the sanction of the minimum price law had in view the stabilization of the prices for our meat. The law having been passed and put into force by the Executive Power, its only effect up to the present has been to paralyze totally all transactions in export beef cattle. The Executive Power is urged to do something to restore normal conditions. If it cannot do so, it will be necessary to admit that in practice the legislation referred to is contrary to the interests of the producers it was designed to protect, and in that case it will be necessary to arrive at the quickest way of repealing it.[3]

Other memorials stated that it was not in accordance with the general interests of the country to push to extremes the restrictive measures against the packing companies, who, in order to carry on their business abroad with success, needed to be free from hindrances which might prevent them from marketing meat successfully.

The pressure brought to bear was finally of sufficient strength to cause the government to withdraw from its

---

[3] *Review of the River Plate*, Oct. 26, 1923, p. 971.

untenable position. About two weeks after the law went into effect, a presidential decree appeared which suspended for a six months' period the authorization of the executive power to fix minimum prices for the purchase of beef and cattle for export purposes. The law itself has not yet been repealed, but there have been no further attempts to set buying prices for cattle, at least formally. Some pressure was exerted after the 1930 revolution; of this more will be said presently.

The second of the regulatory measures was called the Live Weight Law. The implication behind this law was that livestock producers were being dealt with unfairly through the practice of estimating the weight of cattle rather than actually weighing them. The law stated that all transactions in cattle intended for internal consumption or export must be effected at a unit price of so much per kilo, live weight. All purchasers of cattle were required to install weighing machines, the control of which was intrusted to the Ministry of Agriculture. Although compliance with this law involved some additional bother and expense, little objection was voiced by the packers. As a matter of fact, the greatest inconvenience was suffered by the small plants supplying the local trade.

The third and most extensive measure, the Packers Control Act (Number 11,226) contained numerous provisions, all designed to obtain for the government information on the intimate details of the packers' operations. It required among other things that each meat-packing establishment be registered with the Ministry of Agriculture, and such registration imposed upon the establishment the following obligations: to adjust the prices of its services to a tariff approved by the Ministry of Agriculture; to inform the Ministry of Agriculture in detail of the transactions effected in the establishment, according to the form which the executive power ordained in the regulations; to keep a set of books clear and precise, showing its entire business on the basis of the books required by the Commercial Code . . . and to present such reports, accounts, statistics, and other data of general interest as the bylaws might call for; and to facilitate the access of inspectors of the Ministry of Agriculture for the purpose of examining and controlling the accounting, subsidiary books, registers, correspondence, and other documents, except those relating to secret industrial processes or formulas pertaining to the realm of invention.[4] Numerous prohibitions were placed upon the packers in regard to such matters as concealing or falsifying true profits, taking monopolistic action, apportioning among themselves the supply going into the European markets, discriminating among those from whom they purchased, and failing to take sanitary precautions.

The packing companies protested against the provisions of this law, and particularly against the right given to the Ministry of Agriculture to inspect their accounts, correspondence, and all other documents at will. If the law were strictly administered, all independence of action, and undoubtedly all privacy of action, would be withdrawn from the packing companies. Fortunately, conditions in the meat trade improved, agitation subsided, and for nearly a decade there was little attempt to enforce the law. Perhaps the government's inability to enforce the Minimum Price Law aroused some misgivings about its ability to enforce any of the legislation directed at the meat trade. At any rate, nothing was done; in fact, the constitutionality of the law was never tested until 1934.

Between 1923 and 1930 there was little attempt at regulation, but the effect of the recent depression upon the livestock industry again set the pot to boiling. Agitation continued for some years with no very decisive results. The first action taken, in point of time, was in part an outgrowth of the 1930 revolution. The provisional government "suggested" that the price of cattle usable for chilled beef be maintained at 29 centavos per kilo, and conditions

[4] This information was secured from the *Review of the River Plate*, Oct. 5, 1923, p. 799.

were so upset that the request could not well be ignored. The government's action was based at least partially on political expediency, and results might have been unfortunate if any resistance had been offered. But, from the economic standpoint, the effect of maintaining an artificially high price for cattle was likewise unfortunate. Argentine chilled beef in England became relatively dear in comparison to frozen beef from Australia and New Zealand, and in comparison to pork products from Denmark. Furthermore, Britain's ability to buy quality meats at maintained prices was decreasing as the depression became more severe and this necessitated the purchase of lower qualities imported from the Dominions. The net result was that the high purchase price for cattle curtailed the amount of Argentine meat sold in Europe and thus failed to clear the cattle from the Argentine *estancias*. Later there was an overabundance of heavy cattle which should have been sold earlier and which finally were sold at very low prices.

About the middle of 1931 there appeared another piece of questionable regulation, the aim of which was to overcome imagined unfairness on the part of the packers in dealing with the livestock producers. A decree was issued which forbade the sale of livestock on a consignment basis. Previously, when the number of cattle offered by a producer was too small to justify sending a buyer to his *estancia*, or when the cost of so doing was too high because of distance, the packing companies often permitted the producer to send the cattle to the plant, where they were graded and a price was determined. Admittedly, the producer had to depend somewhat on the honesty of the company, for reshipment either back to the *estancia* or to another plant would not have been feasible. Still, the producer had every chance to determine whether the price which he received was in accordance with the market on the day of sale. Forbidding this procedure was harmful to the small producer, for he was denied the possibility of selling direct to the large packers and was thus forced to sell at auction or to dispatch the cattle to the large market at Liniers or other local markets.

It soon became apparent that, as a result of this regulatory measure, the producers were getting less for their cattle than formerly, instead of more. About six months after the decree went into effect, there was a rumor that it was to be annulled. This the Minister of Agriculture flatly denied. However, a new decree did appear shortly which in effect was an annulment. It provided that each packing plant should propose a scale of prices for the various grades of cattle. When this scale was accepted by the seller, the cattle could be dispatched to the plant, there classified, and their value determined according to the scale of prices previously agreed upon. If the prices were strictly adhered to, the value level would be set before shipment; however, the determination of price is so largely a matter of grading that the effect of this decree was largely to reestablish the old consignment system.

During the latter part of 1932 the position of the packing companies was seriously threatened by the attempts of the government to control the meat quota which had been established for Argentina after the Ottawa Conference between the various members of the British Empire. This, in turn, would have given the Argentine government an appreciable measure of control over the packing companies. The conference at Ottawa was held in an effort to establish closer trade connections between the Dominions and the mother country. Imperial preference appeared to be the watchword of the conference, and the Dominions did everything possible to secure a preferential position for their products in the British market. Australia, New Zealand, and British South Africa were exporters of meat, and they were anxious to secure the British market, which was supplied in large part by Argentina. Although the English spokesmen were loath to accede to their demands, still it was a bargaining affair and concessions were needed by all parties. Therefore, an agreement was reached which allowed the Dominions some additional volume, by restriction of imports from South America under a quota system.[5] A further purpose of the quota system was to relieve the crisis in British livestock production which had been caused by low prices and high comparative costs.

Argentina was greatly perturbed during the progress of the Ottawa Conference. It was feared that the Dominions would be given a large measure of preference and that exports from Argentina would thereby be seriously curtailed. In an effort to prevent this, the government and the packing companies had a common objective, and both were active in espousing the Argentine cause before British officials. Of particular aid in this crisis was Sir Edmund Vestey, Bart., the head of the Vestey interests, which included the Anglo packing plant in Argentina. Had it not been for his influence, the South American meat trade with England might have been dealt a much more severe blow by the decisions at Ottawa.[6] After the quotas were set, however, the community of interest between the government and the packing companies was quickly submerged by a struggle for control of the quotas which had been set by the British government. If the Argentine government had been given full control of the apportionment of the quotas, then the packing companies would have been in an unfortunate position, for the government could have determined how much could be shipped by each, likewise what kind of

[5] The quota allowed for Argentina did not decrease exportations drastically. It was based on quantities exported between July 1, 1931, and June 30, 1932. The quota allowed for frozen meats was approximately 80 per cent of the base period. For chilled beef, the quota was the same as the base period. This, however, was a severe reduction compared to exports of other years, for the base year was a period of relatively light exports. For a complete account of the quotas see the *Review of the River Plate*, Nov. 4, 1932, p. 21, or *La Prensa*, June 15, 1933, editorial comment. Later, the quotas were reduced 10 per cent for a limited period of time, originally eighteen months.

[6] Two pamphlets were published by Sir Edmund Vestey, Bart., for private distribution, one of which was called "A Message, Ottawa Imperial Preference and Meat," and the other "Britain's Economic Insanity, Ottawa —and Then?"

meat, and the time of shipments. The packing companies would have been in a large measure at the mercy of the government. Furthermore, at that time the government was considering legislative measures aimed at the acquisition and operation of a national packing plant. With the government having full control of the quotas, this unit could have been given every advantage over the independent concerns. Without such control and in a freely competitive situation, a nationalized plant would have had little hope of successful operation, in view of the strongly entrenched position of the independent companies in the British market.

Since 1914, there has been apportionment of the chilled beef exports from Argentina and Uruguay to England, through mutual agreement between the packing companies. Agreements are highly necessary if such a perishable product is to be marketed in an orderly manner, and if gluts and shortages on the market and deterioration of product are to be prevented. A regular supply of known qualities is needed to meet the demands of the market adequately.[7] Agreements are effectuated by apportionment of refrigerated space on the boats which run on regular schedule between the two continents. Conferences between the packing and shipping interests are held regularly to decide schedules for the meat trade and assign space to the various companies. In view of this developed organization for the control of meat imports, it was only to be expected that the English Board of Trade, entrusted with the administration of the meat quotas, should turn to the packers for aid and cooperation. This the Board of Trade proceeded to do, for it thus was relieved of the need for setting up new administrative machinery, which would simply have duplicated the organization that was already operating effectively.

The action of the Board of Trade in dealing with the apportionment committee of the packers directly, instead

---

[7] For a description and an economic justification of the apportionment agreements between the packing companies see Putnam, *op. cit.*, Chap. 6.

of through the Argentine government, raised a storm of protest in Argentina. Editorial comment in *La Prensa* and *La Nacion* was particularly severe. It was alleged that the English government had usurped the right of Argentina to regulate the activities of its own industries, and had denied to Argentina the liberty to deal as it saw fit with foreign concerns operating within its borders. Commentators asserted that by this act the British government had violated the principle of national sovereignty, and that such procedure was without precedent between sovereign states.[8] The controversy had its repercussions even on the floor of the British House of Commons, through the questioning of Captain Anthony Eden, then Under-Secretary for Foreign Affairs, about the "irregularities" in the methods employed by the government in obtaining provisional meat restrictions from South America. Captain Eden answered that there had been no irregularities, and that a quite normal procedure had been followed in dealing with the question of quota administration.[9]

The controversy was carried on through diplomatic channels and with considerable tact during the early months of 1933. At that time a special Argentine mission, under the able leadership of the Vice-President of the Republic, Dr. Julio A. Roca, was in England, attempting to conclude a new Anglo-Argentine commercial treaty. It appears that this question of administration of the meat quotas was one of the most knotty problems dealt with. Argentina wished full control and thus the power to dictate to the packing companies. Great Britain, on the other hand, was not distrustful of the packers' group, which had been apportioning imports for many years. Evidently the British government realized the advantage accruing to the livestock producers in Argentina, to the packing companies,

[8] For an exposition of the Argentine attitude toward this question, see an editorial comment, "El Sistema De Cuotas Ante El Derecho," *La Prensa*, Oct. 29, 1932.

[9] See an Associated Press dispatch from London published under the heading "No Irregularity," in the *Buenos Aires Herald* of Dec. 8, 1932.

and to the British market, from orderly and systematic planning of imports, and was loath to turn over the responsibility for planning to the Argentine government. Moreover, the British negotiators probably thought that the interests of British capital invested in packing enterprises would be jeopardized if the Argentine government were given control over the quotas. The result was a compromise, but a compromise favorable to the packing companies. The Argentine government was given control of 15 per cent of the total amount of chilled beef imported, but only under the condition that a packing plant was acquired and operated by the government. The following are quotations from the protocol of the treaty:

> At the moment of signing the Convention of this day's date relating to trade and commerce between the United Kingdom of Great Britain and Northern Ireland and the Argentine Republic, the undersigned Plenipotentiaries, being duly authorized to this effect by their respective Governments, declare:
> Paragraph 1. That the Argentine Government, fully appreciating the benefits rendered by the collaboration of British capital in public utility and other undertakings, whether State, Municipal, or private, carrying on business in Argentina, and following their traditional policy of friendship, hereby declare their intention to accord to those undertakings as far as lies within their constitutional sphere of action, such benevolent treatment as may conduce to the further economic development of the country and to the due and legitimate protection of the interests concerned in their operation.
> Paragraph 2. That the Government of the United Kingdom is prepared to cooperate with the Argentine Government in a joint inquiry into the economic and financial structure and working of the meat trade, with particular reference to the means to be adopted to ensure a reasonable return to the cattle producers.
> Paragraph 3. That should the Argentine Government or the Argentine producers, operating under a special Law, own, control, or manage undertakings not conducted primarily for private profit but for a better regulation of the trade, with the purpose of assuring a reasonable return to the cattle producer, the Government of the United Kingdom will be prepared to license approved importers to import meat from such undertakings up to fifteen per centum of the total quantity of chilled beef imported from Argentina to the United Kingdom (such percentage to include the imports now permitted from the Frigorífico Gualeguaychú

and the Buenos Aires Municipal Frigorífico) on the understanding that such shipments are efficiently marketed through the normal channels, taking into consideration the necessary coordination of trade in the United Kingdom, and any licenses granted by the Government of the United Kingdom under the provisions of this paragraph will be issued in accordance with this undertaking.[10]

Paragraph 4. That the Government of the United Kingdom will communicate from time to time to the Argentine Government particulars of all licenses issued in respect of the importation of meat from Argentina. . . . [11]

These quotations need little comment. It is evident that the British government would agree to withdraw to but a limited extent from its original position in reference to quota apportionment. The packing companies thus avoided a large measure of potential control which would have been, in all probability, distinctly inimical to their interests. Furthermore, it is likely that the agreement on the apportionment of quotas was a factor in causing the Argentine government to postpone action in regard to the acquisition and operation of a packing plant in competition with the independent concerns. At any rate, no positive action toward the attainment of such an objective has yet been taken (1935).[12]

[10] Of this 15 per cent assigned to the Argentine government for allocation, 4 per cent was allotted to two Argentine packing plants. A further portion was allotted to a new organization known as the "Corporación Argentina de Productores de Carne" which was established under government supervision. For the handling of its livestock this new company made a slaughtering and marketing arrangement with the Sansinena Company and the Smithfield and Argentine Meat Company. The first shipment from the new organization was made in July, 1935, not, as it happened, to England but to France. Undoubtedly many shipments in the future will go to England and be included under the 15 per cent control privilege granted by the Roca-Runciman Agreement.

[11] "The New Anglo-Argentine Commercial Treaty," *Review of the River Plate*, May 5, 1933, p. 17.

[12] Argentina did receive some important concessions in this treaty. The following quotation from p. 7 of the May 5, 1933, issue of the *Review of the River Plate* is illustrative: "It provides a guarantee against the hazards of slashing interference with the country's chilled beef trade with Great Britain

Meanwhile other attempts were being made to control the packing companies in Argentina. Early in 1932 it became apparent that the government would seek to enforce the various provisions of the Packers Control Act (Number 11,226), which had been largely disregarded since 1923.[13] Among other things, this act empowered the government to make a complete inspection of the accounts, correspondence, and other records of the packers, at will. When attempts were made by the Ministry of Agriculture to obtain information under this act, the packers refused to allow inspection of their books. Their position is indicated by the following public statement:

> As His Excellency, The Minister of Agriculture, announced in his speech at Palermo, the Government is requiring strict compliance with law No. 11226, known as the Packers Control Act, and as the Packers have expressed their objection to furnishing certain data which they consider private, the matter will be taken before the proper courts, which will decide whether the interpretation of this law is erroneous or whether it is in parts repugnant to the National Constitution.
>
> The attitude of the Packers is not one of defiance. They merely seek protection from measures that threaten their very existence.
>
> It is the honest belief of the Packers that this law only requires them to furnish statistical data of public interest, such as they have at no time refused to furnish, as the copious daily reports submitted by the Packers to the Ministry bear evidence. This has been the interpretation given the Law by the distinguished gentlemen who in turn have occupied the Minister's chair since the year 1923, when the Law was passed by Congress.
>
> Today an attempt is being made to give this Law far wider scope, even to the extent of investigating the books of the Packers, ascertaining their contracts and cost of production, all of which the Packers consider

---

and in this sense should have the effect of inspiring renewed hope and confidence in the minds of cattle producers. The treaty puts a limit on the exercise of the Ottawa policy; and, as has been very well pointed out, there have been conceded to Argentina some of the privileges attaching to Dominion status. Any fear of new or increased duties on the principal livestock and agricultural products which Argentina ships to Great Britain can no longer exist, as the treaty is explicit on the point that no new or increased duties or charges shall be levied thereupon."

[13] For a defense of the Packers Control Act see *La Prensa*, editorial comment, "Los Operaciones De Los Frigorificos," Dec. 10, 1932.

violates business privacy and attacks that liberty of trade which is guaranteed by the National Constitution.

The Packers are submitting their case to the equanimous judgment of the Argentine Courts.[14]

On October 21, 1932, a presidential decree was issued through the Ministry of Agriculture, which ordered that the department proceed through the accountants and inspectors of the Meat Control Board (Division de Contralor del Comercio de Carne) to examine, in conformity with the ruling of Article II of Law Number 11,226, the accounts, books, and papers of the packing enterprises. The following information was desired by the Meat Control Board in accordance with a resolution issued by the Ministry: (1) the sale price of each of the products and by-products in the country and abroad, and the stock on hand in each case; (2) a copy of the charter-parties in force; (3) the cost of processing various products and by-products, and the expenses per kilo from the purchase of the cattle until delivery to the local or foreign wholesale dealer, butcher, or consumer.[15] A copy of this decree was sent to each of the seven packing companies. Later, when a government representative appeared demanding access to the accounts and other records he was refused. Then, on December 3, 1932, each of the companies was fined 5,000 pesos for noncompliance with the decree. These fines were paid under protest, and an appeal by the packers to the Argentine Supreme Court followed, this being the usual procedure for placing a case before the court.

For almost two years, while the Packers Control Act was in the hands of the Supreme Court for consideration in regard to constitutionality, all interested parties did little but await the decision. The comparative quiet

[14] "The Packers," *Buenos Aires Herald*, Sept. 22, 1933, p. 10.
[15] See *La Nacion*, Oct. 22, 1932, editorial comments, "Sera Revisada La Contabilidad de Los Frigoríficos."

was broken only by one major incident in the spring of 1933, of which more will be said presently. Finally, however, the Argentine Senate could not restrain itself and proceeded to make further demands on the packing companies before the decision was handed down by the Supreme Court. On October 26, 1934, a special committee of the Senate, appointed to inquire into the conditions of the meat trade, adopted a resolution calling for a complete examination of the records of the packing companies. The resolution stated: "The examination of the books of account of the private companies engaged in the purchase, industrialization, and exportation of meats is necessary in order that the purposes of the Committee shall not prove illusory and in order to establish facts essential for its plan of inquiry."[16] It also stated that the packing companies had been asked by the committee to collaborate in its task and to furnish it with concrete information, and, that, although they had agreed to furnish some data, in the main they had excused themselves either openly or by means of evasive answers. The resolution provided for the appointment of three expert accountants, "who, presenting and invoking this resolution, shall call for and examine, wherever in the country they may be found, and in the conditions of time most compatible with the normal use of the same, the commercial books of the following concerns."[17] Five concerns were listed: two North American, two British, and one Argentine. The accountants were charged with acquiring the most complete information possible on such subjects as the following: purchases, classification of cattle bought, costs of processing, schedules of profit and loss of each section of the factory, assets and liabilities both fixed and liquid, inventories, and number of employees and their remuneration. In addition, some of this information was desired over a five-year period for comparative purposes. A term of forty days

[16,17] "Investigation of the Frigorífico Companies' Books," *Review of the River Plate*, Nov. 2, 1934.

was fixed for the experts to present in writing the results and conclusions at which they arrived.

In accordance with the resolution, three accountants were appointed to secure the information.[18] The packing companies protested, both as individuals and as a group, and were accused of disrespect to the Argentine Senate. Then, the packing companies in a joint letter to the Senate attempted to clarify their position. The letter stated:

> The situation which we maintain at present is far from being disrespectful. We have respectfully said that we are willing to submit all the information possible, providing that it does not contain purely commercial secrets, and we have always insisted on recognizing implicitly the power of the Honourable Senate to make investigations in the same manner as the attributions of the judges. But we have also noted that the judges have attributions within the constitutional warranty, and this has been the judgment which the same tribunals of justice have utilized for the examination of our books and papers.[19]

The packers were particularly concerned because the law requiring them to give the information called for was still under consideration by the Argentine Supreme Court. Their attitude is illustrated by the following quotation from a letter addressed by one of the packing companies to Senator Landaburu, the president of the Senate Investigation Commission of the Meat Trade:

> As the defenses of a juridical and constitutional nature invoked by the Company are still awaiting the finding of the Supreme Court, its attitude now would be contradictory and liable to be interpreted as a cession of its rights if it permitted in this case, with no law to authorize

---

[18] One of these was the accountant for the Frigorífico Municipal, the packing plant owned and operated by the city of Buenos Aires, and a competitor of the companies under investigation. The impropriety of this appointment, in view of the access to commercial secrets which was afforded, was noted by the press, and was a subject of protest by the packing companies.

[19] "The Frigoríficos," subheading, "The Frigoríficos publish the following notes which they have sent to the Investigation Commission of the Meat Trade and to the Honourable Senate of the Nation," *Review of the River Plate*, Nov. 16, 1934, p. 24.

such a measure, what it has resisted up till now in the face of the ruling legal dispositions.[20]

Evidently the Senate, on the recommendation of its committee on constitutional affairs, was convinced that it had the perfect right to commission a special investigation committee to inspect the books of the privately owned packing plants even, if necessary, by the use of force. Therefore, the fact that the constitutionality of the Packers Control Act was then being tested in the Supreme Court was of little moment. Regardless of the outcome of the adjudication, the Senate believed that it still had the right so to act that the data from the packers would be obtained. Accordingly, the accountants appointed by the Investigation Committee presented themselves at the packing plants and asked to see the records. They were refused by all the managements. Later in the same day they again appeared, accompanied by the deputy of the Senate. Since this was a technical use of force, the packing companies submitted to the ruling of the Senate under formal protest before a notary public.

At this stage of the controversy the Supreme Court on November 19, 1934, finally rendered its decision on the Packers Control Act. By a unanimous vote the court declared the Act to be constitutional. Moreover, it said that the right of a committee of accountants appointed by the Senate to inspect the books and documents of the packing companies was consistent with the meaning of the Act.[21] In view of this decision by the final legal

[20] *Review of the River Plate*, Nov. 16, 1934, p. 25.

[21] Although constitutional interpretation is not a major interest in this study, it might be well to observe that "according to the finding of the Court, Article 14 of the Constitution grants 'the right'—not the freedom— to work and carry on in any legitimate industrial undertaking. It is considered, however, that this right must be subordinated to the terms of existing laws and that on the strength of other constitutionally recognized attributes, Congress is fully empowered to exercise control over the operation of the stated rights in the stated spheres of enterprise." (*Review of the River Plate*, Nov. 23, 1934, p. 3.)

authority, there was only one course open to the packing companies, and that was compliance with the demands under the law. This the North American companies realized. The controversy was over, the other side had won, and the only thing to do was to conform with the decision. Consequently, arrangements were made with the Senate Investigation Committee, office space was provided for the work, and the records were made available. Soon afterward, another group of accountants was appointed by the Meat Control Board to see that the provisions relating to records and accounts in the Act were fully complied with by the packing companies.

At this point something approaching comedy entered into the situation.[22] Whereas the North American companies decided to place no further obstacles in the way of the Senate in obtaining the desired information, the British Anglo company still maintained a defiant attitude. After the decision of the Supreme Court, it was only good business policy for the packers to withdraw gracefully from their former position, but evidently the Anglo company thought that the Argentine government would hardly dare risk offending the British government by pressing the matter, in the event that the records demanded were withheld. The Anglo company represented British capital engaged in the meat trade between the supplier and the mother country, and the company thought that enough influence could be exerted to prevent action of a disciplinary character by the Argentine government. As a result, the accountants in the employ of the Senate Investigation Committee reported that they had experienced some difficulty in carrying on their task, especially at the Anglo company, and that they had not been permitted to examine the records showing the cost price of different meats, which was one of the essential facts required in the plan of investi-

---

[22] Information in regard to this incident was partially secured from the article entitled "Inspection of Frigorifico Companies' Books," *Review of the River Plate*, Nov. 23, 1934, p. 19.

gation. The local manager of the company, when interviewed by the Committee itself, stated that, in accordance with custom, one copy of cost sheets was sent to London and the other was destroyed. He also admitted that he had recently suppressed the costs department of the firm's office, apparently to prevent the government from obtaining the requisite data. In view of this attitude, the Senate Committee ordered his arrest until he should exhibit the records required. Accordingly, he was arrested and conducted to the central police department by the deputy of the Senate. This action created great indignation in the British community, and shortly afterward he was "confined" to his own home under guard.

In the meantime someone informed the government that records of the Anglo firm were being shipped from Buenos Aires to England under the marking of corned beef. The government, with the assistance of a contingent of police, forthwith searched a Blue Star liner which was about to sail and confiscated twenty-one cases which were found in the hold of the ship and which contained Anglo records. These were conveyed under guard to the Senate chambers, there to await inspection by the accountants appointed by the Committee. Later, the Anglo company again attempted to send records abroad, and these likewise were seized. Accusations and recriminations passed between Sir Edmund Vestey in London and the Vice-President of the Argentine Republic, Dr. Julio A. Roca.[23] The charge was made that there had been discrimination against the Anglo company. Dr. Roca replied that there had been no discrimination, inasmuch as the other packing companies had not resisted the efforts of the Senate to obtain the desired information after Law Number 11,226 was declared constitutional by the Supreme Court. A member of the Senate Investigation Committee made a further accusation to the effect that the Anglo company

[23] "The Frigorífico Anglo Case," *Review of the River Plate*, Dec. 14, 1934, p. 21.

had failed to return some cost records from England as it had promised. This accusation was flatly denied by the submanager of the Anglo company. A telegram from the English offices of the company stated: "We very much resent report published that cost statements we promised were not returned. This absolutely untrue. The original documents without any replacement or substitution by *Highland Patriot* December 8, 1934."[24] With this final recrimination the outward evidences of the controversy ceased. Undoubtedly the whole incident was uncalled for, and the Anglo company brought discomfiture upon itself by its unwillingness to conform with the decision of the Court. Moreover, considerable ill will undoubtedly remains between the company and the various government entities, and this may have its repercussions in later relationships.

Another test of the Packers Control Act, likewise directed at the Anglo company, occurred in the spring of 1933. Action in this instance was probably brought under a part of Article 6, which stated that a packing company should "refrain from any deceitful action in the conduct of its business and from any procedure creating unfair distinction between persons or places served by the establishment."[25] The action which was considered by the Argentine authorities to be reprehensible involved the classification of a herd of cattle purchased by the Anglo concern. The cattle were purchased as "freezers," a rough, inferior type, not suitable for export in the form of high-grade chilled beef. When the herd was slaughtered, however, it was found to be of higher grade than had been expected, and part of it was eventually shipped as chilled beef. Somehow this fact was discovered by the producer, and he lodged a complaint with the Ministry of Agriculture, which was charged with administration of the control

[24] "The Frigorífico Anglo Case," *Review of the River Plate*, Feb. 15, 1935, p. 19.
[25] *Review of the River Plate*, Oct. 5, 1923, p. 799.

law. Subsequently the Anglo company was fined 30,000 pesos for having bought cattle at a price lower than their actual value through deliberately misrepresenting quality at the time of the purchase. This, at least, was the charge against the company. Exception was taken to the charge, not only by the company, but by all the packers through a joint communication.[26]

The Anglo company's statement pointed out a number of extenuating circumstances in this particular case. The company claimed that classification of this particular lot of cattle had been very difficult, in view of the weather and the lack of help to accomplish the task, that the cattle had been a mixed lot and therefore difficult to classify, and that because of the small size of the herd the company had not reclassified it at the time of loading; in fact, that it was quite possible that the herd had become mixed with other herds between the time of classification by the Anglo representative and the time of shipment. The company also stated that the herd had been classified by other cattle dealers but had been rejected because of its roughness, weight, and age. Furthermore, it was freely admitted that some error might have been made by the company's representative.

The joint statement made by the packing companies covered more general subjects. It pointed out that the terms "chilled" and "freezer" had come to be considered as indicative of value in purchasing, whereas these words actually referred only to the manner of processing for shipment abroad. It was also noted that a chilled-type herd might give as many as five different classifications of chilled meat, each of them of different value, and that it was not unusual for a herd bought in the freezer classification to be processed and shipped as one of the lower values

---

[26] See "Classification of Beef Cattle, a Statement by the Management of the Frigorífico Anglo," *Review of the River Plate*, May 19, 1933, following p. 32, and "Argentine Meat Exportation, Bulletin No. 2," *ibid.*, June 30, 1933, p. 48.

of chilled meat or, on the other hand, to be put in cans. Moreover, it was asserted that a change of intention dictated by business policy in regard to something which has been bought and paid for with no coercion on the part of the purchaser is not a reprehensible act and therefore is not subject to disciplinary measures by government officials. These assertions were of value, for they clarified the position of the packers in regard to purchasing classifications. However, the incident furnished still further proof of the antagonistic and frequently unreasonable attitude of the authorities charged with administration of the measures designed for regulation and control of the packing industry.

When these various regulatory measures are considered as a whole, certain conclusions can be drawn in regard to the objectives sought by the government, the effectiveness of the legislation and other means used to attain these objectives, the extent to which independent decisions by the packers have been curtailed and profitable operation has been made more difficult, and the motivation behind these governmental actions. The objectives appear to have been four in number: the securing of higher prices to producers for livestock, largely through limitation of the profits of the packing companies; the attainment of complete information about the operations of the packers in order to institute and facilitate control; the apportionment of the British meat quotas among the packers; and the elimination of what was thought to be "sharp practice" by the packers in their dealings with livestock producers.

Realization of the first of these objectives was attempted originally through the ill-conceived Minimum Price Law, with which compliance was refused. Under such arbitrary price control by the government, profitable operation by the packers would have been very unlikely. Moreover, controlled prices are likely to be high prices, and high prices for Argentine meat would have diminished exports, in view of the fact that various suppliers meet the needs of the British market. Later, in 1930, the government again attempted direct price control by "suggesting" that a buying price of twenty-nine centavos per kilo be maintained. This price was too high, in view of the competitive situation and the generally declining prices for meats, but the packing companies, because of the uncertain state of political affairs, complied. As a result, exports were curbed and cattle were not cleared from the *estancias*. Finally, to dispose of the surplus of cattle, which had become too heavy for the chilled beef trade, the producers had to accept very low prices. Government tampering with the buying price on cattle was inimical to the best interests of both the packing companies and the cattle producers. It may have had some political advantage, but this likewise can be doubted.

The Packers Control Act was designed primarily to force the packing companies to divulge confidential information on their operations. From this the government hoped to ascertain exactly how much the companies were making from participation in the meat trade. Previous legislative acts had required that all companies with limited liability should furnish the government with an annual profit and loss statement to be published in the *Diario Official*. This requirement was met by the packers, but evidently there was some question in regard to the accuracy of the statements. With complete accounting data available for analysis, it was expected that excessive profits, if there were such, could be discovered and in some manner eliminated. Little was done to enforce the provisions of the law until approximately ten years after its adoption. In 1934, as the result of attempts at enforcement, the law was tested in the Argentine Supreme Court and declared constitutional.

With this authority, there can be little doubt that the government has obtained some additional information about the operations of the packing plants. But even if a thorough analysis has been, or will be, obtained of the data made available on packing operations—which is questionable—the problem remains of translating the information secured into positive regulatory action. If low processing costs are discovered, as they undoubtedly will be in the larger plants, this does not mean that such costs can be duplicated in government-owned and operated plants. Efficient operation has not been the outstanding characteristic of government packing plants in either Argentina or Uruguay. If larger profits are discovered than those currently stated, this does not necessarily indicate that the position of the cattle producer or the country as a whole would be improved by attempting to limit profits or by ousting the foreign interests. Profits are the result of efficiency in management, and such efficiency would have to be duplicated if the country were to benefit from government ownership. Furthermore, profits induce the packing companies to secure supplies from Argentina rather than elsewhere. If profits were limited too greatly by regulatory action, it might be to the packers' interest to stimulate production and exports from Australia and British South Africa, thereby dealing a severe blow to the Argentine. At any rate, information secured must be translated into regulatory action to be effective, and it is too early to predict with any confidence the future action of the government.

Little need be said about the attempt of the government to gain control of the British meat quotas. Had the British government granted the Argentine requests, there would have been opportunity for onerous control measures, and, furthermore, the Argentine government's entry into the meat trade would have been facilitated. Therefore, the refusal of the British government relieved the packing companies, at least for the moment, both from direct regulation and from direct competition.

The Live Weight Law, the Consignment Decree, and the action regarding classification, all had as their objective the elimination of unfair practice by the packing companies.

Whether there was unfair practice is open to question. The policy of requiring purchase by live weight assumed that the buyers were more skillful judges of weight than were the sellers, and that the packers wished to deprive the producers of their just dues by underestimating the weight of the cattle purchased. Perhaps this law created a more healthy situation in buying and selling. At least there were no very severe criticisms. The Consignment Decree was so amended that it was largely nullified. It constituted regulation that was injurious to all interested parties, and the effect was that small producers of high-quality herds were deprived of their best market. The controversy with the Anglo company over classification was of little benefit to cattle producers. It demonstrated a heckling, or "we are watching you," attitude which is hardly conducive to healthy relationships. It did, however, focus attention on the fact that the terms used to designate methods of processing had become too generalized and thus may have been of some benefit to the various interested parties.

From the foregoing it is apparent that the activities of the packing companies have not been hampered greatly by regulatory measures, for the controls attempted have been largely ineffective. We should not, however, overlook the administrative time required, the legal service needed, and other costs incident to the maintenance of a constant defense against prejudicial governmental action. Moreover, it may be true that because of the constant agitation, the margins taken by the companies were somewhat less than they otherwise would have been and that their profits were thus reduced. This comment suggests a whole train of interesting speculations in regard to whether regulation was actually needed or not. While the confines of this study do not permit a thorough treatment of this question, still a few observations may be pertinent. There is not sufficient evidence here to suggest that there was among the packers any collusion which was prejudicial to the interests of the cattle producers, nor that unduly high earnings were being attained. But, on the other hand, the stage was set for high profits in 1933 and thereafter, in the event that the packers wished and were allowed to take advantage of the situation created by the British meat quotas. By means of these quotas, prices were held at a higher level in the British market in which the packers were selling, and at the same time there were heavy supplies in the hands of Argentine producers because of the limitations on exports imposed by the quotas. Therefore, an excellent chance was given to buy cattle cheaply through the competition of sellers and to sell meat at an artificially maintained price in England. Under such conditions, control measures were to be expected. Yet, as we review the control measures, it becomes apparent that the majority of them were uneconomic and that they served no good purpose. As stated previously, it is not the fact of regulation and control which has been subversive to the interests of the packing companies, but the singular ineptness of the attempts at control.

Regulation of the Petroleum Industry

In Latin America there is a wide diversity in oil legislation. Some countries reserve all mineral rights to the federal government, others reserve rights to the various state governments. Some follow the rule that the surface owner is likewise the owner of the minerals which may be found in the subsoil. Other variations abound; for instance, in regard to the right of the surface owner to draw product from under the surface owned by another, in regard to restrictive measures designed to reserve developmental opportunities to nationals, and in regard to the participation of nationals or the government in enterprises started and largely financed by foreign companies.

It is not surprising that variation exists. Prior to the present century, the only legislation in effect was embodied in the old mining laws, which dealt primarily with coal and mineral ores. These laws had been modeled after the legislation of the colonizing nations and had been motivated by the personal whims of the dictators of an earlier period. In fact, there was no body of law applicable to the situation that arose when it became known that petroleum existed in large quantities and was being sought after by the large North American companies. Legislation was frequently passed hurriedly without any clear conception of the probable results of the rules and regulations adopted, at least from the long-run point of view, and this fact led to non-uniformity. Moreover, countries differed in their need for immediate revenue and in the degree of dictatorial power exercised by one government executive, or a few. Power, coupled with the need for revenue, often produced legislation which was fairly lenient in allowing developmental activities on the part of foreign oil companies. Lesser power, coupled with socialistic tendencies, as in Argentina, produced legislation which was inordinately restrictive.

Although the laws of the various countries are widely different, they were predicated upon much the same attitudes, much the same thinking on the part of those empowered to enact legislation. The lawmakers were actuated by fears, misapprehensions, and questionable assumptions. Sir Arnold Wilson, in an article in *Foreign Affairs*, says that oil legislation in Latin America is largely based on the following four assumptions:

First, that petroleum deposits in any given country are the absolute property of the inhabitants, to be utilized or not solely in their own interests, without reference to the needs of the world at large.

Second, that the investment of large amounts of foreign capital in an undeveloped country is a potential menace to that country's independence, whether political or economic; that this applies in a peculiar degree to the capital required for petroleum development; and that special enactments are therefore necessary to prescribe the conditions under which such foreign capital investments may be made.

Third, that there is a probability of a world shortage of petroleum products in the comparatively near future and that each government has the duty in the vital interests of its nationals, *and therefore the right*, to take steps to conserve its own reputed deposits of petroleum for the use of future generations.

GOVERNMENTAL CONTROL OF BUSINESS ACTIVITIES 195

Fourth, that exports of petroleum, whether crude or refined, constitute a drain on the natural resources of the country concerned, without adequate counterbalancing advantages, since petroleum deposits, however vast, are limited.[27]

These assumptions have been quoted verbatim because they have so evidently been the foundation for oil legislation in Argentina, the only country included in this study which has become a large producer of petroleum. This was particularly true of the first major regulatory attempts in 1924, and of the numerous decrees issued in the years immediately following. Sir Arnold Wilson questioned each of the assumptions and decided that they were largely based on false premises. Now we find responsible public opinion in Argentina doing likewise, and the new legislation, both provincial and national, which is in a slow process of formation, will probably be less burdensome and restrictive to independent enterprises than that of a decade earlier. Provincial legislation, particularly that in the province of Salta, has given new hope and opportunity to the private companies. While federal legislation has been proposed in every session of the Argentine Congress in the past few years, no final action has yet been taken.[28] Here we will review somewhat briefly the situation in Argentina and the legislation enacted which has been subversive to the interests of the North American oil companies doing business in that country.

First it will be necessary to present some factual information, in the light of which regulatory attempts can properly be interpreted. With the exception of Russia, Argentina is the only country in which the government is engaged in all branches of the petroleum industry—production, transportation, refining, and distribution. All activities are concentrated in the government-owned and operated

[27] Sir Arnold Wilson, "Oil Legislation in Latin America," *Foreign Affairs*, Oct. 1929, p. 108.

[28] Since this chapter was written, action has been taken through the promulgation of a new petroleum law, Number 12,161, on Mar. 26, 1935. The law is published in the *Boletin Official* of Apr. 1, 1935.

Yacimientos Petrolíferos Fiscales (hereafter referred to as the YPF). This is a powerful organization, whose assets have a book value of about 300,000,000 pesos (about $125,000,000 at par exchange). Administratively, the YPF is connected with the Department of Agriculture, but the officers are appointed by the President of the Republic with the approval of the Senate. Because of the existence of this organization, regulation of the Argentine oil industry takes the form of denying certain privileges to the private companies, or, stated otherwise, of creating advantages for the YPF in its competition with the private companies. Hence, the story of regulation is likewise an account of the competition between private companies and the YPF.

Petroleum was first discovered in Argentina in 1907 by the government bureau of mines in what is known as the Comodore Rivadavia field. From that time until 1916 the industry was entirely in the hands of the government, but in 1916 private companies started production, and by 1921 they were producing about 15 per cent of the national output. In 1924 this proportion had increased to 25 per cent, and in 1925 to about 35 per cent. Little additional progress was made by the private companies, in comparison to the YPF, until 1931.[29] In that year the two were approximately equal in output, and thus the situation remained until very recently, when the private companies took the lead.

By 1924 it had become apparent that the private companies, by virtue of their superior personnel and techniques, would soon, if uncurbed, concentrate control of the industry in their hands. Accordingly, at that time, action to prevent this was taken under the active sponsorship of the Union Civica Radical and directly under the leadership of President Alvear. This action practically forced

[29] Production data were secured from *El Petroleo y Sus Derivados en la Estadistica* by Carlos Guevara Labal (Buenos Aires: Tall. Gráf. Ferrari Hnos., 1932), p. 47.

the private companies to discontinue any attempts to discover and exploit new petroleum deposits. The measures used for restricting the operations of the private companies were the so-called reserve decrees issued on January 10, 1924. These decrees reserved to the government, and thereby indirectly to the YPF, the oil rights in all areas in which it was thought possible that petroleum deposits existed—among others, the territory of Neuquén, part of La Pampa, the western part of Chubut, and the territory which comprises the Comodore Rivadavia field. The action of the federal government was followed shortly by similar action on the part of certain provinces. The province of Salta reserved for public development the greater share of its land, and the province of Jujuy reserved the oil rights in all of its territory. Later, between 1924 and 1929, new decrees appeared at intervals, clarifying the decrees of 1924 and reserving new areas to the government. An additional part of the territory of Neuquén, all of the territory of Misiones, likewise the territories of Formosa and Chaco were reserved for government development. As a result, the private companies have done little geological work since the decrees were issued.

Something was saved from the wreckage, however, for, during the years immediately preceding 1924, the private companies had been active in developmental work and they were able to perfect title to at least a part of those holdings on which work had been started. Yet even this advantage was partially lost, because the reserve decrees enabled the YPF to enter and drill on the immediate outskirts of the private holdings. Moreover, some of the contemplated results of prospecting work were entirely lost, for the numerous petitions before the federal and provincial governments requesting concessions to open new wells were set aside and never acted upon. Additional petitions were not accepted. Thus the development of the private companies was effectively curbed from the standpoint of securing new holdings.

In the distribution of their product, as well as in production, the private companies have been hampered by regulations which, as administered, favor the YPF. In the municipality of Buenos Aires numerous ordinances have been adopted to regulate the retailing of petroleum products. One is to the effect that a gas station may not be established within four hundred meters of one already operating; another provides that a retail gas station and all of its equipment, after being in operation for a ten-year period, become the property of the municipality. The first of these ordinances has been violated repeatedly by the YPF, whereas the private companies have been forced to adhere closely to the ordinance provisions. The second ordinance has also proved to be prejudicial to the interests of the private concerns, for the municipality has proceeded to turn over to the YPF the gas stations which it has acquired from the private companies at the end of a decade of use. The result has been that the YPF has secured the best locations for stations. This fact can be proved by data showing the average volume of sales per station. Furthermore, from the standpoint of taxation, the YPF has been favored constantly.[30] Handicaps such as these have made it difficult for the private companies to operate profitably.

The uneconomic policies of the YPF have also been difficult to cope with. For example, one of the earliest moves made by the YPF, after its La Plata refinery started operation and the organization commenced to market refined petroleum in 1926, was to establish a uniform price throughout the country. This was probably a political move to establish favorable reactions in the interior. There was no economic justification for it, since the supply originated chiefly on the coast, through the refining of Argentine crude oil and through importations, which

[30] For a thorough discussion of the favoritism shown by the municipality of Buenos Aires to the YPF, see "La Politica Municipal en Materia de Petroleo." editorial comment. *La Prensa.* Feb. 22. 1933.

constituted a substantial portion of the total. The price in the interior would normally be the coast price plus transportation costs. In the spring of 1933, the price of gasoline in Buenos Aires was 23 centavos per liter, of which 5 centavos were federal tax and 18 centavos represented the base price. In Mendoza, on the Chilean border, the price was also 23 centavos, of which 5 centavos were federal tax, 2 centavos state tax, and 8 centavos transportation cost from the coast. Thus the base price in Mendoza was 8 centavos in comparison with 18 centavos in Buenos Aires. Under such conditions, people in the coast cities were not given the advantage of their position near the source of supplies. They were forced to pay part of the transportation costs incurred on the supply shipped to interior points. Attempts were made by the private companies to secure a change in this pricing system through cooperative means, but the YPF would not concur. Finally, faced by fly-by-night competition in the form of dumping, particularly by the Soviet government, the private companies reduced their prices on the coast without a like reduction in the interior. The YPF countered with a general reduction throughout the country, and a price war was in progress. This is necessarily a brief account of the incident, but it does illustrate the difficulties of private companies in competing with a government organization, the latter being dominated by political, as well as business, motives.

Notwithstanding the limitations imposed by the government and the favoritism shown to the YPF in administrative circles, the private companies have forged ahead, and in 1931 they became equally important with the YPF as petroleum producers. In the meantime, the Union Civica Radical had been deprived of its power through the revolution of 1930, and the new administrations, under Generals Uriburu and Justo, were less unfriendly to private interests. Intelligent public opinion, of which there is a goodly measure in Argentina, began to question the limitations imposed on the private companies through the reserve decrees. In 1924 it had been stated by government officials that the Argentine would be self-sufficient in respect to petroleum by 1928. But this result had not been achieved. Importations were not being decreased appreciably with the passage of years, for the reason that geological exploration work of a productive nature practically ceased when it was confined, through limitations on the private companies, to the YPF. An editorial comment in *La Prensa* in 1933 stated:

> The result of such an absurd mode of procedure is now open to view. The facts of the situation speak with eloquence. Since the reserve decree was dictated, that is, for nine years, there has been no important new discovery of petroleum deposits.[31]

Editorial comment in both the newspapers and reviews in Argentina argued that the YPF had proven its inability to do careful, painstaking geological work. *La Prensa*, in another editorial, stated the case exceptionally well:

> We repeat that it is necessary to stimulate general activity in all parts of the country without any consideration in regard to the origin of the capital employed, whether it be public or private, national or foreign. The scarcity of resources on the part of the national or the provincial governments should not constitute an inescapable difficulty when there is private capital disposed to employ itself in a similar capacity if shackles and burdens are not imposed which make practically impossible its investment with a commercially acceptable result.[32]

It is thus apparent that intelligent public opinion was beginning to question the whole theory upon which the petroleum legislation was based. Carlos Garcia Mata published an excellent article on the subject in the *Revista de Economia Argentina*.[33] He pointed out that all the

---

[31] "La Busqueda Racional Del Petroleo," editorial comment, *La Prensa*, Jan. 24, 1933. This is a free translation.

[32] "Las Perforaciones en Busca de Petroleo," editorial comment, *La Prensa*, June 6, 1933. This is a free translation.

[33] Carlos Garcia Mata, "El Nuevo Fundamento Economico de la Legislación Petrolífera," *Revista de Economia Argentina*, July, 1933, p. 15.

legislation prior to 1925 had been based upon two suppositions; namely, that there was an immediate danger of scarcity because world petroleum reserves were limited, and that petroleum was an absolute necessity with no acceptable substitutes; also that these two suppositions were no longer tenable, in view of the new discoveries which had been made and the new developments regarding the production of a synthetic product. He then stated that the new fundamentals upon which oil legislation should be based are that mechanical energy is becoming more and more important for contemporaneous economic life, that energy derived from petroleum is the only immediate possibility for Argentina, and that constant importations of petroleum constitute, through the balance of payments, a drainage on the nation which can no longer be afforded. His conclusion was that, in view of the inability of the YPF to develop the industry to such an extent that the country would be self-sufficing, legislation should be enacted immediately which would give reasonable opportunities and assurances to private capital.

These numerous expressions of opinion during the latter part of 1932 and the first half of 1933, friendly to the interests of the private oil companies, may have had some effect on the legislative bodies. At any rate, the trend of events appeared to be much more hopeful from that time forward. The province of Salta, in particular, took action that benefited the private companies substantially. On October 19, 1932, the province had entered into an agreement with the YPF which, if rigidly construed and later enforced, would in all likelihood have excluded the private companies entirely from further exploration, and possibly from further operations of any sort. As a result of this agreement, heavy operating royalties had been imposed on the private companies. These were contested in the courts by the Standard Oil Company. Evidently the Salta officials thought that the company might win the suit, and they therefore decided to negotiate with it. At least, for some reason, the officials of the province did a right-about-face from an unfriendly attitude in the latter part of 1932 to a friendly one in the early part of 1933. Perhaps there were other reasons for this change of attitude. There is some indication that the officials of the province were having difficulty with the YPF. The governor of Salta made various accusations, among which was a statement that the YPF occupied a false position in the province and could not be relied upon to develop its petroleum resources. Another possible reason for the change of attitude was the fact that funds were greatly needed by the province, and these could be secured from the private oil companies.

Subsequently an agreement was reached with the Standard Oil Company resulting in a contractual arrangement whereby the royalties assessed against the private companies were appreciably reduced. Previously the royalties had been set at 5 pesos per cubic meter of crude oil extracted. In the new agreement, the province was to receive 10 per cent of the crude oil output, or approximately 3.5 pesos per cubic meter. Article 8 exempted the company from taxation other than that imposed through the use of stamped paper, municipal taxes, taxes on the retail sales of petroleum products, an annual tax upon the acreage used for petroleum production, and national taxes, if such should be imposed through the Petroleum Law which was then under consideration by the federal Congress. The latter, however, if imposed, were to be deductible from the proceeds of the 10 per cent crude oil royalty. The agreement also contained an important provision relating to pipe lines and some relatively unimportant provisions for administration. Its duration was to be for thirty years.

While this agreement was not an unusual one, it did create a great furor in other parts of the country when the news came out that it was under consideration by the Salta legislature. The province was accused of selling out to foreign interests to the detriment of the whole nation. Undoubtedly the YPF had a hand in this unfavorable publicity, for its prestige had suffered through the controversy with Salta, and through the fact that direct negotiations were taking place with the private companies. In its condemnation of the projected Salta-Standard agreement, the YPF was whole-heartedly supported by the Union Civica Radical party, under whose sponsorship the reserve decrees had been promulgated in 1924. Congressional representatives of the party demanded that something be done to restrain the province, and urged the Minister of the Interior to send an admonitory message to the governor. How much influence the Radical party had may be open to question, but, nevertheless, such a message was sent, and it was greatly resented by the officials of the province. They roundly maintained, both in their own legislative chambers and in the national assembly, that their sovereign state rights were being infringed upon by the national government, and that it was within their power to negotiate with the private oil companies as they saw fit. In a debate on the subject in the national Senate, the position of the province was ably upheld by Senators Sperry of Salta and Villefane of Jujuy.[34] Disregarding the message from the Minister of the Interior, the Salta legislature approved the agreement, and it was put into effect.[35] Later, the agreement was approved outright in a *La Prensa* editorial comment, and the right of the provinces to make such agreements was upheld. Other publications also approved the action, and, therefore,

[34] For the presentation of this debate in the Argentine Senate, see "Los Senadores Representantes de Salta Hicieron la Defensa de la Politica Petrolífera Seguida por el Gobierno Provincial y Criticaron la Gestion de las Autoridades Administrativas Federales," *La Prensa*, May 12, 1933.

[35] Since the negotiation of this agreement, production in Salta has increased appreciably. More than 90 per cent of the total production is by the private companies. There has been intense activity both by the private companies and by the YPF. *La Prensa* says that none of the gloomy prophecies made at the time the agreement was reached have been fulfilled. Furthermore, the income of the province has been materially increased.

much of the unfavorable comment provoked by the agreement was counteracted.

This dispute indicates that the rights of the provinces and the national government in mineral deposits are not clearly defined in the mineral code (Codigo de Mineria). The code states that mineral deposits are the property of the nation and the provinces. Probably the framers of the code meant that minerals were the property of the provinces when such were formed, and of the nation in the case of territories not formed into provinces. In 1927 there was under consideration in the federal Congress a bill providing for nationalization of the oil resources of the country. This bill failed to pass in the Senate. In its discussion, there were long debates on the subject of states' rights in mineral deposits. While bills before Congress in more recent years have evaded the issue, they have apparently assumed that the provinces have the right to negotiate with private parties.

It is thus apparent that the position of the private companies is an uncertain one. It could not be otherwise inasmuch as there is still some doubt in regard to the rights of the provinces and the federal government to determine the conditions under which companies shall operate. For a decade after 1924, governmental policy, both provincial and national, was dictated largely by the feeling that foreign capital in the oil industry was a potential menace to the country. But if the industry was to grow and finally meet the needs of the country, developmental activities had to be performed, either by the government itself or by private interests from abroad. The dearth of capital and of training in the technical aspects of the industry prevented local groups from successfully exploiting the oil reserves. The failure of the government, through the YPF, to increase the output of the country to a self-sufficiency basis, although it had every opportunity to do so, has raised grave doubts in regard to the whole policy of excluding, or at least hampering, the developmental activities of the large foreign oil companies. Recently, the Salta incident and the friendly attitude of the more responsible press have given renewed confidence to the private companies that they will be allowed to operate to an increasing extent, and with reasonable assurance that sufficient leeway will be given for continued profitable operation.

Admittedly, the position of the private companies depends largely on the political situation. Little consideration for private interests engaged in the extraction of major raw materials, particularly petroleum, can be expected from certain political groups if they come into power. There is little to indicate that the Union Civica Radical, which was responsible for curbing the activities of the private companies from 1924 on, has experienced a change in attitude. Yet the healthy doubt which now exists in Argentina, among informed people, regarding the ability of the YPF to develop petroleum resources augurs well for the future of the private companies. Argentina will not continue indefinitely to import petroleum products when it appears that sufficient deposits to satisfy her needs exist within the country. Thus in time the private companies may be allowed to operate in Argentina without restrictions so burdensome as those now in force.

REGULATION OF OTHER INDUSTRIES

This discussion of the regulation to which the packing and petroleum industries have been subjected should not lead to the inference that all branch factories are or will be subject to such regulatory attempts. The influences urging regulation are not of equal strength for other industries. Both in meat packing and in the exploitation of petroleum resources, special reasons provoked regulation. The importance of meat as an export, the fact that livestock producers were a politically coherent group, and the fact that the industry was almost entirely in the hands of North American and British concerns, all were of significance in bringing forward control measures. In the case of petroleum, the factors provoking regulation were its particular importance to Argentina, in view of the lack of other sources of energy, the exaggerated notions which prevailed concerning the need for conservation, the unfortunate publicity given to certain incidents in the history of Mexican petroleum development and recession, and the attempt at virtual government monopoly through the YPF.

Furthermore, it should be recalled that the packing and petroleum industries have not been without regulation in this country. The packing industry in particular, through such measures as the Packers' Consent Decree, has been appreciably restricted in its operations. Recently, a Supreme Court decision refused to set aside this decree. Undoubtedly, legal decisions adverse to the interests of the packers have been motivated in part by the fear that a few large companies would attain too much dominance in the processing and distribution of food products, and would thereby attain an opportunity for monopolistic practices that would be prejudicial to the public welfare. Various legal decisions affecting the oil companies have likewise curbed monopolistic tendencies. Apparently the courts have succeeded in controlling the monopolistic element in the oil industry, but the aftermath has been a large measure of uneconomic production with accompanying waste. With these examples of control and regulation, it is not at all surprising that Argentina decided to do likewise. The same companies subject to control in the United States were also operating in Argentina, and the incentive to restrict their operations was doubly great, for not only was there the possibility of monopolistic practices, but such action would be taken by foreign concerns rather than domestic. If unduly high profits were made, the benefit would accrue, not to nationals of the country, but to foreign stockholders.

The other industries in which North American concerns have branch plants are not affected with a like degree of public interest. From the standpoint of size, the capital investment needed, the extent of dominance which may be exercised, and the opportunity for monopolistic practice, the operations of other branch plants are not of equal importance in the national economy, nor is regulation of them so necessary to protect the public interest. Moreover, the activities of industries represented by other branch plants have not been subject to regulation to a like degree in the United States, and therefore the example of regulation has not been placed before South American governments.

Although these differences are apparent, still regulation of the packing and petroleum industries cannot be summarily dismissed as being of no significance to other industries. So to dismiss it would be to neglect the motives behind regulation. It proceeds largely from a distrust of the power and purposes of all large foreign capitalistic organizations. Furthermore, it has its origin in the socialistic tendencies which are clearly apparent in all South American countries. The aims of such political groups as the Union Civica Radical in Argentina are inimical to the best interests of large foreign companies. Such groups may attain a greater measure of control over governmental activities, and in that event foreign concerns may be hampered to an increasing extent. While it is not likely that companies other than those in the packing and petroleum industries will be regulated directly, still indirect regulation may result through social legislation.

Social Legislation

Unreasonable demands upon employers have not characterized South American labor legislation, at least not until recently. Manufacturers have been allowed a large measure of freedom in dealing with their employees, and the labor legislation in force has been neither strict nor difficult to comply with. North American concerns, in particular, have had little difficulty, for the working conditions in their plants, their wage rates, and their employer-employee relationships in general have been markedly superior to those in the majority of establishments. But recently, decisions of the labor courts in Chile, the administration of the pension law and other laws in Uruguay, and a modification of the commercial code in Argentina have placed upon business concerns additional demands which, in some particular instances, have jeopardized their existence. Because of the wide divergence in the legislation of the various countries, the situation in each country will be considered separately.

Argentina.—In Argentina, labor legislation is enacted both by the federal government and by the various provincial governments. Usually, that of the federal government applies only to the ten national territories and to the federal capital—that is, the city of Buenos Aires—although on certain subjects the federal government may enact legislation which applies to the entire nation. On other subjects, the power of legislation resides in the provinces. In general, this distinction is not of importance, for the legislation passed by the federal government is likewise adopted by the provinces by means of regulatory decrees. These decrees provide for the application of the law within the territory of the province. There is, consequently, a large measure of uniformity in labor legislation throughout the Republic. For instance, the Workmen's Compensation Law has been put in force through regulatory decrees in nine of the ten provinces, only the province of Tucuman being outside the fold.

The first Argentine law directly affecting labor, which was known as the Sunday Rest Law, was passed in 1905. Except in a few industries—among them, domestic service—this law prohibited Sunday work. From 1915 on, there have been a number of important acts. The first of these was the Workmen's Compensation Law, passed in 1915. This law defines the liability of employers in case of accidents to workers causing death or disability. The law is not particularly severe, for the maximum payment demanded for the benefit of survivors is approximately

$2,500 (at par exchange). Provision is also made for discharging obligations under the law by means of insurance.

Four laws have been passed which entitle employees to retirement annuities and pensions. The first two of these are unimportant in this review, since they apply only to government employees. The latter two, passed in 1923, cover employees of private streetcar, telephone, gas, telegraph, electric, and radio-telegraph companies and banks. Each law provides for contributions into a government-administered fund. In 1924 a law was passed regulating the employment of women and children in both industry and agriculture. This was followed in 1925 by a law relative to the payment of wages, which, however, did not provide for minimum wages. In September of 1929 a law was passed which provided for an eight-hour day and a forty-eight-hour week. This applied to all manufacturing establishments but not to agricultural or domestic service. An important piece of legislation, it radically changed working hours in many plants. Similar laws were enacted by seven of the ten provinces.[36]

The most recent change in the demands of government on business relative to labor occurred in 1934 through a revision of Articles 154–160 of the commercial code (*Codigo de Comercio*). This section of the code dealt with employee-employer relationships in regard to: (1) continuance of pay when unavoidable circumstances hindered execution of duties in the usual manner; (2) notice before discharge and pay during such period; (3) arbitration when disputes arose; and (4) special grounds for discharge without notice or indemnification.[37] After revision, the provisions were much more severe.[38] Formerly, the employee who was

[36] For a general summarization of labor legislation in Argentina, and a translation of the laws, see *Labor Legislation in Argentina*, U. S. Department of Labor, Bureau of Labor Statistics, Foreign Labor Law Series, Bulletin No. 510.

[37] *Laws of Argentina* as compiled and translated by J. A. and E. De Marval.

[38] See *Comments on Argentine Trade*, September, 1934, p. 27.

unable to perform his customary duties because of accident or illness was to receive pay for three months at the usual rate. Under the new ruling, employees with a service of ten years or less are to receive the same treatment as formerly, but for those with service of more than ten years the payment period after interruption of work is extended to six months. A new article provides for annual vacations ranging from ten to thirty days according to the length of service.

Furthermore, an article is included (Number 157) which provides that a discharged worker shall receive indemnification of not less than half of his monthly remuneration for each year of service or fraction thereof exceeding three months—the remuneration figure used to be the average wage of the past five years or the entire period of service, if it is less than five years. Bonuses and payments in kind are to be included in the wages used in computing the indemnity. The total indemnity is not to be less than one month's salary nor more than 500 pesos for each year of service. Moreover, either suspension of work for more than three months in the period of one year or unjustifiable reduction of salaries, not acceptable to the employees affected, is to place such workers in the position of discharged employees and to make them subject to the indemnity payment.

Other provisions of the code, as revised, relate to employee transfers, payment to survivors in case of the death of the principal, and the nullification of contracts which seek to reduce the obligations imposed by the law. The last article states, among other things, that a fraudulent act or abuse of confidence on the part of an employee, doing business as an agent without explicit permission from his principal, or incapacity to fulfill the duties and obligations to which assigned will be considered sufficient ground for discharge without indemnification. Periods of service prior to the sanction of the law were recognized, but not to exceed five years. By the passage of this law, industry was forced to assume additional burdens for the benefit of employees. Whether additional profits can be made to cover the expenditures required under the law is open to question.

Uruguay.—Of all South American countries, Uruguay is the most socialistically inclined. There has been no attempt to exclude those individuals with socialistic or communistic attitudes, and the result has been that such people, often excluded from other countries, have flocked to Uruguay. The country has frequently been described as the theatre for social experiments in South America. Measures first adopted in Uruguay later find favor elsewhere. But it is to be sincerely hoped that other countries do not follow the lead of Uruguay in all particulars, for its socialistic legislation has been carried to an extreme. Private business in some lines has been almost excluded through laws creating government monopolies. Furthermore, compensation and pension laws have placed a heavy burden upon all business establishments.

Prior to 1928, labor laws in Uruguay were not much different in type from those of Argentina, but the demands of the government under the laws were uniformly more severe.[39] The compensation law passed in 1920 provided for life annuities in case of accidents causing death or partial or permanent disability. In case of death of an employee through accident, survivors are granted annuities ranging from 20 to 40 per cent of the previous annual wage, according to the number of dependents. Permanent disability allows the employee a life annuity of two-thirds of the previous annual wage. The Argentine law, in contrast, provides for a total maximum payment of not more than $2,500 as previously noted. Other laws establish regulations for the prevention of accidents, a minimum wage for

[39] For general information on labor legislation in Uruguay and a translation of the laws, see *Labor Legislation in Uruguay*, U. S. Department of Labor, Bureau of Labor Statistics, Foreign Labor Law Series, Bulletin No. 494. This bulletin was published in 1929 and does not include the important new laws enacted in 1928 and thereafter.

rural workers, an eight-hour working day, a compulsory weekly rest, and old age pensions which are financed partially by a small monthly tax on employers. In 1919 a retirement and pension law was enacted which applied only to public service employees and laborers. In 1925 another law embodied a similar plan for banking and stock exchange employees, and in 1928 the plan was extended to employees and laborers of limited liability companies and unincorporated businesses. Thus branch plants were brought within the scope of the retirement and pension system.

The Retirement and Pension Law provides for a contribution from employers of 9 per cent of salaries and wages paid, and, in addition, a three-mill tax on gross sales. Five per cent of the workers' pay is deducted by the employer for the workers' contribution to the fund. The total amount paid to the pension fund frequently reaches as much as 25 per cent of the total wage payment. The right to benefits under this law is acquired after ten years of service, whether it is continuous or not. Full benefits are acquired after thirty years of service, or, for the following classes of persons, after ten years of service: (1) those who are discharged by their companies, (2) those who have been declared physically or mentally incapable of continuing their work, and (3) those who reach fifty years of age, whether or not they are then in the active service of the companies in question.

There is general disapproval of the pension law, at least by North American companies with branch plants. Objection is voiced particularly on three counts. The contribution required is a heavy one, and there is little possibility of so operating that profits will be increased sufficiently to offset the contributions made. The law is not based on actuarial data. One executive stated in conversation that his company would have no objection to a pension law if it were based on actuarial data initially, and if it were capably administered later. The third common objection regards administration, which apparently is very inefficient. In one instance, an individual thirty-seven years of age was discharged after several years of service. His wage at the time of discharge was 108 pesos monthly. He was awarded a pension of 87 pesos monthly and has not worked since. Another individual, a sales manager, was discharged in 1930. He was forty-five years of age. Since the law was enacted in 1928, he had been contributing to the reserve fund for only two years. Nevertheless, he was awarded a pension of 230 pesos per month. His salary had ranged between 500 and 750 pesos per month. It has been a common practice by the government to grant pensions, somewhat indiscriminately, to the numerous persons who have made application. In fact, a large portion of the volumes containing new legislation is used to record the fact that pension grants were made to specific individuals. When, through legislation, business concerns are forced to contribute heavily to a scheme so imperfectly constituted and so incapably administered, little but active disapproval could be expected.

Socialistic legislation has not been confined to unemployment and old age benefits, but has been extended to provide for direct government ownership and operation in a number of industries. In public utilities, there was precedent for such action, for the production and distribution of electric current were monopolized by the state in 1912. The first significant new step in the direction of state industry was taken in 1928, through the acquisition by lease of a packing plant owned by the Argentine Sansinena company. Immediately, a partially monopolistic situation was created by a ruling that all meats sold in the Montevideo market should be slaughtered in the state plant.

Later, on October 15, 1931, a law was passed providing for a government monopoly in the production of alcohol, combustibles, and cement. Strictly speaking, a monopoly was not created in the cement industry, but authority was given for the building of factories to manufacture cement and similar products "for the accomplishment of public works." If this power was acted upon, a virtual monopoly would be accorded, since the greater share of the cement output goes into public works. For carrying out the provisions of this law, an organization was set up, the Administración Nacional de Combustibles, Alcohol, y Portland, familiarly known as the ANCAP. First, the alcohol-producing companies were taken over from private interests. This move did not involve negotiations with foreign companies, for the alcohol plants were owned by Uruguayan concerns. In 1934 the ANCAP was producing alcohol and soft drinks, importing and distributing petroleum products in direct competition with private companies, and producing some heavy chemicals, such, for instance, as copper sulphate. Bids had been asked for the construction of an oil refinery. Since the law stated that the government monopoly on petroleum products would not go into effect until 50 per cent of the entire consumption was produced in government refineries, the private companies were not immediately excluded. No steps have been taken either for the construction of a new cement plant or for acquisition of the plant operated by the International Cement Corporation.

One further move was made by the government in its program of state industry. The telephone system, which had been owned and operated, first by British and then by North American interests, was nationalized in 1931 and placed under control of the government organization which administered the electric power monopoly. A contract was let to a German concern to construct a new system in Montevideo, and by now this system is probably in use. At the time this information was secured, there was doubt as to whether the government would attempt to operate the telephone system or whether it would turn over the operation to a private concern.

This movement to socialize industry has been distinctly prejudicial to all foreign business concerns operating in the country. Even if a company, such as the International Cement Corporation, has not yet been affected, it nevertheless is threatened, and the resulting situation is one of uncertainty. Direct competition by the state with the packing companies and the oil companies, accompanied, as is always the case, with special favors to the state entities, makes profitable operation by the private companies difficult. Withdrawal of the foreign concerns might be in order if it were not for two considerations: first, that the state enterprises are almost invariably operated ineffectively; and, second, that political changes may in time give more latitude and thus more chance of profitable operation to private organizations.

Because of inefficiency, the competition which the private companies must meet is less than it otherwise would be. The national packing plant, for example, has never been operated successfully, and, if they did not fear political repercussions, Uruguayan political leaders might decide to discontinue its operation. Political changes have already partially altered the situation. In the troubled years since 1930, the Batllista, the political group which has sponsored nationalization of industry, has lost power through the death of its leader, Brum, and the events which brought President Terra into power. Although Terra was formerly a Batllista, there is evidence that he did not completely approve of its policy of socializing industry, nor of its rabid anti-foreign-capital sentiments. Therefore, some informed individuals believe that Uruguay has passed the crest of its socialistic program, and that private concerns, particularly those of foreign origin, will be less hampered in the future. A complete retraction is not to be expected, of course, for the people of the country are addicted to socialization of industry, and, even if some political leaders realize the advisability of abandoning the socialization program, they are powerless to institute changes in view of public opinion.

Brazil.—Social legislation in Brazil, in contrast to that in Argentina and Uruguay, is of comparatively recent date. Before 1930 there was little legislation concerned with labor, and the laws in force were largely disregarded by business enterprises. But after the revolution of September, 1930, by means of which Getulio Vargas was made provisional president of the Republic, numerous attempts were made, some of them of questionable character, to improve conditions for workers. A Ministry of Labor was created which embarked upon an ambitious program, including the unionization of all workers under government auspices. A decree by the government, early in 1932, provided for the registration of all workers in commerce and industry. A later modification provided for the registration of all workers who rendered remunerative service. Unless they were so registered, workers could not have their complaints and claims inquired into by the Ministry. This arrangement suggests the idea behind the plans of the government. Evidently the government intended to organize the workers and then serve as an intermediary for arbitration between employers and labor groups. The Ministry of Labor was also expected to administer the provisions of the numerous labor laws in the process of formation.

The first decree relative to labor, known ultimately as the "two-thirds law," appeared less than three months after the revolution. It provided that, for all concerns hiring more than five individuals, not less than two-thirds of the employees should at all times be native-born Brazilians.[40] This decree was later modified as the result of protests made, particularly in regard to the status of foreigners. For the purposes of the law, the modifications provide that any

---

[40] For a complete translation of the law, see the *Monthly Bulletin of the British Chamber of Commerce in Brazil, Inc.* (Rio de Janeiro, September, 1931), p. 309.

foreigner shall be considered as a Brazilian who is married to a Brazilian and has children by this marriage, and who has resided in Brazil for more than ten years. All other foreigners who have resided in the country for more than ten years are also considered as Brazilians for a period of five years from July 29, 1931, forward. Various industries are exempted from the provisions of the law, among them farming, animal husbandry, and the extractive industries. If the employer can prove to the Ministry of Labor that Brazilian workers are not procurable, or that the work to be done is of a technical nature and demands unusual abilities and training, he may be exempted from adherence to the law. The law also provides that, in the event of lack of work, foreigners must be discharged before native-born Brazilians. There are numerous other provisions which deal chiefly with administrative features.

The next move of the government consisted of the promulgation of a decree on March 28, 1931, suspending the execution of the Employees' Holidays Law, which had been in effect but apparently not enforced since 1925, and establishing new measures for the concession of holidays. Annual leaves with pay were to be granted to employees who had twelve months of uninterrupted work in one establishment.[41] Other provisions dealt with remuneration during holidays, claims and indemnities, official supervision, and penalties.

On October 1, 1931, a decree was issued (Number 20,465) which established "The Retirement and Pension Funds Act."[42] Because of numerous objections from business concerns, this Act was later modified appreciably by a decree on February 24, 1932 (Number 20,081). Although the Act aroused a great deal of objection, still, in compari-

[41] For a complete translation of the Employees' Holidays Law, see the *Monthly Bulletin of the British Chamber of Commerce in Brazil, Inc.*, September, 1933, p. 401.

[42] For a complete translation of the Act, see the *Monthly Bulletin of the British Chamber of Commerce in Brazil, Inc.*, a Special Publication, and for the later modifications see the same publication, March, 1932, p. 110.

son with the pension system in Uruguay, it is a very mild measure. Funds are secured by a levy against the workers' remuneration of from 3 to 5 per cent, the exact amount depending on the condition of the fund, and by an assessment against employers of 1½ per cent of gross revenue. In no case may the employers' contribution be less than that of the employees. Some contribution is also made by the state. In order to receive payment from the fund, workers must be at least fifty years of age and have had thirty years of service. In special cases, the lower age limit may be reduced to forty-five years and the service period to twenty-five years. In addition, workers must have contributed to the fund for at least five years. Pensions are fixed at from 70 to 100 per cent of the average earnings of the last three years of service but may not be more than two contos nor less than 200 milreis per month (equivalent in United States money to a maximum of approximately $150 and a minimum of $15 at the exchange rate ruling at the time the decree was issued). Various other provisions of the law are concerned with retirement because of incapacity, dismissal, and the procedure for administration.

One further important measure was put into effect, a decree which established working hours in commercial establishments. This decree, Number 21,186, appeared on March 22, 1932.[43] Later, on May 4, another decree appeared, Number 21,364, which established the same hours for industrial workers, with but slight variations—for example, in connection with rest periods. This decree provided for a basic eight-hour day and a forty-eight-hour week with a compulsory weekly rest period of twenty-four consecutive hours. The normal duration of work might be increased to as much as nine hours daily or fifty-four hours weekly, if the change was agreed upon by employees and

---

[43] For a complete translation of Decree Number 21,186, see the *Monthly Bulletin of the British Chamber of Commerce in Brazil, Inc.*, April, 1932, p. 171.

employers, by payment of an additional percentage of the remuneration. Agricultural work, places of amusement, and service establishments, including public utilities and transport, were excepted from the provisions of the decree. Business concerns were required to keep complete records relative to hours worked, interruptions to work and their cause, and remuneration.[44]

As a whole, this labor legislation in Brazil is not particularly severe nor difficult to comply with. Although the desirability of the "two-thirds law" is open to question, particularly in view of Brazilian attempts to stimulate immigration, still from the standpoint of branch plants it has had but little effect. The managers of some branch plants stated that no changes were needed since they were well within the law before its enactment. Another executive stated that it was literally impossible for his concern to acquire enough Brazilian workers of the right abilities to make up two-thirds of its force but that no difficulty was expected, since the law was not being enforced. All concerns experienced less difficulty after the law was modified to allow inclusion as "Brazilians" of those people who had resided within the country for ten years. Neither the laws relative to holidays nor those establishing working hours should unduly burden business enterprises. The law pertaining to retirement and pension funds contains more dynamite, for its effect depends greatly on the manner of its administration. If moderation is exercised and the government does not bring forth additional demands upon employers by unwisely yielding to illegitimate demands of workers and thus depleting the fund, the pension plan should not be prejudicial to the interests of foreign companies operating branch plants.

Chile.—Chile has proceeded further than any other South American country in laws designed for the protection

---

[44] A national health and unemployment insurance scheme was likewise proposed. Perhaps some definite action has been taken, but it has not come to the notice of the author.

of workers. Various interpretations might be given of the motivation behind such extensive legislation, but one significant fact is that Chile depends largely on the extractive industries, in which there are large numbers of workers employed chiefly by foreign concerns. A feeling that such workers were being exploited would give rise to extensive legislation. Argentina, Brazil, and Uruguay, in contrast, have been chiefly engaged in agricultural pursuits, with lesser congregations of labor under one employer, and that employer in the vast majority of instances has been an individual rather than a corporation and a native rather than a foreigner. On the other hand, in all industrial activities except those of an extractive nature, Chile has proceeded less rapidly than her neighbors on the eastern seaboard; hence, there has been less need for labor legislation.

In contrast with the labor legislation in Argentina and Uruguay, which has been enacted over a period of three decades, that in Chile has been a product of the past ten years. In fact, a whole program of legislation designed to protect labor was instituted in 1924 and was practically completed through additions in 1925 and 1926. Since that time, relatively few changes have been made in the legal structure, although administration of the measures has varied greatly from time to time. The legislation consisted of a number of separate laws (Numbers 4053 through 4057) followed by several decree-laws. These will not be considered in detail, but a few facts will be given to indicate the nature and scope of the legislation and the responsibilities which it placed upon business enterprises.[45] The first law (Number 4053) prescribed the contractual relationships between employers and employees. It was amplified by a decree-law (Number 857) issued in 1926.

[45] All the important laws and decrees, with the exception of Number 4054, can be found in a compilation published in 1931, *Texto Definitivo de las Leyes Trabajo* (Talleres Gráf. de "La Nacion," Santiago de Chile). Law Number 4054 can be found in a separate publication, *Ley 4054 Sobre el Seguro Obrero Obligatorio* (Imprenta Nacional, Santiago de Chile).

The law requires that employers' contracts either with individuals or with labor groups be made in writing. Holidays are provided for, and also a month's notice in case of discharge. Furthermore, if the employee does not leave voluntarily, if his incapacity to perform the task allotted cannot be proved, if there has not been malfeasance in employment, and if the enterprise is not to be terminated, indemnification upon discharge must be given. In order to be eligible for such benefits, the worker must have been in the employ of the company for at least one year. The rate of indemnification is one month's salary for each complete year of employment for all workers earning less than 1,000 pesos monthly. These, of course, constitute the vast majority. Other provisions of the law require that 55 per cent of the workers in each establishment shall be Chileans and that 85 per cent or more of total salary payments, those to technical experts being excepted, shall be assigned to Chileans. In these provisions we see the pattern used by Brazil some years later.

A further provision of Law Number 4053 merits especial attention because it indicates more clearly than those previously mentioned the socialistic philosophy behind Chile's labor legislation. Article Number 146, freely translated, is as follows:

> Commercial and industrial establishments which obtain profits from their operations shall be obligated to distribute to employees as extra remuneration not less than 20 per cent of such profits. The amount distributed to an employee shall not be more than 25 per cent of his annual salary, special agreements excepted. . . . [46]

Subsequent articles indicate the manner in which the employees' share in the profits shall be determined and give some rules regarding the determination of the profit figure. The profit figure determined by the Department of Internal Revenue for taxation purposes is used as a basis, and from it business enterprises are allowed to

---

[46] *Texto Definitivo de las Leyes Trabajo*, pp. 53, 54.

deduct 8 per cent on capital invested for return to capital and 2 per cent upon the same capital figure for contingency reserves. Of the remainder, 20 per cent is assigned to the employees. Although the allowance of these deductions for capital costs and reserves will appreciably lower the amount left for division with employees, still the intent of the law is clearly to force the payment to employees of remuneration more nearly in proportion to the profit returns of an enterprise. It is thus socialistic in intent, and it serves as a drawback to capitalistic endeavor. The article, in effect, provides a method for improving the position of workers through confiscation of profits for their benefit. Uruguay, with the same objective in mind, decided that the proper means for its attainment was through state ownership and operation of important industries.

The second law of the group, Number 4054, provides for an obligatory employee insurance scheme, funds for which are obtained through assessments upon the employee of 2 per cent and upon the employer of 3 per cent, and through contribution by the state of 1 per cent of the weekly salary of the insured. For mining enterprises, the rates are set at an appreciably lower figure. Administration of the fund created is in the hands of a governmental agency. Sickness and death benefits are provided for, also medical care, which may be extended at the option of the worker to other members of his family. Another law, Number 4055, sets forth the obligations of the employer in case of accidents to workers. In case of temporary incapacity to serve, the worker receives 50 per cent of his usual wage. Permanent disability calls for payment at the rate of 70 per cent of the previous wage.

The other two laws of this labor group have as their objective the formation and regulation of labor unions (*sindicatos*), and the establishment of governmental bodies for arbitration and conciliation in the event of disputes between employers and employees. One of these laws,

Number 4057, called the "Organización Sindical," gives workers the right to organize either on the company basis or as a group of workers performing like tasks. After organization, which must be in conformance with various provisions expressly stated in the law, the union obtains legal status by action of the President of the Republic. If the union is thus recognized by the government, and if it includes not less than 55 per cent of the total number of workers in a company, all the workers in the company are to be considered as part of the union (*sindicalizados*) and must be included under any arrangements which may be made between the union and employers. The objectives of the union organization are given as follows: to bargain with employers collectively, to represent the workers in the exercise of their rights, to represent the workers in labor conflicts and especially in arbitration and conciliation, and to oversee any mutual benefit schemes of an insurance or educational nature which the union may decide to initiate. The law also provides that the union shall participate in the profits made by the enterprise to which it is attached, to an extent of not less than 10 per cent, although the amount shall not be more in total than 6 per cent of the salaries paid to the workers during the year. The business concern is allowed to deduct 10 per cent on its invested capital from the profit figure before determining the amount to be allotted. One half of the amount is given to the union, the other half to the workers directly. It is expressly stipulated that the funds placed in the hands of the union shall not be used in any manner which would endanger the interests of the business concern to which the union is attached.

Under Law Number 4056 a system of labor courts is established, including courts of first instance and those of appeal, and provision is made for bringing cases before the Supreme Court. Permanent labor conciliation boards are also provided for, and their use is required before strikes are allowed to occur. Other parts of the law deal with the procedures for handling different types of cases which may arise, the manner in which appeals to higher courts shall be made, the execution of penalties provided for in decisions, and other subjects attention to which would be expected in this type of law.

This brief summarization gives some indication of the completeness of labor legislation in Chile in comparison with that in other countries of South America. Chile is also unique in its provisions which force business to share profits with labor groups. Furthermore, no other country in South America has made such complete provision for the formation of labor unions and the creation of tribunals for the settlement of labor disputes. Although this legislation shows unmistakable socialistic leanings, still, if it is reasonably administered, business concerns should be able to operate under it successfully. The difficulty lies in the fact that so much chance is afforded for maladministration. If there is no possibility of securing just decisions in the labor courts, if the decisions always favor the worker instead of the business enterprise, as appears to be the case, then this labor legislation is prejudicial to the interests of North American companies. Moreover, there is evidence that the labor courts are none too free from political influence, and that, consequently, political considerations frequently are influential in the formation of decisions. Among business executives there is almost universal condemnation of the labor courts and of the favoritism shown to the labor unions. Prior to the enactment of Law Number 4056, no provision was made for appeal of labor cases to the Chilean Supreme Court, a body in which foreign interests have confidence of fair treatment. But through the efforts of the newspaper *El Murcurio* and other reform agents, the possibility of such appeals was included in the law. This may in time improve the situation. However, until there is more evidence to the contrary than now exists, the conclusion cannot be escaped that the manner in which labor legislation is administered in Chile is a potential, if not an actual, menace to the activities of all business concerns, particularly those of foreign origin.

Summary.—When these four countries are considered jointly, it is apparent that the heyday for labor legislation came in the years 1923 through 1926. Prior to that time, few demands were made upon business concerns in the interest of labor. The years since 1926 have witnessed some new laws and various modifications of those previously enacted. In Brazil, labor legislation is largely a product of the years since 1930. With legislation, many new demands have been made upon business enterprises, and there is a very general feeling that even further demands may be in the offing. Both in the provisions of the various labor laws and in the manner in which they are administered, Argentina has created fewer obstacles for business than have the other countries. The Brazilian laws have been enacted so recently that it is as yet difficult to determine the position of business under the law, but most companies with plants in Brazil are apprehensive because, in certain respects, the laws are modeled after those of Chile, the administration of which has been prejudicial to all employers. In Uruguay, unreasonable demands have been made upon business, and in addition steps have been taken toward active state participation in business. This creates additional uncertainty. Chile, in contrast, presents a situation in which the state requires some employee participation in profits, if there are such; moreover, a system of unionization is fostered by the state and is favored to such an extent by both political and legal entities that the interests of the employer are not protected in a reasonable manner.

Business concerns are not out of sympathy with the objectives of labor legislation in these countries, nor, in the majority of cases, are the laws so framed that the interests of business are necessarily prejudiced. It is true that the pension systems are seldom based on actuarial data, and thus the situation is far from desirable from the standpoint of those who are forced to contribute. And there are other questionable features with which business executives are not in entire accord. This is only to be expected. But the content of the law does not, in general, provoke active opposition. Most of the dissatisfaction has been with the administration of the laws. Unless moderation and good sense characterize the administration, those to whose actions the laws apply are bound to suffer. Unfortunately, moderation and a reasonable consideration for the rights of business enterprises have not characterized the administration of labor laws in South America, particularly in Uruguay and Chile. Legal interpretations and decisions should be divorced from political affairs, and they should be impartial. Frequently they are neither, especially in the lower courts. The growth of social legislation and the nature of its administration must therefore be viewed as an unfavorable factor in the situation of branch plants in South America.

Means of Protection against Governmental Regulation

From the foregoing discussion it is apparent that business concerns, either individually or as a group, frequently need to protect themselves against governmental action which is inimical to their interests. When so many of the restrictions and demands arising from legislation are prejudicial in effect, it is especially important for business concerns to know whether any means of self-protection are available. This section will consider, not only the possible measures that business concerns may take to protect themselves, but also certain factors in the situation which serve as protection and which are not the result of a conscious exercise of will by branch plant executives. Furthermore, the question arises as to what attitude companies of foreign origin should take toward regulatory attempts.

It is obvious that the need for protection in some manner or other depends very largely on the extent to which a regulatory measure affects branch plants. Where conditions are such that it is possible to meet demands without undue injury to the company, it has been the policy of North American concerns to comply strictly, realizing that there is little to be gained and much to be lost by an antagonistic, noncooperative attitude. When there is no important right or principle at stake, or when there is the likelihood that an uneconomic measure will eventually be withdrawn or modified because of its own characteristics, compliance without too much objection may be the course of wisdom. Antagonism created in government officials by habitual unwillingness to do that which is suggested or required only leads to more and more objectionable demands. If, however, there is an important right at stake, and, particularly, if a demand which is given compliance without protest is likely to become the precedent for many others, then self-protection is called for.

The methods used to combat unfavorable action in South America are little different from those used elsewhere, but their application differs. Forceful objection, publicity, appeal to the courts, the aid of friends in positions of authority, and, perhaps, more direct and possibly less ethical means—all are used frequently. Finally, of course, all other means failing, the branch organization has the possibility of appeal to its own government, through accredited representatives of that government, if its rights are flagrantly violated.

Group protest against regulatory action has been resorted to frequently by North American companies. The packing companies, in association with those of British and Argentine origin, have sent numerous petitions and protests to the Argentine government during the years since regulation was inaugurated. Moreover, the case of the packing companies has been taken before the public on numerous occasions. Large advertisements, often a full page, have been run in Buenos Aires newspapers over the signatures of all of the large companies, setting forth the position of the industry and the reasons for objection to legislation or its enforcement.[47] The International Telephone and Telegraph Corporation, when under attack in Uruguay, used the newspapers extensively in order to inform the public of the actual state of affairs from the company's viewpoint. This mode of attack is used much more frequently by companies in South America than it is in this country. Publicity by business concerns for the purpose of influencing public opinion is more direct, less subtle than it is here. Furthermore, the source of the publicity is openly stated and not carefully concealed as is usual in this country.

Another method of protection is that of appeal to the courts, perhaps to adjudicate some current difficulty, perhaps to test the constitutionality of a control measure. Its efficacy depends in no small measure upon the administration of the courts. In general, North American companies have high regard for the integrity and the ability demonstrated in the supreme courts of these countries. The caliber of these bodies is of itself a protection against unreasonable demands. Much less respect is entertained, however, for the lower courts. Frequently, as in the labor courts in Chile, little real protection is afforded.

Practically all of the larger firms retain native lawyers, not for the trial of one case only, but as more or less permanent legal advisers. Men of excellent training, great ability, and high standing are retained, and through their influence and their ability to interpret shifts in public opinion and in the course of political events, some protection, or at least forewarning, is secured. The importance of this type of assistance cannot easily be overstressed.

[47] The *Buenos Aires Herald* of Sept. 22, 1932, carried a full-page communication from the packing companies protesting against the enforcement of the Packers Control Law. The same communication was carried in *La Prensa* and other newspapers.

These are Latin countries, and often the Anglo-Saxon mind is at a loss to understand the Latin, the motivations behind his decisions and actions. Unless the same thought-patterns are followed, unless it is possible to realize the emotional elements which have influence, the decisions reached may be entirely incomprehensible. Individuals of standing in the country, probably from influential families, can do much to improve a foreign company's position, particularly if they occupy influential positions and are favorably disposed toward the company. "Business is business" to a lesser extent in Latin América than in the United States. Friendly relationships mean more to business enterprises, and these may be secured by having as business associates natives of the country in which the organization is operating. Native lawyers serve as interpreters or go-betweens, and, as such, are invaluable. Of course, it is not necessary that for this purpose legal talent be used. One of the large packing plants has as its manager an able Argentine gentleman, and in all probability he serves much the same purpose.

There is some dissenting opinion on this question of hiring native lawyers and major executives. The doubt is frequently expressed whether a native will have complete loyalty to an organization which some consider as an interloper in the country and not worthy of loyalty. Then, some North American concerns have been unfortunate in their selection of legal talent, although as a rule the concerns operating in South America have had satisfactory experience in this respect. In other instances, it has been thought that native lawyers keep the pot boiling for personal reasons instead of getting controversies or legal disputes finally settled. It appears that such reprehensible practice would be much more likely under a short-time relationship than under a permanent arrangement.

Protection of a similar nature is afforded by the existence of native companies and by the presence of branch plants owned by British, German, or other European concerns.

The meat-packing situation is again a good example. Control measures restrict not only the North American packing firms but also the Sansinena Company and the Smithfield and Argentine Meat Company, the first of which is completely, and the latter at least partly, owned by Argentines, and the Frigorífico Anglo, S.A., which is a part of the English Vestey concern. These companies fight their battles in common, and their combined influence may defeat unfavorable action under circumstances in which North American concerns alone might be powerless to do so. The presence of local firms in the same industry is very likely to be a protective influence. British firms, also, have more influence than their North American counterparts, because England is the chief market for Argentine products, and the need to protect the seller-buyer relationship not only deters hasty action but frequently is a positive influence as well. The influence of the Vestey concern has been a bulwark to the packing industry in Argentina against governmental encroachments.

Chapter 7

OPERATING DIFFERENCES AND DIFFICULTIES

It has been stated previously that uncertainty, arising from the many unpredictable elements involved, appears to be the outstanding characteristic of branch plant affairs. This statement was made in reference to external influences, such as the actions of government, but it is equally true in reference to internal management problems. Contingencies of one sort or another are constantly arising, particularly in the earlier years of an enterprise, and the operating problems which present themselves are perplexing and difficult of solution. The chief reason for this multiplicity of problems is that the branch plants are in each case a part of a relatively new industrial situation. In Europe, the branch plants of North American concerns became part of an old industrial economy, and their establishment followed the general industrial development of the country, but in South America it preceded such development.

One handicap to which South American plants have been particularly subject is the lack of auxiliary industry, upon which other industrial establishments depend heavily for having machinery and equipment repaired on short notice and for securing machine parts, containers and labels, and a host of other supplies. Although such auxiliary industry is growing rapidly, both in the number of products manufactured and in the quality of those products, especially in Argentina, it is still inadequate, and many supplies have to be imported. As a result, preplanning is necessary if shortages of material are to be avoided. Frequently, machines have been forced to remain idle for many weeks while some part was being secured from the United States or Europe. Had the machine been located near its original source, a day or so would probably have been sufficient for putting it into operation again. In branch plants there is simply less likelihood of successful, uninterrupted operation.

Furthermore, personnel problems are different in character from those encountered in the factories of the parent corporations, and they are more troublesome. Labor in all of these South American countries is cosmopolitan in nature, and the workers often lack the requisite training. They react differently to the various stimuli which may be used as inducements for greater production. Not only in the labor group, but also among the executives, additional problems arise. If minor executives are chosen from the native population, they may be incompetent, but importing individuals from the United States for such positions is costly, and frequently the Americans who are hired fail to adapt themselves readily to the changed conditions.

It is the purpose of this chapter to consider the internal management problems of branch plant organizations, with particular attention to the differences observed in operation and the reasons for those differences. Attention will likewise be given to the difficulties which are practically inevitable, in view of the conditions under which these branch plants operate. First, there will be a discussion of the operating differences and difficulties encountered in relation to machinery and equipment, and, later, of those which arise in connection with raw materials and supplies, labor, and the personnel for executive and minor executive positions.

Machinery and Equipment

The machinery and equipment used in branch plants may be practically identical with those used in the home factories of the parent corporation. Manufacturing processes may be such that no change in equipment is possible.

An example is the production of automobile tires, with the exception of the rubber-mixing process. Likewise, in the procedures used in the processing of livestock and the manufacture of cement there are no great differences between the North and the South American plants. But in the majority of instances, branch plants use much less machinery and more hand labor than their North American counterparts. There is but limited use of the time- and labor-saving devices which are so pronounced a feature of manufacturing in this country. Packaging of food and pharmaceutical products is often a hand instead of a machine process. Less conveying machinery is used. Numerous other examples could be cited, for they are noticeable in almost all branch plants. Moreover, the equipment and machinery which are used have frequently been discarded by factories in this country as being obsolete and of little further usefulness. The entire equipment of a branch plant producing food products in Brazil had been discarded some years earlier by a Chicago plant of the same concern. A heavy machine tool which had served the parent organization for eight years in the United States was finally sent to Argentina, where in 1933 it was in its fifth year of use. When new and improved machinery is imported and installed in these countries, the reason given is rarely the reduction of labor costs. Rather, it is stated that the quality of the finished product can thereby be improved, or that raw materials can be conserved. At times, even the prospect of appreciable savings in raw materials has not been a sufficient inducement to bring about additional capital investment in machinery and equipment.

The reasons for a greater use of labor and a lesser use of machinery than in this country are not difficult to ascertain. Labor is cheaper, in many instances, even when differences in productivity are taken into account. On the other hand, machinery is much more costly, for all of it must be imported, and its cost therefore includes heavy transportation charges and, in most cases, tariff charges. As the economist would express it, South America is working under a condition of cheap labor costs and heavy capital costs, while exactly the opposite is true in the United States. Then, also, North American concerns consciously attempt to limit their more or less fixed capital investment in these countries, and advisably so. The outlook for profitable operation over a long period of years is always uncertain, and, if at a later date withdrawal appears to be advisable, the concern with a relatively low fixed investment is in the best position to withdraw without undue losses.

A further reason for limiting the use of improved technical equipment, and, perhaps, the most effective one, is the relative scarcity of demand. Without a certain volume of business, it does not pay to install equipment with high productive capacity. Examples are numerous. In the production of automobile tires, the mixing of the rubber is done by a machine called the Banbury mixer. One of these machines will mix enough rubber in eight hours for three to five thousand tires, the exact number depending on the size of the tires. In a factory such as those in South America, in which daily production is less than one thousand tires, the use of the Banbury mixer is not feasible, even though it conserves raw materials as well as time, for the original investment required is too heavy to permit part-time or part-capacity use. Another example of conditions in which it has proved inadvisable to install expensive equipment is found in the smelting process. Whereas in Argentina a certain operation required $1\frac{2}{3}$ man-hours per ton, in the United States, where larger and better equipment was in use, the same operation was performed by $\frac{1}{10}$ man-hours per ton. Still, with the limited tonnage in Argentina, it would not have been advisable to install the perfected equipment. Perhaps the best example of this inability to use the latest technical equipment, because of limited demand for the finished product, is found in the manufacture of light bulbs. The blowing of bulbs by a hand process was abandoned in the United States nearly two decades ago, when a machine was perfected for blowing bulbs for the smaller sizes of lamps, but in Brazil the hand method is still used. The equipment required for the new process is very costly and, if it were installed in Brazil, enough bulbs could be produced in two or three months to last the entire country for a full year. Under such limited demand conditions, the obsolete equipment continues to be used, and probably will still be in use for some time to come.

Companies likewise hesitate to install new equipment because errors in the purchase of such equipment are so much more costly. For instance, a Budd welder was brought to one of these South American countries, the landed cost being about $5,000. After the welder had been used for a relatively short period, it became obsolete, as far as operations for that branch plant were concerned. The welder could not be sold advantageously and was to be shipped back to the United States. It is doubtful whether, when the machine was finally disposed of, the concern would realize over 25 per cent of its investment in the welder, which included its packing, transportation two ways, tariff charges, insurance, and other costs. In the United States, if a machine was no longer needed after a limited use, it could probably be returned to the maker at but a nominal loss. In branch plants the manufacturing operations are so remote from the centers of production of technical equipment that additional risk is involved in the purchase of such equipment, and this risk acts as a deterrent to its use.

Raw Materials and Supplies

Many of the raw materials and supplies used in branch plants must necessarily be imported. Quite evidently, assembly plants were set up with such a procedure in view, but the statement applies also to other plants. In some cases importation is necessary because the material cannot be produced in the country, in other cases, because auxiliary industry has not as yet developed sufficiently to meet requirements. For example, crude rubber must be imported because rubber is not cultivated in Argentina, whereas high-grade corrugated pasteboard boxes must be imported because the Argentine box industry is not as yet producing a really good box which will carry the necessary weights without breakage.

When reliance is placed upon imports, there must be more preplanning in regard to future wants if production is to be carried forward successfully. Branch plants, to be on the safe side, must anticipate their needs from abroad by at least ninety days, and perhaps longer. Errors in judgment in regard to when product will be needed and how much will be needed are more unfortunate in their after-effects than similar errors would be in this country. Even though the branch plant executives do their part and order sufficiently early, those responsible for shipment, perhaps the home office of the concern, may err, and the result may be interrupted production in the branch plant. A few years ago, forty-five unassembled automobiles of a certain model were sent to one of these South American countries. When assembly was attempted, it was found that one part was missing. Attempts were made, without avail, to have it produced locally, and the forty-five cars stood in storage for many weeks, awaiting the missing part. Even when no errors have been made, either in time of ordering or in shipment, still contingencies may arise which cause production to be interrupted. Very few branch managers have not, at some time or other, badly needed some materials and found themselves unable to get the materials cleared through the customs with any reasonable degree of promptness. Since such difficulties are a natural outgrowth of dependence upon importations, they will in all probability continue to be experienced by branch plant organizations.

The use of locally manufactured products, such as parts for assembly, repair parts, and supplies of all sorts, has been constantly increasing. With a greater measure of industrial expansion, which has been the outstanding feature of the economy of these countries since 1930, usable products are becoming increasingly available.[1] Furthermore, the exchange situation has furnished a strong incentive to purchase locally, instead of importing, whenever the opportunity presents itself. Because of this incentive, branch plant executives have aided local suppliers to perfect their products so that they will be acceptable for use; in fact, it is the announced policy of some organizations to substitute a locally manufactured product for importations whenever the former is so perfected that it becomes acceptable from the quality standpoint, if the price is within reason. Many locally manufactured parts and accessories are submitted to the automobile companies each year. Some items are purchased, but many more are rejected because they are not of sufficiently high quality and because they do not conform rigidly to standards.

In the purchase of parts and supplies, uniformity above all else is required, and therefore difficulties are frequently involved in purchase from those small independent companies whose entrance into manufacturing activities has largely resulted from the presence of branch plants. In the first place, the executives of these companies often lack the technical abilities which are necessary for the manufacture of an acceptable product. Moreover, their small-scale production and limited output are not conducive to uniformity of product. A good example of this situation is furnished by the Argentine paper industry, which produces only limited amounts of some types of paper. Those who purchase paper manufactured in Argentina state that it varies in color, thickness, and tensile strength; in other words, it is not sufficiently standardized.

[1] D. M. Phelps, "Industrial Expansion in South America," *American Economic Review*, Vol. 25, No. 2, June, 1935.

Because of the limited demand, perhaps only three to five tons of a certain grade of paper are produced at one time. The first 25 per cent of this amount is likely to be imperfect, for some time is required to get the mixture right and to secure acceptable operation of the machine on the new batch. Since the run on a three-ton batch takes only three or four hours, there is constant changing over and readjustment. Moreover, in view of the limited demand and the shortness of the runs, the purchaser is likely to secure, in one order, product from more than one run. The result is still greater non-uniformity, since the product from different runs is less standard than that from any one run. Another reason why locally produced supplies are likely to be inferior is the fact that frequently the machinery and equipment used make it impossible to produce as high-quality products as those manufactured in industrial nations. Although a greater variety of parts and supplies can now be furnished by local manufacturers than could be procured from them a few years ago, and although local concerns are making appreciable advances in production techniques, still branch plants cannot rely wholly on auxiliary industry to furnish the products needed in the desired qualities. Many supplies will continue to be imported, and occasional interruptions to production will be experienced because of unforseen contingencies, the result of the absence or ineffectiveness of auxiliary industry.

Labor

Effectiveness in manufacturing operations depends in no small measure upon the availability of labor that is experienced and trained in industrial pursuits or, at least, is able to acquire facility in the performance of industrial tasks. Furthermore, it depends in part upon the presence of a nucleus of trained industrial workers, capable of teaching the larger group how various tasks should be done. In all four of the South American countries here considered, there are many skilled workers, trained in the manufacturing establishments of Germany, Italy, and Central European countries, and also a much larger group of natives with little if any industrial background. But in the proportion between skilled and unskilled workers and in the background of the workers available, the four countries under observation differ markedly. First, in order to secure a rough picture of the labor group from which selection must be made, let us note briefly the make-up of the population of these countries as to race and nationality.

Each country presents a composite of races and nationalities, much like that in the United States, but it is more truly a composite, for there has been less racial segregation and color discrimination, and the blending process has been carried much further. Particularly is this the situation in Brazil. The basic stock was Indian, whereas the early colonists were the Portuguese. Large numbers of Negroes were later brought in as slaves. These were subsequently freed, toward the end of the nineteenth century. In the last fifty years, many Italians, Germans, and some Central Europeans have emigrated to the south of Brazil, mostly to the states of São Paulo and Rio Grande do Sul. The most recent development has been the emigration of some 150,000 Japanese to Brazil. Here we find taking place one of the most interesting racial admixtures which the world has known, but as yet it is too early to determine just what the admixture will produce from the viewpoint of abilities for industrial pursuits. The number of individuals who were trained in industrial activities prior to their emigration is comparatively small.

Argentina, in contrast, has a much larger body of workers with some industrial training acquired in Europe. Of the total population, about 25 per cent emigrated from Italy, mostly from the northern provinces of Lombardy and Viamonte. Many have had some experience in industry and are able, industrious workers. There are also many Germans, Anglo-Argentines, and Central Europeans. The Spanish, although not so likely to possess training, do well at the heavy jobs which require more brawn and less technical ability. Moreover, the native Argentines are able to work more effectively than the Brazilians. On the average they are of better physique, stronger, and less nervous than the Brazilian workers. The basic stock was Indian, the colonists were Spanish. There is neither an Oriental nor a Negro element in the population. It is a mixture of Indian and Spanish, with a very heavy admixture of Italian in the past fifty years. Whereas the situation in Brazil might be termed a fusing of races, that in Argentina might be considered an admixture of nationalities.

Little need be said of Uruguay and Chile beyond the fact that their populations are very largely a mixture of Indian and Spanish. There are proportionately fewer Italians and Germans than in Brazil and Argentina. As in Argentina, there is neither a Negro nor an Oriental element. The number of individuals possessing industrial training or experience is less in proportion to the total than in Argentina but probably somewhat greater than in Brazil.

One branch plant in Argentina, with a labor force of something over three hundred in 1933, presented the following nationality breakdown. It was estimated that approximately 20 per cent of the men were of Italian origin, another 20 per cent were of Central European origin, including Germans, Lithuanians, and Poles. There were also a number of Spaniards and some Russians and Scandinavians. The remainder, much less than 50 per cent, could be considered of Argentine descent; that is, descendants of families which had been in the country for three generations or more. Practically all of the workers possessed Argentine citizenship. This cannot be considered a typical breakdown, other than in its distribution of workers with European origin, for the organization of which these men were a part had shrunk appreciably after 1930, and undoubtedly the best workers had been retained. Presumably, the company kept a greater proportion of the European-trained group than of the native group, since the former were the most valuable employees. At one time another branch plant, with a labor force of between five and seven hundred, was employing men of twenty-six different nationalities. This diversity was partly a matter of intent, however, for the concern had experienced difficulty with cliques among workers of the same nationality, who forced the elimination of workers of other nationalities. To prevent such action, the company had attempted to secure workers of many nationalities. In Brazil the labor forces of branch plants are more predominantly native, with fewer Europeans of recent immigration. In Uruguay and Chile, likewise, the labor groups are less international in character.

Supervisory Labor.—Despite the presence in these South American countries of a nucleus of trained and experienced industrial workers, there is an insufficient number of the right type of individuals for supervisory labor. There is a real shortage of the energetic, responsible foreman type, trained in industrial tasks, and with sufficient ability and forcefulness to train other workers and so to manage them that work will be done with a minimum of time and materials. Workers do not develop and become able to supervise others so rapidly as they do in this country. The production manager of one branch plant stated that in his entire labor group of more than one hundred there was not one individual able to step into a newly created supervisory position. The position in question did not require technical abilities, but only the direction of workers in relatively simple operations. Moreover, supervisory workers are particularly needed. Since many of the native industrial workers have been trained only in pastoral and agricultural activities, they possess little familiarity with machines and machine processes, and consequently need careful training by experienced people. Neither do the South American workers visualize their place in the production scheme to the extent that workers do in this country. Their background has made them individualists, and they do not understand the relationship between economy in production and the need for continued effort on their part. The worker in the United States acquires, partly from reading, a knowledge of the unity of an industrial enterprise and the reasons for high productivity and low-cost production, and he thus realizes that inadequacy in his particular job will cause suffering on the part of other workers. South American workers do not possess a like comprehensive knowledge of industry, and consequently require more training.

Although some concerns after many years have succeeded in culling from their labor force enough individuals with the requisite abilities for supervisory work, still most concerns are dissatisfied with their foreman group. The foremen are said to lack initiative, and, even though they are willing to accept responsibility, they fail to perform acceptably the duties which that responsibility entails. The fact that they do not follow standards well probably indicates that they are not sufficiently familiar with industrial practices. There is also some belief that the inadequacy of the foremen can be ascribed, in part, to their fear of the rank-and-file workers. Certain it is that many individuals among the workers in these countries are none too stable emotionally and that they are not particularly tractable nor amenable to instruction by strong-arm methods, particularly by people of their own nationality. Workers in these countries, especially in Argentina, are very independent and can be "urged" much more successfully than they can be "driven." Two branch plants in Brazil, which had formerly used Germans in supervisory positions, gradually changed to Brazilians, as they found that the harsh methods used by the Germans caused active ill will and were productive of trouble. The ineffectiveness of supervisory labor may thus be considered the result of a number of contributory factors, among which are the essential difficulty of such work in these countries and the unwillingness of workers to accept dictation, as well as the lack of training and experience on the part of those in supervisory positions.

Branch plants in Argentina use many Germans and Italians and comparatively few Argentines as foremen. One automobile assembly plant uses four Germans, two Argentines, and two Scandinavians; another, two Anglo-Argentines, one Italian, and one native Argentine. It is said that one of the British-owned Argentine railroads employs Czechs, Germans, and Italians as foremen, and that the reason it does so is that the native Argentines of the class available for such positions are not sufficiently responsible and do not direct other labor well. Individual case studies of foremen, in this instance employed in an automobile assembly plant, will give some idea of the sort of men who are being used. The foreman of the commercial body assembly line is an Austrian. After spending some time in primary school, he was apprenticed to a shipbuilding firm and stayed in that employment for a number of years. His work was largely carpentry. He came to Argentina in 1925 and began to work for the North American concern in 1927. He is an energetic, intelligent workman. The assistant shop superintendent is a young German who, after securing a good education, spent a year's apprenticeship in a machine shop. This work was followed by two years in the Krupp works and an additional two years in a factory that made spinning machinery. He came to South America in 1925 and soon afterward started employment with the automobile company. He is a valuable employee, can do anything of a mechanical nature, is imaginative and inventive, and, in addition, handles men excellently. Men of the type of these two are all too scarce, and, as a result, in the great majority of cases less able individuals must be used. There are still fewer trained workers of supervisory caliber in Brazil, Chile, and Uruguay, and consequently a greater proportion of natives are found in supervisory work.

Rapidity in the acquirement of industrial skills by the great mass of workers is hindered by the relative scarcity of those with previous industrial training. But there is little doubt in the minds of branch managers in regard to the ability of these people to acquire such aptitudes if they are given a reasonable opportunity to do so. There is a general consensus of opinion on this point. The works manager of a plant employing 1,200 men in Brazil stated that Brazilians were good, dependable workers; that, although the Brazilian required long and careful training, he did possess the necessary attributes to become a good factory worker. The production manager of an automobile assembly plant in Argentina stated that he would have no hesitancy, so far as labor was concerned, in opening any type of factory in Buenos Aires; that, no doubt, difficulties would be experienced initially but that they could be overcome in time because there is a nucleus of trained industrial workers and because the people in general acquire industrial skills easily. The measures of comparative productivity, which will be presented in the next section, will at least partially substantiate these statements.

Companies migrating to these countries follow various plans in regard to training workers. Most of them rely on securing in South America individuals who will be able to train others. Whether or not this policy is followed depends largely on the nature of the manufacturing process. If it is complex, there is more need for careful training procedures. The automobile and tire companies sent numerous individuals from this country to instruct workers. The Goodyear Tire and Rubber Company has what is known as its "flying squadron," which goes wherever a new factory is established. After new workers are trained and become proficient, the squadron returns to its base. This proved to be a very satisfactory method in Argentina, for the men trained by these expert workers have become most satisfactory employees. Another method is to select nationals and send them to the United States for a training period. This plan has been used to a limited extent by two of the packing companies and has been successful. However, it involves a substantial investment in specific individuals, who may see fit to leave the company shortly after their return. Hence, it must be considered a risky method of training, although it may produce excellent results if the training period is followed by a long tenure of employment.

Productivity of Labor.—The productivity of workers in these countries is much higher than it is usually supposed to be. Companies establishing branch plants have, in practically every instance, been agreeably surprised at the performance of workers after a training period of reasonable length. Both the quickness of the workers in acquiring skill and the records which they have made in production afterward have been much better than expected. A number of factors, however, make difficult any direct comparisons of productivity between branch plants in South America and factories of the parent corporations in this country. In the majority of cases there is a difference in the machinery and equipment used, that in the branch plant being older and more obsolete. As has been observed previously, the volume of business is frequently too small to make feasible the installation of labor- and time-saving devices which are currently used in the United States. There is also less specialization of work. A man may perform a number of operations, instead of just one. There are often differences in the materials used by the workers and in the conditions under which the work is done. All of these factors make direct comparisons of productivity difficult to secure, for, obviously, differences in output reflect the comparative capacity and effort put forth by the worker, only in so far as the operations performed and the conditions under which they are performed are the same. However, some idea of comparative productivity can be secured at times, if an attempt is made to allow for the differences noted. In some cases, enough for the purposes of this study, the conditions of work and the operations were sufficiently alike to permit direct comparisons. These comparisons, although not entirely conclusive, serve to substantiate the general conclusion that workers in these countries are capable of fairly high industrial output.

First, some comparisons will be noted which involved relatively simple industrial operations. In the making of a certain type and size of reinforced concrete tile for roofs, the standard in the United States was forty-five per day per worker. For performance above this standard, a bonus was given, but workers seldom produced many more than fifty per day. In the making of the same tile in Rio de Janeiro, workers frequently reached fifty-five or fifty-six per day, and the average output was fully as high as in this country.

Another example involved the manufacture of paper valve bags, which require cutting and sewing operations by the use of power equipment. For this work girls and women are employed, principally. In this case allowance is necessarily made for the fact that the equipment used in Argentina is not so new or up-to-date as that used in this country. After the difference in equipment is taken into consideration, those employed were about 90 per cent as productive as those employed for similar operations in the United States.

Another comparison is drawn from service work rather than from manufacturing operations. In the servicing of its technical office equipment, one company has service costs of about 11 per cent of its returns for the equipment, whereas such costs in the United States are only 8 per cent. A number of reasons other than the ability of the workers may explain this difference in service costs. Apparently there is a greater turnover in service men, and there are fewer machines in use. Evidently the men do acceptable work and are imaginative in their conceptions of what the machines will do and what may be amiss when they fail to operate successfully, but they work more slowly and deliberately than do service men in the United States. Hence, costs are higher.

Some comparisons from the automobile assembly plants indicate that the number of man-hours required for the assembly of automobiles is no greater than it is in countries such as Norway and Holland; in fact, at times, when the number of automobiles assembled has been high, the number of hours required has been appreciably lower. This has been the case in both Brazil and Argentina. Another measure often considered of significance in judging the capability of a labor force is the relationship between productive and nonproductive labor. Nonproductive labor includes such workers as janitors and watchmen, maintenance men, electricians, material men, inspectors, and salvage men. In one Argentine automobile plant, there were 204 productive and 66 nonproductive workers, or one of the latter to three of the former. The comparable figure in the United States is one nonproductive worker to four productive workers. Oftentimes, this figure runs as high as one to two, but there is an appreciable saving where the ratio is smaller. The ratio of one to three in this Argentine plant may be considered an indication of an efficient labor force.

The experience of the tire companies, although of much shorter duration than that of the automobile companies, appears to be markedly similar. Productivity has been much higher than was expected and compares favorably with productivity in plants located in other parts of the world. In specific operations, workers have equaled, in some instances even broken, existing records held elsewhere. Effort, however, is not sustained over a long period, and apparently the workers do not have sufficient interest in earning additional income to continue a high rate of output.

The examples given indicate that the productivity of workers in these countries is relatively high. In making a final judgment, however, two things should be borne in mind. The labor force of many of these companies has been in a process of continual selection for a number of years, and, through selection and training, a well-coordinated, reasonably efficient force has been brought together. Another significant fact is that some concerns, the construction firms and the automobile companies in particular, had appreciably reduced their forces after 1930. Obviously, the least acceptable workers were released, and the average efficiency was thereby improved. When the tire companies entered Argentina and assembled their labor forces in 1930–1931, there were many more semitrained workers available than there had been a few years previously. It is not probable that a company entering Argentina or Brazil today for manufacturing purposes would find as acceptable workers available as did the tire companies in 1931. Nor would such a company immediately attain the degree of labor productivity that has been attained by the automobile assembly plants.

Managers of practically all the North American branch plants, and of some European branch plants as well, were asked their opinion of the relative productivity of workers in these countries and workers in the United States or Europe. The general consensus of opinion was that workers engaged in manufacturing operations in Argentina are from 80 to 85 per cent as productive as workers in the United States, Germany, or England, due allowances being made for differences in volume, equipment, and so on. Likewise, it was the consensus of opinion that productivity is lower in Brazil, Uruguay, and Chile, and that, of the Brazilian workers, those in São Paulo approach the Argentine level most closely. Perhaps it would be somewhat more accurate to call this an average of opinion or estimates, rather than a consensus of opinion, for some people thought that about 60 per cent was a more accurate figure, while others thought that there was little if any difference. A large number, however, drawing upon some specific comparisons of particular operations and upon many years of experience, without being influenced by the estimates of others, arrived at the 80 to 85 per cent figure for Argentina.

Of course, variation in the estimates would be expected, for it is only reasonable to assume that the workers available would be more proficient at some kinds of tasks than at others. The Italians in particular are very proficient at hand work, such as upholstering automobiles or furniture, or doing the knife work in packing plants. It is very doubtful whether workers in any part of the world are more effective at such tasks. Furthermore, an estimate as to relative productivity is the product of personal, and hence limited, experience. If a firm has been particularly effective in assembling a labor force, then the manager is likely to think that all labor is as productive as that in his plant. It must be remembered also that the opinions quoted were those of branch plant managers and that branch plants in all probability have secured better labor forces than have the native concerns. Therefore, the estimates may be too high for industrial labor as a whole in these countries. The figure given should be accepted, not as a general estimate, but as one for the labor in branch plants only.

Some of the reasons for lower productivity are apparent. The majority of workers have no industrial background and but limited training, and the scarcity of individuals who are capable of directing others in the capacity of foreman is not conducive to high output. Another reason, and a telling one, is that the workers lack the physical stamina needed for continued work at high speed. This fact is probably more true of workers in the warmer climates—Brazil, for instance—than of those in more moderate climates. The lack of stamina is not wholly a matter of climate or working conditions, however, but also of innate bodily resources, which on the average are unequal to those possessed by workers in the United

States. Observation, used as an imperfect substitute for the quantitative records which are not available, leads one to believe that South American workers in general are smaller, less heavy, and more nervous than a typical group of workers in this country.

Some light is shed upon this question by the experience of the Brazilian Traction, Light & Power Co., Ltd., in Rio de Janeiro. In the company's shops, some 1,200 men are employed. Of this number, one-half to two-thirds take their noonday meal in the company's restaurant, where they are served all they can eat of good hearty food at a nominal cost. Whether the restaurant was started with the hope of increasing the productivity of the workers is unknown, but it has had that effect in a truly notable measure. Previously, output had slumped about three o'clock in the afternoon and remained low until quitting time. Evidently the men did not have sufficient luncheon, were undernourished, and thus were physically incapable of maintaining output in the late afternoon hours. The output of boys winding coils increased 20 per cent after they were fed at the factory during the noon period, and absenteeism, which had often been as high as 15 to 20 per cent, decreased to 3 or 4 per cent. It is likely that the meal received at the plant is the only good, hot meal of the day for many employees. Certain other companies have established similar eating facilities for their workers.

The experience of this company suggests that part of the difficulty lies in the conditions under which workers live. Living conditions in general leave much to be desired. Few houses have central heating, sanitary facilities are inadequate and obsolete, and as a result there is much sickness and disease. That living conditions can appreciably affect output has long been recognized, and it is amply demonstrated in South American countries.

Poor working conditions also account for low productivity. This is not the situation in branch plants, for there the working conditions are fully equal to those in this country in the factories of the parent corporations. But in the factories of native concerns, conditions at times are unbelievably bad. Ventilation and light are not properly provided for. In one factory visited, manufacturing operations were being carried on in the cellar of an old building, the rooms being damp, ill-lighted, without heat, and totally unfit for workers. While such conditions appear to be the exception more often than the rule, still they are sufficiently numerous to merit comment. Manufacturing can be carried on under the handicap of such locations, but there is little chance of high productivity on the part of workers, and detriment to their health under a long tenure of employment is inevitable.

One further condition limits productivity. It is the attitude of workers toward increased earnings which might be achieved through additional effort on their part. A number of plants have instituted incentive wage schemes, but they appear to be less effective in stimulating production than they usually are in this country. The workers do not seem interested in increasing their incomes, but apparently prefer to proceed at a leisurely pace. Particularly is this true of the peons—that is, the lower grade workers. In one plant, a large group of peons who had been receiving between four and five pesos daily were put on piece work which, with additional effort, would have yielded them as much as eight pesos. These peons disregarded the possibility of higher earnings and worked along slowly for eight hours, thereby earning their usual wage. The higher grade laborers, known as *mecanicos*, are stimulated to a greater extent by incentive wage schemes. The Swift International Company, which has a thirty-year history in these countries, uses an incentive wage scheme, and thus it seems that such a scheme may be used effectively after a thorough trial. Still, it is reasonable to believe that the easy-going Latin temperament in general is not particularly subject to prodding through the incentive of higher wages, and that incentive schemes will be less productive of greater output in South America than in the United States.

The question now arises whether the productivity of workers in these countries is likely to increase as time goes on. In all probability it will, for there is agreement among those in close association with the workers that they are able to acquire industrial skills with relative ease. Industry in these countries has been expanding during the past two decades, and thus workers have been gaining additional experience. Natural ability, combined with accumulated experience and training, should bring about increased productivity. On the other hand, there is some question whether the physical stamina of the workers will permit a high average output. That even this can be increased has been amply demonstrated by the experience with Brazilian workers previously described and by the effect which improvement in living and working conditions has had upon output elsewhere. Finally, it has been questioned whether workers of Latin and Indian origin are temperamentally of a type which will achieve the high level of productivity reached in the United States and certain European countries. And, indeed, this factor is likely to be the most serious drawback to the achievement of high productivity among workers in these South American countries.

Labor Costs.—Labor costs in these countries are low, both in comparison to other types of cost and in comparison to labor costs in the United States. Other costs, particularly for heat and power, are high. Coal must be largely imported, and there is little hydroelectric power of consequence except in Brazil. Many raw materials must be imported, likewise the greater share of the capital for productive effort. Capital goods, such as machinery and equipment, must be procured abroad. Management costs are high in so far as the individuals in charge are nationals of another country imported for the express purpose of directing productive operations. All of these factors contribute to relatively high production costs. Labor, on the contrary, is less costly than in the United States even if comparative productivity is taken into consideration. A number of concerns estimated that labor costs were only about 50 per cent as high whereas productivity was nearly equal. In one particular instance, an employee receiving a sum in Argentine currency equivalent to approximately $1.75, at the current exchange rate, was performing the same task, with about the same output, as a man receiving $6.50 in this country.

This fact appears to be in direct contradiction to the generally accepted theory that comparative wages in different countries are roughly in proportion to the productivity of the workers. But there are numerous factors which, temporarily at least, obviate this theory as far as industry in South American countries is concerned. Taussig says that high money wages are the consequence, not of general effectiveness, but of effectiveness in the production of exported goods.[2] Agricultural products are the goods generally exported from the east coast, where the greater share of industry is located. Moreover, the analysis behind this theory presupposes a more or less static condition, whereas South American industry lately has expanded with some rapidity. With continued industrial activity and with higher wages in agricultural areas, which may follow higher prices for exports, it is not unlikely that competition for the limited group of trained workers available will lead to a higher level of wages and thus higher labor costs in branch plants.

Labor Disturbances.—Only in Argentina have North American concerns had noteworthy trouble with organized labor groups. Labor in Brazil and Uruguay has not presented any particular problems. Until recently there has been little organization of workers in Brazil, and the

[2] F. W. Taussig, *Selected Readings in International Trade and Tariff Problems* (Boston: Ginn and Company, 1921), p. 125.

workers there appear to be more tractable and less disposed to create disturbance than elsewhere. Little difficulty with labor has been reported in Uruguay, despite the fact that this country has been the gathering place for people with radical tendencies. In Chile, the situation in respect to labor has not been an altogether favorable one because of the trouble occasioned by maladministration of social legislation.[3] The labor groups in branch plants are small, however, and adjustments have been made without long-protracted disturbances, such as those experienced in Argentina.

In view of the number of branch plants in Argentina and the length of time over which each has operated, there have not been many serious controversies between management and labor. Some concerns have experienced no difficulty worthy of mention. Others, when subjected to demands on the part of workers, have been able to make adjustments and have thus avoided further difficulty. But in 1933 a number of concerns were figuratively holding their breath in anticipation of labor troubles, largely, no doubt, because of the strikes between 1929 and 1932 by workers associated with the General Motors Corporation, the Ford Motor Company, and the International Telephone and Telegraph Corporation. The first of the controversies, that involving the General Motors Corporation, lasted from the middle of 1929 to the middle of 1930. Before this dispute was entirely settled, a strike was declared at the Ford plant on July 10, 1930. This strike lasted about three months, or until the revolution on September 6, 1930. The International Telephone and Telegraph Corporation strike also lasted about three months, from early spring to midsummer in 1932.

All of these strikes had marked similarities. The issues were much the same. They pertained to union recognition and the rehiring of individuals who had been discharged, rather than to wages or working conditions. In each case,

[3] See Chap. 6, pp. 224–225.

the strike was not an attack of the workers on company policies, but an attempted intimidation of the company by outside labor organizations with a sprinkling of members within the plants. Moreover, strikes in these countries are of a peculiarly vicious nature, and these three were not exceptions. Intimidation, sabotage, destruction of the property of third parties, the use of the boycott, and even physical injury, were resorted to frequently during the strike periods. Actually, the strikes resembled guerrilla warfare more than an orderly protest against real or imagined wrongs. More will be said of these characteristics presently, but first attention will be directed to the background necessary to this discussion.

Each of the three companies, because of the change in general economic conditions, was forced to discharge an appreciable number of workers. Between 1929 and 1932, the telephone company, being unable for financial reasons to continue with its program of new construction, found it necessary to discharge about three thousand employees. At the time of the strikes involving the automobile companies, labor forces had not been so drastically reduced, but the number employed was considerably below the peak. Then the selection process, so necessary in any South American country to the acquisition of a capable body of workers, in itself created a numerous group which at some time had worked for the corporations. These men, when employed, had received wages somewhat above the going rates, and, when approached by labor agitators with a promise of reemployment as the reward for cooperation in a strike effort, readily agreed to participate and voice their claims through a labor union. In each instance the number of actually employed workers who participated in the strike was comparatively small. According to the *Standard*[4] of July 12, 1930, 1,037 men out of a total of 1,106 came to work at the Ford plant the day that the strike was called, and many of the rest probably stayed

[4] A Buenos Aires newspaper published in English.

away only through the fear of personal violence. The situation was accurately stated in the *Buenos Aires Herald* of July 5, 1930: "Things are going too well and too easily in the Ford establishment for the liking of outsiders." The strike, in all three cases, was forced upon the workers and was not a product of their own volition.

The automobile companies, in particular, were not in conflict with the vast majority of their workers. Rather, they were in conflict with the Chauffeurs' Union—a powerful, undisciplined group which espoused the cause of the few agitators and malcontents in the factories and of those who had been discharged. Evidence that this union did not actually represent the workers is furnished by the fact that a group of Ford workers, estimated at 1,000 men, marched to the capital building and asked the government for protection. A manifesto was also directed to the government, stating that the workers were not in sympathy with the strike. *La Nacion* of August 8, 1930, stated:

> The attitude of the workers of the Ford Motor Company who gathered yesterday in front of the Casa de Gobierno [capital building] in order to manifest their desire that the authorities assure them the liberty to work demonstrates that the agitation which is pretended to be in said personnel is entirely artificial and contrary to the true interests of the workers.[5]

In the telephone strike, also, there was little evidence that the workers then employed were discontented with the treatment accorded them by the company. The opposing party, however, was not an outside union, as in the case of the automobile companies, but the Union of Telephone Employees (Federación de Obreros y Empleados de Telefonicas). This union included among its members the majority of those persons who had been discharged because of the cessation of new construction, and it was this group that carried the strike action forward. So, as in the case of the automobile strikes, agitation and inter-

---

[5] This is a free translation.

ference from without were the primary cause of the labor troubles.

Condemnation of the methods used by the unions in these strikes cannot be too severe. Malicious destruction of property was resorted to in numerous instances. The telephone company strike, after an exchange of communications between the union and the company but without official declaration of a strike, began with simultaneous bombings in various company offices located in different parts of Buenos Aires. The Palermo exchange was put entirely out of commission, and broken water pipes caused the damaging of supplies and equipment elsewhere. After this initial outburst, the strike was a well-organized one, characterized by periodic sabotage. Cables were cut, likewise poles and outside wiring. Manholes were blown up, physical assault on workers was not uncommon, acid was thrown on girls' clothing, and other acts of violence were perpetrated. In order to protect employees who continued on the job, the company provided meals and sleeping quarters in or near the exchanges. Finally, after the strike had lasted about three months, the government stepped in and said that the strike must stop. A settlement, the terms of which were largely dictated by the government, was effected within forty-eight hours. Although the settlement terms might be considered a draw, still there can be little doubt that the workers' federation lost a prestige which it had formerly possessed.

The methods used by the union against the automobile companies also involved property destruction, but they were directed to a greater extent at third parties. Dealers were threatened if they continued to handle the products of the company against which the strike action was directed. Members of the Chauffeurs' Union controlled the purchase of many cars, and the boycott was invoked. This was carried even further, through a policy of preventing the purchase of cars by individual buyers. Tires were mutilated, acid was thrown on cars to destroy the finish, fenders were purposely smashed, cars were stolen; all in all, it became hazardous to operate a car made by the company involved in the strike. Most of these acts were carried out with impunity, little restraint of any sort being exercised. The obvious purpose of such acts is to destroy the demand for a company's products.

Although this method of procedure cannot be countenanced in any way, still it must be recognized as constituting the only method, other than arbitration, whereby the unions could impose their will upon the companies. The usual method of refusing to work until demands are met would have been ineffective, for usually many applicants were waiting for the vacated positions. Both wages and working conditions in branch plants are well above the average in these countries, and workers are attracted. As a matter of fact, the vast majority of workers are satisfied and are fully cognizant of the favorable conditions under which they labor. It is thus apparent that there was little legitimate reason for strike action in the first place. The evidence obtainable indicates that the three strikes under consideration were largely the product of disturbing influences from without, rather than of dissatisfaction on the part of those employed.

The vicious nature of these strikes is difficult to explain with any measure of assurance. In contact with the workers, however, one becomes aware of a certain instability, an emotional characteristic not present to a like degree among workers in this country. This instability may be a product of a changing racial admixture, with Latin and Indian elements predominating. Partly, it is a product of class hatreds and the undercurrent of lawlessness found in all South American countries. Moreover, the socialistic and radical tendencies which have gained momentum during the past two decades are in no small measure responsible for the attitude taken by the workers. The Union Civica Radical party, which is by far the most numerous group politically, is strongly opposed to foreign capital, and it must be remembered that the strikes described were directed against North American companies. The Radical party was in power prior to the revolution of 1930 and during the time that both the General Motors and the Ford strikes occurred. The intimidation and lawlessness which characterized this period in Argentine history were largely due to a governmental regime that was entirely ineffective and unable to cope with the existing situation. After the revolution, conditions improved markedly and have continued to do so under the Justo administration.

Therefore, it is apparent that the nature of labor disturbances is in part the outgrowth of instability and weakness of government. The Ford strike terminated with the 1930 revolution. Undoubtedly this political upheaval, with its aftermath of rigid military control, saved the Ford company from a long-protracted and costly struggle such as that experienced for a twelve-month period by the General Motors Corporation. The telephone strike was allowed by the Justo government to run for only a three-month period. But even with this relatively strong government in power, little real protection was given to the company. Either the police were unable to prevent willful property destruction or they made only half-hearted attempts to do so, for the company was forced to incur heavy expense for the repair of its properties. During the automobile strikes which took place while the Radical party was in power, practically no police assistance was given. Strike leaders would be arrested one day and released the next. People caught attempting to damage the factory were taken a few blocks away by the police and released. From the experience of these companies, the conclusion cannot be escaped that little real protection is accorded by government to business of foreign origin in the event of labor disturbances and that even less can be expected if the Union Civica Radical party happens to be in power.

Perhaps the appearance of labor difficulties in the first place, as well as the failure of the government to give the companies full protection, arises from the fact that the companies attacked are of foreign origin. Even in conservative groups there is an undercurrent of anti-foreign-capital sentiment, and among the parties of the Left, which include many workers, this sentiment becomes rabid. Then there is some question whether the management of branch plants deals as effectively with labor as does the management of native concerns. There appears to be little labor disturbance among the latter, even though the wages and working conditions are less acceptable from the worker's standpoint than in the branch plants. Of course, the fact that the native concerns are usually much smaller means that they are less subject to labor trouble. In view of the size of the labor forces employed in branch plants, the anti-foreign-capital sentiment, and the socialistic and communistic leanings in Argentina, it is likely that labor disturbances will continue and thus contribute an element of instability to all branch plant operations. Conditions in Chile are much the same as those in Argentina, but in Brazil there are likely to be fewer labor disturbances, as there is less labor organization and the workers appear to be more tractable. Still, too much optimism on the part of management in regard to the stability of labor in any of these countries would be a failure to recognize the potentialities of the labor situation.

Executive Personnel

Branch plants have three main sources from which to choose their executive personnel: the organization of the parent company in the United States, the Europeans who have migrated to these countries, and the nationals of the country in which the plant is located. Companies differ markedly in the extent to which each of these sources is used. One company, although of North American origin, has not one North American individual in its employ.

The manager is a Scotchman, and his chief assistant is an Argentine citizen whose father was an Italian and whose mother was a North American. In contrast, another small branch plant has brought nine men from the home office in this country. In yet another, the manager is a North American, his assistant is an Anglo-Argentine, and some of the minor executives are Argentines and some are Europeans.

There are numerous reasons for the differences observed. One of these is the degree of technicality of the product manufactured or assembled. However, in all three of the cases mentioned, the product is a technical one. This would suggest that the degree of technicality of the product has little to do with the source of executive personnel. In general, however, more men from the offices and plants of the parent corporation are likely to be used in the branch factories if the products manufactured or assembled are technical in nature. Another factor accounting for differences in the nationality of the executive personnel is the length of time in which the branch plant has operated. In the earlier years of a plant's operation, one frequently finds many North Americans in executive positions. Later, the North Americans tend to be replaced by individuals of other nationalities who have gained proficiency in executive tasks and who, perhaps, are more willing to continue to live in South America. Again, if companies have branch plants in Europe, they sometimes import men for South American executive positions from these plants, instead of from the home office. Before the men are sent to South America, they are usually given a period of training in the United States. Finally, the nationality of the executives may be the expression of differences in the policy of various companies. Those in authority express a wide diversity of opinion in regard to the capability and dependability of individuals from the different sources. These opinions are based, no doubt, upon their several fortunate or unfortunate experiences in selection. Here an attempt will be made to analyze the strong and weak points of executives chosen from the various sources.

The majority of branch plants have two or three key men, some of whom were sent to South America for the express purpose of starting and supervising operations. These key men are usually the branch manager, a comptroller, and a production man. While they are likely to be North Americans, there are numerous exceptions. Any one, or all, of the three may be either national or European. Usually, however, this executive nucleus to whom the fate of the enterprise is intrusted consists of men who have been with the company for many years and who are thoroughly trained in company policies and methods. Their selection for responsibilities so far removed from the home office indicates that they have the complete confidence of their superiors. For such major positions very few nationals with the requisite training and experience are available, and, even if they are available, it might not be good policy to place them in a position to know all the affairs of the concern or to intrust them with intimate details of the company's policies. Moreover, it is necessary, at times, for a concern operating in a foreign country to have relationships with the government representatives of its own country. The advice of its legation may be sought on matters which involve the protection of company interests, for difficulties do arise between governments and foreign concerns operating within a country. Obviously, in cases of this type, members of the legation could not talk freely before the executives if the latter were nationals. In general, it seems questionable whether a concern should risk the chance of divided loyalty and consequent biased decisions by hiring nationals for major executive positions.

Europeans with the requisite abilities are more numerous, and the question of divided loyalties or of a national viewpoint which may be at variance with company interests does not arise to a like extent. In numerous branch plants, Englishmen hold major executive positions with great success. Among these concerns are the branch plants of some of the packing companies, the Otis Elevator Company, and the United Shoe Machinery Company. A German is doing an excellent job as manager of a North American branch plant in Brazil. Not only in branch plants, but also in financial institutions, merchandising organizations, shipping companies, and public utilities, all owned and operated by North American concerns, a large number of Englishmen, Germans, and Italians are found in managerial positions. This extensive use of Europeans is not difficult to explain. The United States has but recently become a large capital-exporting nation, and as a result there are but few individuals trained for work abroad. European countries, on the contrary, and England in particular, have been heavy capital exporters for many years. In each of the countries under observation, English capital was the chief factor in the development of public utilities. As a result, there are in these countries many Europeans who are well versed in the problems connected with migration of capital and the most effective methods for their solution. Their employment has done much to strengthen the executive personnel of North American companies.

Between the executive nucleus of which we have spoken and the foreman group, individuals are needed who are called upon to assume a goodly measure of responsibility. Some of the positions are in sales, some are of a semi-technical nature, and others might be termed secondary production jobs. As a class, they are called minor executive positions. It is in the source of men for these positions that firms so markedly differ. There is, however, a general tendency to use fewer and fewer North Americans. A number of branch managers stated emphatically that they did not wish North Americans for semi-executive positions and that, if they had complete authority to make the decision, they would not bring people from the United States for such jobs. The basis of this attitude is partly a matter of comparative cost, partly a matter of adaptation. First, we will dispose of the simpler question, that of cost.

When firms are able to secure competent individuals for semi-executive positions, either from among the nationals of the country or from the Europeans already residing there, the cost is appreciably less. People brought from the United States are used to a standard of living which is higher than that in South American countries, and they must be paid enough to allow them to take their place in the North American community. The very fact that they are North Americans in the employ of one of the well-known companies places a responsibility upon that company to pay them salaries which will allow them to maintain their accustomed standard of living. Otherwise the company, as well as the individual, loses face. In addition, there is the cost of bringing them down, and the return costs if either the individual or the company becomes dissatisfied with the arrangement.

Individuals are never left stranded in these countries. Even when they are discharged for good cause, they are returned to the United States with expenses paid by the company. Moreover, vacations must be arranged for, again at company expense. It is the common practice to give vacations every three to five years, the majority of which last two or three months. A shorter vacation would be of little value to the individual, for, if travel is by boat rather than by airplane, the time taken in travel alone is between five and six weeks. In view of these expenses which the company assumes, in addition to the higher initial salaries needed to maintain an accustomed standard of living, the efficiency of the imported individuals must be considerably higher than that of nationals to justify the expense. For some positions, it undoubtedly is higher, but for others there is considerably more question.

If the imported individuals always adapted themselves readily to the conditions under which they were expected to work, there would be more reason for their employment.

Frequently, however, they do not adapt themselves and must either be sent back to the United States or retained, even though they are unacceptable employees. One difficulty is that the individuals selected for positions in these countries frequently are unable to learn the language required (Spanish or Portuguese), or else are unwilling to exert enough energy to learn the language thoroughly. They acquire a smattering of the language, just enough, perhaps, to enable them to get along without too much difficulty, but not enough to enable them to comprehend exactly the meaning intended by those speaking. If a person is unable to tell whether a customer has said, "I can pay," "I will pay," or "I would pay," he is of little use to a sales organization. Without a thorough knowledge of the language used, a North American cannot control a sales force of Brazilians or Argentines who do not know English. Also, unless he has a workable knowledge of their language, he loses the respect of the sales force. One of the most able branch executives in South America stated it to be his opinion that not one out of ten North Americans acquires a sufficient knowledge of the language of the country in which he is located. In addition to the language, customs and manners must also be learned. Although there is much more similarity than is commonly thought in the manner of conducting business in the two Americas, still there are variations, and a failure of the individual to acquire a knowledge of these variations may make him a less valuable employee than he otherwise would be. A receptive, analytical mind has much to commend it, particularly in these South American jobs.

Failure to adapt one's self readily is in part a matter of general attitude toward work in foreign countries. In this respect, the contrast between the Englishman and the North American is a revealing one. The former, when sent to South America by his company, expects to stay there indefinitely. He may hope to return in his later years, but his working years are to be spent abroad.

With such expectations, a man conducts himself, not as a transient, but as a permanent member of the community in which he is placed. He purchases a home, makes other definite commitments, and adopts a conciliatory, friendly attitude toward the nationals with whom he comes in contact. Moreover, he learns the language thoroughly; in fact, he probably learned it earlier, in anticipation of work abroad. North Americans, on the contrary, usually come to Brazil or Argentina with the fixed idea of returning permanently in from two to five years—with no intention of making these countries their permanent home. They avoid definite capital commitments, their attitude toward nationals leaves something to be desired, and they study the language only a few months—not long enough to secure any mastery of its details.

The dissatisfaction frequently felt by North American executives is to some extent caused by the attitude of their wives, who are discontented at being located in a foreign country. The man might be contented, and thus an efficient employee, if his wife were willing to remain within the country indefinitely. But constant agitation at home for return to the United States is not conducive to successful adaptation and enthusiastic participation in company activities. If all individuals, prior to leaving the United States, could be imbued with the idea that they were making at least a fifteen-to twenty-year commitment, they would become more acceptable employees for migrating companies.

This question of permanence assumes additional importance when it is realized that new men, unless in purely technical positions, are of little value for the first year or two. In the greater share of semi-executive positions in this country, a new man, particularly if his business experience is limited, is more of a burden than an asset for at least the first six months. It is not uncommon for executives to state that $1,000 to $1,500 is still invested in a newcomer at the end of the first year. In branch plants, because of the greater difficulties of adaptation, the period before real usefulness begins is longer, and, furthermore, the company assumes not only training costs, but also traveling expenses. Hence, the amount invested in a man destined for a minor executive position in a branch plant is nearer $5,000 at the end of the first year, and conceivably a like amount at the end of the second year. It is doubtful whether any tenure of employment of less than three years nets the company any gain on the individual's services. Only when the individual stays five years or longer, is the company's "investment" in him a really productive one.

Because of the amount invested in executives imported from North America, the problem of initial selection is an important one. That the selection process is not easy is demonstrated by the mistakes which have so frequently been made. The experience of one branch manager is revealing. He made a trip to the United States with the major purpose of selecting five young men for his expanding organization. After innumerable interviews, five men were selected and brought to Argentina as future executives. Despite their careful selection, only one of these men made the necessary adaptation successfully and was in Argentina five years later. One individual who had an excellent record in the United States, and of whom much was expected, failed signally to learn Spanish and was soon sent back to the parent organization. He muffed his opportunity, for excellent positions are available in branch plant administration. Frequently one hears comment to the effect that a certain person did well with the company in the United States, but that he was of little use in South America.

Failure can be ascribed basically to the fact that there were few men in this country with any foreign business experience when the heavy demand for such men appeared during the period from 1915 on. Moreover, selection was hurried and consequently careless. It appears also that there has been a lack of understanding in regard to the type of individuals needed for executive positions with migrating companies.

Unfortunate errors have been made in selecting individuals for branch operations by attaching too much importance to a knowledge of the Spanish or Portuguese language. Proficiency in the language needed is a valuable asset, but that it be acquired prior to departure from this country is not entirely essential. Despite our previous insistence that the language must be learned, and thoroughly, it must be recognized that, by continued effort, the language can be acquired in a relatively short period of time, and especially so while the individual concerned is in South America. Secondary requisites should not be confused with primary ones, and in this case the primary requisite is not a knowledge of language but a knowledge of business. Too many younger men, lacking a thorough business experience and the judgment which comes with maturity, have been sent to foreign positions. On the other hand, some men who went to South America after they had passed the middle years have been very successful. It is reasonable to conclude that the place for branch executives to learn business procedures and attain business judgment is the United States, not Brazil or Argentina. Moreover, when the essential difficulty of the problems presented to executives in branch plants is taken into consideration, it is evident that seasoned businessmen are needed rather than younger men who still are in the apprenticeship period.

One further characteristic is necessary in the individuals selected for either major or minor executive positions with branch plants. This is the ability to meet unexpected situations fearlessly and without too much indecision. Uncertainty has been referred to as the outstanding feature of branch plant administration. A diversity of problems arise, many of them entirely unforeseen, and the individual in authority must possess the necessary fortitude and be willing to accept the responsibilities which his position entails. It should be recalled, moreover, that branch plant executives are not surrounded with legal, technical, and sales advisers as are executives in this country. Thus, the responsibilities assumed are greater, since action must be based largely upon independent judgment. Comparative isolation from the home office makes necessary the selection of higher caliber executives if branch plant operations are to be carried forward successfully.

In view of the greater cost of employing minor executives brought from the United States and their comparative lack of adaptability, branch managers have been using a greater number of nationals and Europeans for sales, accounting, and secondary production jobs. Even for positions involving some technical knowledge, substitution is taking place. Nationals, in particular, lack training, but they learn readily and are especially strong in all of those characteristics which have been considered under the head of adaptation. Northern Europeans, when available, appear to combine the favorable characteristics of each of the other two groups. Many have become adapted through long residence in South America. Others have migrated more recently, but, with the background afforded by a colonizing nation, they become adjusted to the new environment with relative ease. In addition, they are likely to possess some knowledge of industrial processes and of the problems which frequently arise in branch plants.

Despite this tendency for branch plants to use more nationals and Europeans, there are opportunities with the migrated concerns for comparatively youthful North Americans. Many of the major executives will continue to be North Americans, and concerns dislike to intrust some of the lesser executive positions to other nationalities. Then, also, more North Americans would be used if they were adequately trained for the positions in South America and if ready adjustment was made after arrival. Business experience should first be acquired in this country, and the assignment to the branch plant should not be thought of as an interval of two or three years. The idea of impermanence is destructive of morale and prevents the thorough adaptation without which the individual is of little use to his organization.

CHAPTER 8

POLICIES OF MIGRATING COMPANIES

The policies followed by business concerns must in the great majority of instances be inferred from their actions. A policy is often defined as a plan which states an objective, but only infrequently are these plans specifically stated and rigidly adhered to. They are used chiefly for instructional purposes, and instruction in major policies is more likely to be verbal than written. When speaking of company policy, a business executive is likely to say that in general his company thinks it advisable to do certain things or to do things in a certain way. Nevertheless, the carrying out of certain policies, however indefinitely they may be stated and however obscure they may seem, does provide the distinguishing characteristics of a business enterprise, from which may be discerned the attitude taken by those in positions of authority toward labor, government, other business organizations, and, in general, toward the social and economic picture of which the concern is a part. Here we are concerned primarily with the policies of migrated companies which distinguish them as a group. Not all of the policies considered are followed by all companies. They are, however, followed with sufficient frequency to differentiate North American companies, as a group, from others operating in South America.

It will be observed that many of the policies discussed are not particularly new, nor do they arise from the fact that business is being done in a foreign country. Rather, they are policies developed, followed, and found acceptable in the United States. They are not unusual here, but in South America they are sometimes sufficiently unique to set off the migrated companies from the native concerns.

This discussion of business policies is presented with various purposes. One of these purposes is to indicate how certain policies that are widely used in this country work out in South American countries. Perhaps it is needless to say that some policies have been found just as effective there as here, and others much less effective. Other policies are the product of migration and of the problems which migration entails. These are generally unknown and thus need presentation. A further and more general objective is to give some idea of the manner in which migrated concerns have fitted into the economic life of the countries in which they have located. In addition, the discussion should furnish some evidence that will tend to disprove the often-repeated allegations that migrated concerns are unmindful of their social responsibilities in lesser developed foreign countries—that they strive to profit unduly by exploiting both labor and raw materials and by taking advantage of native concerns.

When a branch plant attempts to inaugurate some policy habitually followed in this country, there frequently is misunderstanding on the part of those affected. The carrying out of the policy may necessitate changes in firmly rooted habits or customs and thus may arouse antagonism. An example in a minor policy is furnished by the change in the noon period allowed to workers. In South American countries the customary noon period has been from twelve o'clock until two o'clock. Some branch plants shortened this two-hour period to one of thirty minutes and allowed the men to finish work at four-thirty in the afternoon. At first there was much objection, but later the men became reconciled to the change and some even openly approved it. Yet some firms, unwilling to defy national customs and thus risk the disfavor of employees, have hesitated to make such changes. While this is a minor matter, it does illustrate the type of changes which, if accumulated, may create a disgruntled labor force. Such changes may also bring forth the criticism that a company has failed to adapt itself to local habits and customs.

Among the policies most generally followed by branch plants are many in reference to labor. These include the payment of wages above the going rate, the use of incentive wage schemes, advancement on the basis of merit only, and the establishment of employee benefits. On the average, branch plants pay from 10 to 15 per cent more than the going rate of wages. This figure is based on estimates of comparative wage scales which were secured from numerous individual companies. Some companies estimated that they were paying as much as 20 per cent more than the going rate, and others little, if any, more. While the "going rate" itself is difficult to determine, various checks which were made give confidence in these estimates. In South America, as in the United States, the automobile companies are leaders in the payment of high wages.

Relatively high wages are paid for much the same reasons as in this country, but the fact of foreign location makes these reasons more cogent. When workers are paid well, more is required of them, and the general philosophy is that high wages are both a cause and a result of high productivity. Also, high wages are of particular aid in the selection of workers. Because of their higher wage scales and better working conditions, branch plants have little difficulty in securing the best workers. This advantage is of particular importance in view of the fact that the number of individuals with industrial experience and with those characteristics which will make them acceptable employees is relatively small. High wages might be considered the means by which branch plants secure a reasonably proficient, contented, and loyal labor force.

Furthermore, branch plants pay wages above the going rate partly as a method of control. If wages are high, less control of other types is needed to keep workers in line. Intimidation and other high-handed methods of controlling labor, which at times are resorted to in South America, could not and probably would not be used by North American companies. They are in too vulnerable a position for such tactics, even if moral scruples did not restrain them. High wages are usually preventive of strikes, and the nature of strikes in these countries leads one to believe that even a considerable increase in labor costs might be a small price to pay for either the absence or the mitigation of labor difficulties. On the other hand, high wages were, at least in part, a cause of the strikes mentioned in the previous chapter. People who had been employed at wages above the going rate were prompted by labor agitators to attempt by forceful means to regain their former positions. Those still employed were apparently satisfied. Fortunately, such precipitous reductions in labor forces as were occasioned by the economic reversal of 1929 are not common, and, therefore, the payment of high wages to prevent labor disturbances is generally a good policy. One further favorable result of high wages is the avoidance of litigation in labor courts. Foreign concerns at times fail to secure justice in these courts, particularly in Chile. Summarizing, the payment of relatively high wages is good business policy in terms of productivity, selection of workers, control, and the avoidance of disturbances and litigation which otherwise might arise.

A direct interconnection between wages and productivity is furnished by incentive wage schemes. Such plans are not used in branch plants to the extent that they are in this country, although some of the larger concerns do use them extensively. Apparently these companies are satisfied with the results obtained. The fact that some concerns with long and successful business experience use incentive wage schemes gives confidence in their adaptability for use in South America. Yet, other firms which have tried such schemes report unsuccessful experience. They state that the workers are less attracted by the opportunity to increase their earnings than are workers in this country, that there is not the same urge for an improved economic position. It is also true that complicated wage plans are not likely to be thoroughly understood, for the workers have not had the opportunities for education that are offered here. For these reasons, it is not probable that incentive wage plans will be commonly used.

Little need be said about the policy of advancing employees upon the basis of merit only. This policy, while infrequently stated, is usually followed by companies in this country. Indeed, it has often been referred to, especially by European writers, as a distinguishing characteristic of our industry. The policy has been carried by migrating concerns to their South American operations, and there it has likewise been productive of loyalty to the company and increased productivity.

One further labor policy to be considered is that of establishing employee benefits. Such benefits are seldom provided in South America except by firms of foreign origin. The International Cement Corporation in Uruguay and Argentina and the General Electric Company in Brazil have been particularly active in the promotion of education, the preservation of employees' health, and the introduction of insurance and savings schemes. They have also attempted to encourage social gatherings by forming clubs and promoting athletic competitions. The selection of two companies for special mention should not be taken as an indication that others are inactive in this respect. Practically all of the migrated companies engage in at least some of the activities to which reference has been made. However, because of its varied character, the employee benefit work of the International Cement Corporation in Argentina will be reviewed in some detail.

The International Cement Corporation's plant is located in a small community with a population of 2,700. Since between 500 and 700 persons are employed in the plant, it is evident that the plant "makes" the community.

Therefore, employee benefits are partly in the nature of community betterment work. When the plant was built, there was no acceptable school; so the company built one and later presented it to the government. In 1933, 295 children were in attendance, mostly the children of employees. The lack of adequate housing led the company to construct many houses, which it rents at nominal rates to department heads, foremen, and workers. Single men are housed in dormitories. Each employee's family, whether living in a company house or not, is furnished free of charge a sufficient amount of electric current to assure effective residential lighting. A workers' association was formed, for which an auditorium was built by the company. This building serves also as headquarters for an athletic club. Athletic facilities include tennis courts, football fields, and "conchas de pelota" (courts for playing a form of handball). For social gatherings there is a clubhouse in which dances and motion pictures are held regularly. A small library has been assembled and made available to the workers.

Ever since the plant was established, the company has taken an interest in the health of its employees and of their families. A doctor is employed as a staff member of the company. It is his responsibility to maintain the health of the community. Attention is not confined entirely to workers at the factory. Homes are inspected periodically, and sanitation is supervised. At the plant a small hospital is maintained, to house the medical service. Baths with hot and cold water, lavatories, and individual lockers have been installed at the plant, and the workers have been encouraged to use them. At first, these facilities were the subject of derision, but now a large number of men use the baths at the end of each day's work. As a result of the company's health program, this community is, in all probability, one of the most healthful in the country.

Group insurance is carried by the company, although there is no legislation requiring such action. At the end of six months of service, each worker is given an insurance policy of 500 pesos oro—about $500. The insurance is increased at the rate of $100 annually up to a maximum of $1,000. Some other concerns have taken a further step by starting stock subscription plans for workers, in an attempt to encourage savings. As in the United States, these plans have had a checkered career, but they do, nevertheless, evidence company interest in personnel. The effect of such a plan is indicated by the change which took place in the attitude of an employee who was something of a socialist and an agitator. He received a small dividend check on his stock, the first money, no doubt, which he had ever received other than from direct labor. From that time forward, he was a capitalist rather than a socialist and, incidentally, a much more tractable employee.

Although from such work the company undoubtedly reaps indirect benefits, highly immeasurable but nevertheless real, yet branch plant managers generally expressed more than a slight doubt as to whether the benefits received were commensurate with the expense incurred. Some favorable effect may be secured upon productivity, particularly from the medical work; perhaps a larger measure of loyalty on the part of workers is attained; but whether a company improves its position in the eyes of the government and thus prevents unfavorable action is open to question. Governments change so frequently that the problem of bringing employee benefit work to the attention of officials is a continuing one. Such work draws attention to profits, and profits by foreign companies are always deprecated. A socialistic deputy, when visiting a plant where benefit work was stressed, remarked that the company was making too much money, for otherwise such work could not be done. He was reminded that the company could not improve the community and care for the interests of workers unless it was making money by its operations. There is, however, a goodly measure of intelligent and articulate public opinion in all of these countries, and thus a company has some public approval as a reward for its efforts in employee benefit work.

Other policies which are an integral part of business in this country, and which are likewise followed by branch concerns in South America, have to do with the quality of products, their pricing, and servicing. The policies, while common enough here, often appear distinctive in South America because they are not practiced by business as a whole. One of these is the policy of manufacturing a quality product—one which is manufactured rigidly to standard specifications. Sometimes, when purchasing power has declined, it appears necessary to lower the quality of a product, in order to reach a market in which customary prices play an important role. North American concerns are often unwilling to do this, whereas both local firms and importers from Central European countries are more likely to vary quality and leave the price stationary than to maintain quality and let the price vary. Insistence on the maintenance of quality appears to be a firm policy on the part of North American and English manufacturers, wherever their plants are located.

People in South America have often failed to understand or to expect this insistence on quality. When local manufacture of a product in a branch plant is substituted for importation from the parent corporation, there is generally skepticism as to whether the locally produced article is of the same quality. Both the pharmaceutical companies and the tire companies have had difficulty in convincing buyers that their products, as manufactured in Argentina, are of the same high quality as those previously imported.

Market research work has not been neglected. While, in general, the demand in South America is for products much the same as those sold in this country and but few changes are necessary to adapt products to consumer desires, still the assumption that products which suit purchasers in the United States will also suit buyers in South America has not been followed blindly. Rather, the merchandising point of view—that is, the point of view which recognizes the need of research prior to manufacture, in order to determine the desires of consumers—has been kept clearly in mind by the majority of companies.

Service policies which assure purchasers that the utility of a product will be maintained are largely taken for granted in this country. We expect that when a mechanical device fails to function properly repair service and parts will be freely available. But behind service, as it is known here, there must be careful training of individuals, supervision, and the distribution of tools and parts so that they will be available when needed. Branch plants work under difficulties imposed by a difference in language, distance from the seat of production, the indifference of dealers, the relative dispersion of product-owners, and a scarcity of mechanically trained individuals. Yet they have attempted to give adequate service and to follow the policies formulated in this country.

A final policy in this group deals with price. A single-price policy is generally followed by large corporations in the United States in connection with sales to dealers. Bargaining or "haggling" over price is seldom practiced. But in Latin countries, haggling is much more the accepted mode of procedure, and when concerns insist on a single-price policy—that is, the same terms to all buyers who purchase in like quantities—they are often misunderstood. Following a single-price policy may result in some competitive disadvantage, at least, initially. Nevertheless, this policy is practiced generally by branch plants in their dealings with customers, and after an interval which varies in length with the individual, it is accepted without too much objection. Perhaps it is needless to say that the policy improves relationships with dealers, and that the time needed for consummating business transactions is materially reduced.

The policies which have been mentioned possess one characteristic in common. All are the fruit of experience in this country, and, having been proved successful here, they have been adopted by subsidiary companies abroad. Now we turn to another group of policies, the origin of which can be traced to the fact of migration and to the experience gained in the country of location rather than to the previous domestic experience of a concern. Although, for most companies with branch plants, business experience in these South American countries is comparatively short, still trial and error has led to the formulation of some policies which are quite generally adhered to. Obviously all policies are not equally applicable to the affairs of all concerns, but most of those to be considered are of such broad import that they can be a part of the general policy of practically all concerns engaged in foreign subsidiary operations.

The first of these policies may be expressed as the attempt to adhere as closely as possible to the laws of the country in which the company is operating. In matters of taxation, rules and regulations in respect to labor, license arrangements, and a host of other respects in which legal restrictions affect business, there is the opportunity for lax compliance, possibly suggested by lax enforcement by government officials. Moreover, laws have, at times, been so poorly constructed and of such uncertain meaning that companies, even when aided by native legal talent, have been unable to determine just what was demanded by the government. In such a case, noncompliance is not a matter of intent but one of confusion. Other laws have been so uneconomic and so prejudicial to effective operations that compliance would have been tantamount to relinquishing all control over factors vitally affecting company interests. An illustration of this type of law was the Minimum Price Law for cattle.[1] Rather than comply, the packing companies stopped purchase until the law was rescinded.

[1] See pp. 168*ff*.

However, legislation so restrictive in nature appears but seldom, and it therefore calls for little comment in this connection. In general, adherence is possible, except when there is some question in regard to what the government wishes.

The policy of adhering to the law is not followed purely as a matter of principle. Rather, the exact compliance practiced by migrated concerns is necessary as a means of self-protection, for, being of foreign origin and considered by many as intruders, these companies are in a vulnerable position. There are always some individuals who are seeking grounds on which to attack foreign concerns successfully. Moreover, such concerns are more severely dealt with than are native concerns, if they are found to have violated the law or engaged in any form of irregular practice. In some doubtful cases, exorbitant fines have been imposed, prompted apparently by anti-foreign-capital sentiment and by the knowledge that the company could pay. Decisions which have been made lead one to suspect that foreign companies are always at a disadvantage when legal difficulties arise. Under the circumstances, it is good policy, when operating in South American countries, to adhere closely to the laws which touch business affairs. Carelessness may leave loopholes for legal action, and the penalties inflicted may be severe.

Subsidiary companies made a practice of having little, if anything, to do with political matters. For some concerns, this is a clearly formulated policy in the minds of executives, and undoubtedly it is a good one. Attempts to influence pending legislation are deeply resented by nationals. Such activity, if discovered, furnishes particularly effective ammunition for those opposed to foreign concerns, and it is played up beyond all reasonable limits. In all probability, the harm done through participation in political affairs—unless such participation is very circumspect—is greater than any good accomplished thereby. The hands-off policy favored by most branch executives appears to be most wise.

It has been the policy of most companies to refuse the various favors which are frequently offered by municipalities, provinces, or, perhaps, by the central government. Firms contemplating migration are usually the recipients of numerous offers, which are extended as a bait for attracting industry to certain locations. Or, if favors are not freely extended, they can usually be secured by appeals to government officials. Among these favors the most common is the waiving by a government of the taxation right for a specified period, or at least a restriction of the right to certain clearly defined limits. A municipality, for instance, may agree that neither the property of a company nor the products which it manufactures shall be taxed for a ten-year period after production facilities are established. A similar favor is the waiving of tariff charges on machinery and equipment imported for use in manufacturing operations. Supplies and repair parts may likewise be exempted from tariff charges. Municipal and provincial governments frequently offer free land and water for industrial use. At times, they even go so far as to offer financial aid in the establishment of industry. For example, the province of Salta in Argentina offered land for industrial enterprises, and, in addition, 10 per cent of the amount which would be invested in machinery and equipment.[2] A few conditions were made, the chief of which was that the concern receiving the aid should have a total investment of not less than 200,000 pesos. Other favors extended are more in the nature of assurance than of direct benefits. A concern might be given the assurance that tariff duties on imports of competing merchandise would not be lowered for a given length of time, or, perhaps, that the duties on needed raw materials which could not be secured locally would not be raised. Concessions given to public utilities are in the nature of the assurance that the right to operate for a period of years will not be

---

[2] "El Fomento Industrial en Salta," editorial comment, *La Nacion*, Feb. 6, 1933.

withdrawn. Likewise, the gold clauses in public utility contracts are an assurance that the government will not forbid rate increases if the value of exchange falls.

While the various favors that may be extended are markedly dissimilar in nature, they fall roughly into three categories: (1) gifts of money or property, (2) exemption from taxes or tariffs, and (3) assurance of the maintenance of satisfactory conditions for operation in so far as those conditions are a product of governmental decisions. Favors of the first kind are but rarely accepted by migrating companies. Only infrequently is the municipality or province which makes the offer the most acceptable place for location. The province of Salta, for example, would be a wholly unacceptable location for branch plants. And even if the location decided upon for business reasons and the location offered happened to coincide, the migrating concern would be likely to refuse the favor. Too often, such offers carry conditions which make their acceptance inadvisable. Then, also, favors are likely to beget favors, or, at least, those who are instrumental in extending the favor in the first place think that they should, and North American companies do not like to have governments or individuals believe that any obligation exists.

Favors of the second type are accepted much more frequently by migrating companies. In fact, such favors have at times been requested of government officials. Of course, it should be recognized that favors of this class are not homogeneous. The waiving of tariff charges and exemption from taxation are dissimilar in nature. The first is extended only by a central government, whereas the second comes within the sphere of the municipal and provincial governments. Exemption from taxation for a period of time is projected into the future, while permitting machinery and equipment to enter free of duty is a privilege granted for only a short period. Tax exemption, because of its duration, is likely to cause later difficulties, particularly if political upheavals change the personnel of the executive branch of government. The remission of duties is soon consummated and forgotten. For these reasons, the waiving of tariff charges is a concession that is more likely to be accepted, perhaps striven for, by migrating companies.

Branch managers are doubtful whether attempts should be made to secure exemption from taxes. The consensus of opinion seems to be that no favors of this type should be requested—that a completely independent attitude is to be preferred. If there could be assurance that the property or products of a company would not be taxed excessively, few attempts would be made to secure exemption as a condition of migration. And excessive taxation has not as yet been a feature of business experience in these countries. Furthermore, when exemption has been accorded, it has been ineffective. In one case in Brazil, an exemption given was followed by taxation in less than a year. The tax was not excessive, however, and, although a protest was filed as a matter of record, no serious attempts were made to have the tax withdrawn. Agreements relative to tax exemption have as their purpose the prevention of excessive and unreasonable taxation, rather than exemption from all taxes. Very few North American companies are now securing exemption. Either the time agreed upon for such exemption has expired, or policy has dictated that the company shall not accept or request such favors.

The third class of favors—namely, written assurance of satisfactory conditions for operation, in so far as those conditions are a product of governmental decisions—is usually secured by public utilities, rarely by manufacturing companies. Long-term contractual arrangements are to be expected in the public utility field, but some form of concession which gives the right to operate must usually be secured by all companies. Such a concession might be considered an assurance that the right to operate would not be summarily withdrawn. But, in addition, concerns might conceivably obtain assurance to the effect that certain moves prejudicial to the interests of a company would not be made by the government. For instance, the tire companies might have attempted to secure a written statement from the government that import duties on tires would not be lowered for a certain length of time, also that the duty then in force on crude rubber would not be raised. Perhaps, if such an agreement had been consummated, it would have served as a protection against the unfortunate changing of tariffs in 1932.[3] At least, the tire companies would have had a stronger case to present to the government in protesting the changes. The contention which they actually made was that the government had acted in bad faith by instituting the changes. If a written agreement had been violated, there would have been undeniable proof of bad faith, unless the agreement was secured in the first place by fraudulent means. Perhaps, in view of the frequent and not always orderly governmental changes in these countries, an agreement such as this would not have been respected if it had been made. Still, public-utility concessions in Brazil were not disturbed appreciably as a result of the revolution and the subsequent changes in government personnel in 1930.

This discussion may cast some doubt upon the wisdom of the whole policy of neither asking for nor accepting favors. It is true that companies are better off without the gift type of favor, and there is some question whether any real advantage is gained from tax exemptions. But some written assurance that the basic conditions under which a firm migrates will not be radically changed might be of value in later negotiations and thus worth securing in the first instance. Still, there is much to be said for the independent attitude exhibited by the majority of concerns with branch plants in South America.

Another policy to be considered is that which migrating concerns follow in establishing cordial relations with other business enterprises in the country where they are operating.

[3] See Chap. 5, pp. 128–131 and pp. 139–145.

Evidently the policy followed is to do everything possible to aid other business concerns, sometimes even when the concerns are directly competing. Stated more broadly, the policy is one of stimulating the general economic development of the country. Here again, the motivation behind the policy is not necessarily an altruistic one, for each branch plant has a tangible stake in such things as the improvement of individual incomes, the development of means for transportation, the growth of auxiliary industry, and the local production of raw materials.

This policy of cooperation finds expression in numerous ways. Technical assistance is given to smaller concerns which are striving to manufacture parts or supplies of quality suitable for inclusion in assemblies or for general use. If the desired quality standard is attained and the price is no greater than that of imports, the product is purchased locally. Research work is being carried forward in an attempt to adapt local raw materials to needs. For instance, the tire companies are attempting to find some means by which Argentine short-staple cotton can be used in the manufacture of tires. In this country the fabric used is made from long-staple cotton. Finally, branch organizations frequently join industrial associations, such as the Union Industrial Argentina. Through association, industry as a whole is given coherence, and common problems can be dealt with through group action.

Association with other companies for mutual benefit may likewise be considered as an expression of another general policy which is followed by numerous companies. This is the policy of becoming as national as possible. Various means are employed to achieve the desired result. The name of the company may be nationalized so that there is no reference to the name of the parent corporation. For public utilities, in particular, this appears to be a desirable procedure. The employment of nationals, rather than of North Americans, for semi-executive positions is another means of achieving the desired end. Inclusion within the national economy may also be emphasized by incorporation within the country of location. A company thereby becomes legally a business organization of the country in which it is operating. Continuity in management is likewise desirable for those concerns which do not wish to call attention to their foreign origin unnecessarily. After a person has lived in another country for a decade or more, understanding and tolerance may characterize his dealings with nationals, and thus the foreign aspects of the business which he represents may be obscured.

A firm which attempts to stimulate the economic development of a country, which attempts to become as national as possible, which, in a sense, merges its interests in the national economy of which it is a part, is more likely to enjoy successful, long-continued operation. It will be considered a part of the national economy, rather than an extraneous element, even though it is of foreign origin. By following these policies, a company strengthens its position against prejudicial action by governmental agencies.

CHAPTER 9

RESULTS OF INDUSTRIAL MIGRATION

The subject of this chapter is of sufficient breadth to warrant its constituting a separate, self-contained study. A statement must therefore be given of the extent to which the inquiry will here be carried and of the subject matter that will be included. Obviously, the impact of an industrial civilization upon one in which agriculture, pastoral pursuits, and the extraction of raw materials predominate has important social results. The establishment of branch plants has caused changes in the habits, the customs, and the manner of living of many people in South America. An analysis of the changes in culture patterns, however, no matter how significant they may be, does not come within the confines of this study. On the other hand, the economic results of industrial migration, some of which have already been mentioned in various connections, will be discussed and summarized in this chapter. An attempt will be made to indicate the effect of migration, not only upon the economy of South American countries, but also upon industry in the United States, of which much has been said that needs further analysis and, at times, refutation.

While many of the effects of migration upon the countries from which and to which migration takes place are indefinite in character and cannot be proved by exact quantitative measurements, there are results of a more tangible nature which are of immediate interest to the business community. Among these results there is one of primary importance—the financial success of branch organizations. This may be measured by the rate of mortality among branch plants and by the earnings of these plants. Attention will first be given to these more tangible results of migration.

Mortality among Branch Plants

Few of the companies which have placed branch plants in Brazil and Argentina have later withdrawn. To the writer's knowledge, only two companies have withdrawn from Argentina in the past few years. It should be remembered that reference is made in this connection to branch plants, not to merchandising organizations. The Brunswick-Balke-Collender Company, which had produced phonograph records in Argentina for a number of years, liquidated and withdrew in 1933. During the present year (1935) the International Printing Ink Corporation has withdrawn from Argentina, after operating a combination wholesale paper and ink-mixing business for more than a decade. In Brazil no casualties among branch plants came to the notice of the writer. Experience in Uruguay and Chile has been less satisfactory. Both the General Motors Corporation and the Ford Motor Company had ceased assembly operations in Uruguay in 1933, and complete withdrawal was contemplated. Many branch plants liquidated their holdings and withdrew from Chile after 1929. Others stopped manufacturing operations but remained as merchandising institutions. Among the concerns which made changes of one type or the other were the Otis Elevator Company, the United States Steel Corporation, International Bitumen Emulsions Corporation, and Warren Brothers Company.

The fact that a company has not withdrawn is, of course, no positive indication that it has operated successfully. If a substantial capital commitment has been made, there may be no feasible alternative to continuing operation. A number of concerns have doubtless been in the position of regretting their original decision to migrate but have realized that withdrawal would occasion heavy losses whereas continuance of operations might ultimately result in reasonable profits. The low mortality among branch plants should be considered only as an indication that conditions have seldom been deemed hopeless for profitable operations. In Chile alone have economic and political conditions become so unsatisfactory that there has been a general exodus of branch plants—or, at least, a general cessation of activities. Such was the situation there in the early years of the present decade.

Profits

Profits data, it must be recognized, are largely estimates, for they are based upon property evaluations, and these are the product of someone's judgment. Conservatism or optimism on the part of individuals in executive capacities plays an important part in the determination of the final profit figure. Conditions may influence executives to conceal part of their assets or to recognize insufficient depreciation, thus either understating or overstating profits. Under the circumstances, there is plenty of opportunity for release of profits data which fail accurately to depict the actual monetary results of operation. Confidence in the released data is afforded only by the general reputation of the company or by a knowledge of the accounting procedures used. It is thus apparent that data on profits in this country are sufficiently open to question and that data on the profits of subsidiaries abroad are even more so.

Much of what was said about the difficulties encountered in the determination of capital investment in branch operations applies equally well to profits.[1] Here again, the exchange problem enters in. For example, one company, by diligent work and good management, succeeded in earning 200,000 pesos over a six-months period. But before exchange could be secured for remitting funds to the United States, a lowered exchange rate had entirely wiped out the profit margin. Since more pesos were required to make a dollar, a profit was earned in pesos but not in

[1] See Chap. 1, pp. 16–18.

dollars. After 1929, as the exchange value of South American currencies declined, dollar profits from the operation of branch plants declined likewise. When the United States abandoned the gold standard, however, peso balances immediately became more valuable in terms of dollars. United States concerns are primarily interested in the dollar profits of subsidiaries abroad. Unfortunately it is not practicable to convert the earnings of branch plants to a dollar basis because the rate of exchange to be used depends upon the time at which exchange was secured for transfer of balances. Consequently, the profit data presented here must be in native currencies rather than in dollars.

The profit data presented leave much to be desired from the standpoint of an accurate presentation of the returns on the capital used in branch operations. As mentioned previously, a 10 per cent profit in pesos on the total of capital and reserves in pesos does not necessarily mean a 10 per cent profit upon the dollars invested by the North American company. The problem of transfer remains, and in recent years it has been a most troublesome one. Then, also, in the years since 1930, profit computed as a percentage figure has probably been understated for all concerns except those engaged in processing raw materials or pastoral products for export, because, through inability to secure exchange, the capital and reserves figure has been higher than it would normally have been. Funds which would ordinarily have been transferred to the United States were necessarily retained in these countries and swelled reserve balances.

Furthermore, there is the question of where profits are taken—in Argentina or Brazil or, perhaps, in the United States or Europe. Suppose that one of the automobile companies failed to show a profit on its Brazilian operations. Let us suppose, likewise, that five thousand cars were sold in Brazil. It is far from a safe assumption that the company would have been better off if these cars had not been sold. On the contrary, there is much more reason to presume that a substantial net gain was realized, even though the Brazilian plant showed a loss. The amount of profit or loss depends upon the prices at which assembly parts are billed to the branch plants. Questions of overhead costs also enter the picture. In all probability, parts would be invoiced to the branch plants at a figure which would show a profit to manufacturing units in this country. Surely the invoiced prices on assembly parts would be high enough to cover more than mere out-of-pocket costs. If the sales in Brazil yielded any margin above out-of-pocket production costs in this country, plus all expenses incurred in transportation, assembly, and marketing, the business in Brazil would be profitable to the company.

Those companies which process raw materials or pastoral products for export may likewise understate their profit on South American operations, as such, by taking profits elsewhere. If meats, for instance, are invoiced to branch selling organizations in Europe at low prices, those organizations show high profits and the profits of the packing plants are correspondingly reduced. Moreover, there is more than a slight predisposition to take profits elsewhere, because of the fact that economic exploitation has so often been charged by national groups. In general, profits are misunderstood and resented by nationals. Taking into account the risk factor—the numerous uncertainties which beset all foreign subsidiaries in South America—an annual return of around 15 per cent on invested capital is none too much. But such returns provoke unfavorable comment and even active resentment. Consequently, there is an incentive to understate profits, and this should be kept in mind in any perusal of profit data.

Data on profits were secured only for companies operating in Argentina.[2] While figures were not obtainable for

[2] Data for Brazilian concerns could not be secured. While North American companies operating in Brazil are required to submit annual earnings statements to the Internal Revenue Office for the purpose of assessment of income taxes, such statements are treated as confidential and are not published.

all companies, they were secured for the majority, and for practically all of the larger concerns. Profits of certain companies for specific years were not available. Yet a representative sample for each year was obtained, and one which includes the majority of companies and a preponderance of the capital investment. The source of most of the data was the official publication of the Argentine government, the *Boletin Official*. All manufacturing concerns are required to submit to the government an annual balance sheet and earnings statement. These are later published in the organ mentioned and thus become public property obtainable by any interested person. In addition, some data were furnished by certain companies upon request.

TABLE 6.—PROFITS OF NORTH AMERICAN BRANCH PLANTS IN ARGENTINA, 1923–1932

Year	Number of companies	Capital and reserves, in paper pesos	Profits, in paper pesos	Rate of profit, per cent
1923	4	141,776,757	27,505,684	19.40
1924	5	158,443,742	18,751,998	11.84
1925	5	147,487,536	514,296	0.35
1926	7	153,434,186	6,185,689	4.03
1927	11	166,854,055	6,760,039	4.05
1928	15	199,228,768	31,261,090	15.69
1929	18	216,022,889	32,365,291	14.98
1930	15	214,218,759	33,966,134	15.86
1931	19	247,802,025	26,786,980	10.81
1932	15	230,769,983	18,611,560	8.06

Table 6 shows the profits of North American branch plants in Argentina from 1923 to 1932, inclusive, also the number of companies included in the computations, and the total of the capital and reserves of those companies. Prior to 1926, data on the profits of only five companies were obtainable. However, since there were only eight branch plants in Argentina before 1924, a reasonable sample for the earlier years is included. In the years after 1925, a greater proportion of the total number of companies is represented.

The earnings of only one company are lacking in 1928, and of only four companies in 1931. Therefore, the profit data shown, although not entirely complete, are sufficiently comprehensive to permit of conclusions. The capital and reserves figure ranges from $60,000,000 in 1925 to $105,000,000 in 1931, and profits from $215,000 in 1925 to more than $15,000,000 in 1929 (at par exchange). Profits, it will be observed, were very low in 1925, being less than one-half of 1 per cent, but in no year was there a loss by the companies considered as a group. The high point in percentage profits was reached in 1923, when 19.4 per cent was earned on invested capital. For the decade, the average of the annual profit percentages is 10.5 per cent.

TABLE 7.—PROFITS OF NORTH AMERICAN BRANCH MEAT-PACKING PLANTS IN ARGENTINA, 1923–1932

Year	Number of companies	Capital and reserves, in paper pesos	Profits, in paper pesos	Rate of profit, per cent
1923	3	134,217,473	27,024,650	20.13
1924	4	150,292,112	17,214,868	11.45
1925	4	139,305,311	−1,103,045	−0.79
1926	4	141,144,930	2,115,125	1.50
1927	4	147,007,187	2,620,524	1.78
1928	4	149,780,490	14,794,841	9.88
1929	4	146,680,340	16,997,254	11.59
1930	4	149,633,691	19,624,002	13.11
1931	4	157,803,958	19,843,117	12.57
1932	4	161,525,137	16,401,989	10.15

The greater share of the capital and reserves figure is that of the packing companies. As a result, the profit rates on investments other than those in the packing industry tend to be obscured. It has seemed advisable, therefore, to break down the data further and consider the packing companies and all others separately. Table 7 presents the data for the packing companies for the 1923–1932 decade. The data given here include all of the three large packing companies—Swift International Company,

Wilson & Company, Inc., and Armour & Company—and, in addition, the La Blanca Company, which is largely, if not completely, owned by Armour & Company. The data for Wilson & Company, Inc., are lacking for 1923. Only in one year, 1925, did the packing companies fail to make profits. For the entire decade, the average of the annual percentages is 9.1 per cent. Since and including 1928, the packing companies have had a steady earnings rate which averages about 11.5 per cent.

TABLE 8.—PROFITS OF NORTH AMERICAN BRANCH PLANTS IN ARGENTINA, 1927–1932
(Meat-packing Industry Excluded)

Year	Number of companies	Capital and reserves, in paper pesos	Profits, in paper pesos	Rate of profit, per cent
1927	7	19,846,868	4,139,515	20.86
1928	11	49,448,278	16,466,249	33.30
1929	14	69,342,549	15,368,037	22.16
1930	11	64,585,068	14,342,132	22.21
1931	15	89,998,067	6,943,863	7.72
1932	11	69,244,846	2,209,571	3.19

Table 8 shows the profits of branch plants, excluding those in the packing industry, for 1927 to 1932, inclusive. Prior to 1927, data were available for too few companies to constitute a representative sample. For the years 1927 to 1930, inclusive, business was active, and the branch organizations averaged better than 20 per cent. In 1931 and 1932, as would be expected, there was a pronounced decline, although an actual loss was not experienced. Even in 1932, more than one-half of the companies for which data are included made reasonable profits, and only three showed losses.

The information contained in these tables demonstrates quite conclusively that, despite the difficulties encountered and the hindrances which are frequently placed in the way of successful operation, branch plants are profitable business units. In view of the risk incurred, the profits are not exorbitant, but they are substantial. For the group as a whole, reasonable returns have been achieved, even in view of uncertainties, difficulties, and now and then what might be termed a lack of sound business judgment. The failure of individual companies to earn a profit can at times be ascribed to questionable policies and unwise decisions, rather than to the absence of profit possibilities. And it is equally true that sound business procedures have been adequately rewarded.

Variation of profits between industries could be expected, particularly between those engaged in processing and exporting raw materials and pastoral products and those manufacturing products for sale within the country. The automobile companies and those connected with the building trade were very profitable in the years between 1925 and 1930, but they have suffered more in recent years than have some others. Companies manufacturing food products and small-value consumers' goods have operated on a profitable basis all during the world depression. They were a part of the general industry which thrived as imports became more costly through the application of higher tariff rates. A greater measure of self-sufficiency was forced upon these South American countries by the action of industrial nations, and from this trend toward self-sufficiency certain branch plants benefited.

The profits of branch plants are, in general, appreciably higher than those of native concerns which manufacture the same commodities. The North American packing plants have been profitable, whereas the native companies have usually failed to achieve profits. In the building trades, the difference in profits has been noticeable. The higher earnings of the branch plants must be due to their better management and greater capital resources, for other advantages, if there be such, lie with the native concerns.

In closing this discussion of profits, it should again be noted that the data presented come entirely from companies located in Argentina. A pertinent question is whether plants in the other three countries considered have been similarly profitable. While no actual data are available to substantiate conclusions, still a knowledge of the general conditions under which operations have been carried forward and conversation with branch executives lead to the conclusion that branch plants in Brazil have likewise been profitable, but to a lesser degree than those in Argentina. Brazil is a smaller market. Only about one-half as many automobiles and trucks and a smaller quantity of all sorts of materials and equipment have been sold. Argentina has provided branch plants with a greater volume of demand and thus more opportunity for profit. Moreover, some companies apparently expected as much business in one country as in the other, for there appears to be little difference in the size of the plants which have been built for the manufacture of similar products in the two countries. As a result, overhead costs are similar, even though in Brazil there is less volume over which to spread these costs. There are a number of plants in which, for the time being, at least, capacity is much larger than necessary, and this situation must prove a handicap to the making of profits.

In Uruguay branch plants have had difficulty in achieving acceptable profits. The two packing companies—Swift International Company and Armour & Company—have been handicapped by the government order which prohibits them from furnishing meats to the city of Montevideo. This market is reserved to the government-operated packing plant. The automobile assembly plants, although active and profitable at one time, were practically closed in 1933, and withdrawal was contemplated. The other plant —the one operated by the International Cement Corporation—has been reasonably profitable.

Branch plants in Chile were, in all probability, profitable ventures, prior to 1930. But the economic and political breakdown of the early depression years played havoc with all business enterprises, and particularly with those of foreign origin which needed exchange in order to procure parts or supplies from abroad. There was practically no market for the products manufactured, or assembled in branch plants, and, in addition, losses appeared through the steady depreciation of the Chilean peso in relation to the dollar. Between 1930 and 1935, branch plants had little or no chance of profitable operation. As a result, many of them withdrew, and others suspended operations for an indefinite period.

A statement of profits on invested capital such as the one just given leads to some interesting questions upon the subject of comparative returns on capital invested in different ways. Industrial migration is but one form of capital investment in foreign countries; there are others which are much more widely used. Public utilities, particularly railroads, usually draw their initial investments from abroad, and this was the situation in South American countries. In addition, a large volume of European and North American capital has been invested in mineral and other raw-material deposits and in the bonds of various governmental units. An appreciable quantity of British capital has been placed in agricultural properties in Argentina and Brazil. It would be inadvisable to attempt here a thorough comparison of these different forms of capital investment, for the subject is much too broad and a great deal of the necessary data are not immediately available. But some of the bases of comparison will be suggested, and some opinion will be expressed of the relative success of investment in branch plants.

On the basis of earnings, it is doubtful whether other forms of capital investment have been equally successful. North American investments in public utilities have not been particularly profitable. Many of these investments were made, however, only shortly before the break in 1929; thus the earnings record to date may not be typical. During the last few years something has been earned on preferred issues, but little, if any, on common stock. The returns—or, rather, lack of returns—on South American bonds are widely known, and thus little further comment is needed. Of the countries here considered, only Argentina has paid all of the interest on its national indebtedness and, in addition, has kept up amortization payments. On the greater share of the bond issues of the other countries, likewise on some of the provincial and municipal Argentine issues, interest and amortization payments are far in arrears. Whether returns from investments in raw-material deposits such as those of the copper companies in Chile are more or less than returns from branch plants cannot be stated with any degree of certainty.

Safety of principal is another criterion for judging the various forms of investment, and closely connected with it is liquidity—the ability to withdraw investments without undue losses if conditions change appreciably or if withdrawal is forced by governmental action. While safety of principal has not been a conspicuous virtue of South American bonds, on the other hand, bonds obviously have more liquidity than investments in public utilities, raw-material deposits, and branch plants. Investment in them can be promptly liquidated if withdrawal becomes advisable. As among the other three types of investment, it is probable that withdrawal could be effectuated with a smaller capital loss in the case of branch plants than in either of the other two. Utilities and raw-material deposits are affected with a greater degree of public interest, and more plausible reasons could be concocted for something approaching confiscation. In reference to raw-material deposits, questions have arisen regarding state rights as opposed to individual rights. Investment in public utilities may be other than "safe," because of the regulation of rates by governmental bodies. Although this is, perforce, an incomplete analysis, it appears that funds invested in branch plants are at least comparatively safe.

The foregoing suggests another factor which should be considered when foreign investment is contemplated. It is the probability of attempted regulation by government. Branch plants, as the discussion in earlier chapters amply testifies, have not been free from control and regulation. But when the degree of regulatory action is compared to that suffered by the foreign oil companies in Argentina, the nitrate companies in Chile, and the public utility companies in all of the ABC countries, it is evident that branch plants have been subjected to much less regulation—that they have been relatively free to operate in accordance with the dictates of freely determined individual policy. In other words, a greater degree of individual control, as contrasted with governmental control, has been permitted.

On this basis of comparison, investment in government obligations is the least satisfactory. Such investment is not controlled by men trained in this country and with the interests of the investor in mind. Funds are simply passed over to governmental officials, frequently with no understanding as to how they will be used. Even when agreements are made in regard to the source of interest and amortization payments, they are frequently violated, and, moreover, such agreements are productive of active ill will. Questions of sovereignty enter in to complicate the situation. It is evident that, in security investments, control is largely released, and the soundness of the investments depends almost entirely upon the stability and administrative abilities of the governments involved.

A final basis upon which the various types of our investments in South America might be compared is of exceedingly broad import. It is the extent to which each type is likely to engender ill will toward the United States and its citizens in the country in which the investment is made. Not only active ill will, but even strained relations between governments, may be the offspring of investments and of the policies pursued by investing groups. In this connection it should be recalled that it is not foreign trade which has given rise to the charges of attempted domination and "dollar diplomacy," but capital investment and its attempted protection by diplomatic procedure. Most of our Latin American difficulties spring from too great an inclination to protect foreign investments by diplomatic action. Perhaps some of the investments never should have been made in the first place. More enlightened executive policy might have ironed out difficulties and thus precluded the need for appeal to diplomatic agencies. Investments in branch plants, apparently, have involved less ill will, fewer instances of discord between business enterprises and national groups, and less recourse to diplomatic agencies than other forms of capital investment. Although sufficient research work has not been done to permit of a conclusive statement on this point, still the history of our capital investment in Mexico and a knowledge of events relating to investments in South America during the past decade lend support to the contention made. As yet, the United States government has not been aggressive either in the stimulation or the retardation of foreign investments by its citizens. Still, in the event that some positive action was taken in this direction, a knowledge of the extent to which different forms of investment were likely to be productive of ill will and misunderstandings would be invaluable. On that basis, investment in branch plants should be favored.

Effects of Migration upon Industry in the United States

One of the results often attributed to industrial migration is that it decreases the volume of exports and thereby the output of industries in this country. Proceeding on the assumption that this is the fact, the American Federation of Labor and other labor organizations have stated that migration results in a lesser volume of employment and thus is a detriment to American workers. In some instances, it is true, the establishment of a branch plant has resulted in an immediate and appreciable diminution of exports from this country. Argentina had for years been one of our best export markets for tires, and when the tire companies placed two plants in Argentina, tire exports to that country, with the exception of odd sizes, practically ceased. As a result, there was less work for employees in our own tire plants. Also, a duplication of manufacturing facilities was created, for undoubtedly the plants in this country had sufficient capacity to take care of Argentine needs, in addition to the demand from other sources. Thus the immediate result of migration by some companies is that there is less work for laborers and an excess of manufacturing capacity in the United States.

We must not forget, however, that the export business which foreign production displaces would probably have been eliminated, or at least drastically reduced, regardless of the fact of migration by any one company. Those who object to industrial migration mistakenly assume that exports would have continued at the former level if migration from this country had not been effectuated. But this is far from true. It should not be supposed that manufacturers voluntarily decide to eliminate a portion of their foreign trade by the establishment of a branch plant, or that they would not be satisfied with the existing situation if that situation were likely to remain static. But under certain circumstances the likelihood that a situation will remain static is remote indeed. If a market is "ripe" for local production, either through increased tariffs or through increased demand, the position of a foreign manufacturer who has supplied a portion of the demand by exports is seriously threatened. The threat may come from native concerns, from other concerns in his own country, or from concerns of other countries. For example, the position of the Goodyear Tire & Rubber Company as chief supplier of Argentine tire needs, prior to migration, was threatened not only by the Goodrich and Firestone companies but also by Dunlop of England and Michelin of France.[3] No clear-cut instance has come to the notice of the writer in which a manufacturer substituted production in branch

[3] See Chap. 3, pp. 58–60.

plants for a heavy volume of foreign trade, unless his position in the foreign market was jeopardized—unless the decision to establish a branch plant was forced upon him by competition. Many factors, chief among which are the uncertainties attached to migration and the duplication of production facilities, lead to a preference for continued exports, if it can reasonably be expected that other companies will not seize the market by local production.

The effect of foreign assembly, as contrasted with complete manufacture, has been to increase industrial output in this country rather than to decrease it. Some of the industrial process is shifted to the branch plant, but on the other hand demand is so stimulated by the lower prices to consumers which foreign assembly makes possible that the net result is to increase exports, and not to lessen them. It is freely admitted by most observers that industry in this country has been stimulated, rather than depressed, by the assembly within foreign countries of such products as automobiles and trucks, scales, elevators, and radios.

Effect of Migration upon the Economic Development of South America

The establishment of branch plants has contributed measurably to both the industrial and the agricultural development of the countries considered in this study. When it is recalled that there are sixty-six plants, with employees numbering between thirty-five and forty thousand, in countries which are industrialized to but a limited extent, the truth of this statement becomes apparent. Moreover, native entrepreneurs possessed neither the capital nor the manufacturing experience and technical abilities necessary to carry forward the industries in which branch plants are represented. Without foreign participation from both England and the United States, it is very doubtful whether the Argentine packing industry would have developed to its present size and high level of proficiency. Only through the experience gained from many years of activity, plus ample capital resources and developed markets in Europe, were the packing companies able to develop the meat trade from Argentina, Uruguay, and Brazil. It is even more evident that assembly plants were the direct outgrowth of operations in this country, and that they could not have been duplicated successfully by native business organizations.

The trend of events in the past decade has made the contribution of migrated industry greater than it otherwise would have been. Agricultural and raw-material-producing countries have had need for a greater measure of self-sufficiency than formerly because of the nationalistic tendencies of industrial nations. Since 1930, South American industry, with the exception of that which is engaged in processing agricultural and mineral products for export, has been active, and in each of the countries considered there has been a notable industrial expansion. Branch plants have made possible the attainment of a greater self-sufficiency when it was particularly needed. In these plants many goods have been produced which otherwise would have been imported. In addition, the educational effect which branch organizations have exerted has made possible a more ready adaptation to the new conditions, which demanded more local manufacturing in lieu of foreign trade.

The educational effects of industrial migration will bear further comment. Industrial training has been given to numerous individuals. Since, in the development of an effective labor force, the question of training is of paramount importance, a number of training squads were sent from the United States to instruct workers, and also nationals were sent to the United States to gain experience and ultimately to return and train others. Through the mobility of labor between plants, this training has served as a leavening force, raising the average level of industrial skills. Training has also been given in office management, accounting, sales methods, and, to a lesser extent, in business policy. This likewise has been diffused among other concerns. Many of the business procedures habitually used in these countries are obsolete, when judged by our standards. Business management has not been taught in the schools and universities, and thus the experience gained by the individuals who have worked for migrated companies has been doubly important. Unless nationals actually go abroad for training and experience in business, the best way for them to secure such knowledge is as employees of branch plants.

Economic development has likewise been furthered by the policies of branch organizations mentioned in the preceding chapter. Advice and counsel have been given to native business enterprises, particularly to those which furnish parts and supplies. It has been to the interest of branch plants to aid local industry because, to the extent that they could substitute local purchases for importations, their requirements for exchange were lessened. Branch plants have also had a stake in the stimulation of agriculture and the local production of raw materials. Finally, the development of foreign markets has been a major concern for those branch establishments, such as the packing plants, which are engaged in the processing of products for export, and efforts in this direction have been advantageous, not only to the companies themselves, but also to the economy of the countries in which they are located.

Industrial migration as a part of the general industrial development has had a favorable effect upon the standard of living enjoyed by numerous individuals. Whether the total national income has been raised or whether there has been only a greater diffusion of income may be open to question, but either effect would be desirable. Whether the total income has increased depends in part upon the degree of economic justification for new industry. It is possible, by protection, to foster industry to such an extent that the national income is lowered rather than raised. But many of the products now being manufactured in these countries, or partially manufactured through mixing, packaging, or assembling, should be produced there rather than imported. In other words, production can be justified from an economic standpoint. Moreover, reliance upon agricultural and raw-material exports to produce an acceptable standard of living is not in accordance with tendencies in a world seemingly ruled by nationalistic ambitions. Recourse to industry may be the only alternative for agricultural countries if industrial nations so act that exports to them are reduced. In these later years, maintenance of the standard of living has depended upon increased industrial activity, and in this, branch plants have played an important role.

Industrial growth has also resulted in greater diffusion of national income among the population. Such a result is of great importance in the economy of South American countries, where wealth in agricultural lands, equipment, and livestock, also in raw-material deposits, is held by a small sector of the population and where there is no middle class of any appreciable size such as we have in the United States. Increasing industrial activity is creating such a middle class in South America, and for this change branch plants are partly responsible. In fact, over a period of many decades, the effect which branch plants have on the diffusion of income and the creation of a middle class will probably constitute their greatest single contribution to the well-being of those countries in which they are located.

CHAPTER 10

SUMMARY—FAVORABLE AND UNFAVORABLE INFLUENCES

The question of whether it has been feasible for North American concerns to migrate to South America is partially answered by the data presented in the preceding chapter. But it is only partially answered, for the data are a compilation of the results of many companies' operations, and these companies are diverse as to type, product manufactured, and the conditions under which they operate. Not all concerns have been profitable, and some have actually withdrawn. Moreover, the data cover operations in only one country—Argentina—which is, in many respects, the most favorable location for migrated concerns. For the packing companies, the data are more homogeneous and complete, and they can, therefore, be relied upon to answer more conclusively the question as to feasibility of migration. Also, the packing companies have been operating in South America for so long that there can be little doubt of the correctness of their original decision to purchase or build plants. In certain other cases there is considerably more doubt, for the length of time during which operations have been carried forward is too short to permit of conclusive statements. There is need of yet more proof, which only time can produce, to enable us to determine whether the decisions to establish branch plants were sound or otherwise. Furthermore, profit data constitute merely a record of past successes or failures, and they are not necessarily an infallible indication of results in the future. Because of these limitations on profit data for the purpose in view, something additional will be attempted in the present chapter. This might be described as a logical test of migration and of the factors which have a bearing upon it. Of course, the time limitations imposed by quantitative data are not present in a deductive analysis.

One manner of testing migration is to consider the reasons advanced for the action. If the incentives, the motivations, behind the action were sufficiently cogent, the original decision to migrate can be justified. In Chapter 3 these reasons are considered at length and at least partially tested. Another approach to the problem is to determine under what circumstances and for what companies the difficulties which have been discussed in some detail are likely to be encountered. On this point, also, some evidence has been presented in preceding chapters, either directly or by implication. So this concluding chapter will be in part a review of the whole study, with particular attention to those factors whose presence lends feasibility to the establishment of branch manufacturing operations, including those which, for lack of a more adequately descriptive term, might be called environmental conditions.

First it should be recognized that when the establishment of a manufacturing plant is being considered, much the same analysis is required, whether the plant is to be located in the domestic market or in a foreign market. Quite evidently, the important questions are in regard to the presence or absence of needed raw materials, the availability of labor, the degree of competition which is likely to be met, the extent of the market, and, possibly, tariff protection. Quite aside from the issue of migration, as such, these are pertinent questions in connection with the undertaking of manufacturing operations in any location. The approach which should be taken is that migration is, primarily, a business problem and, secondarily, a problem which is characterized by the fact that both the capital and the management come from abroad. The first question to be answered is this: "Should the product in which we are interested be produced in Brazil or Argentina, in view of the raw materials available, the extent of the market, and so on?" The second question might be stated as follows: "Can our concern manufacture the product in that country on a profitable basis, or is there something in the fact of being a foreign concern which precludes the likelihood of successful operation?" Unless the first question can be answered in the affirmative, and with a reasonable degree of certainty, there is little hope of success for a migrated company. The fundamental bases for an industry must be entirely sound, there must be good and sufficient economic reasons for production, or the disadvantages accruing from the fact of foreign ownership and management will constitute altogether too serious a handicap to operation. For most of the branch plants which have been established, the economic bases for manufacturing activities were of sufficient validity, and profitable operations resulted even despite the appearance of numerous hampering factors. One executive with long experience in South America said that a migrated company has little to fear if a really strong case can be made for the local manufacture of the product in which it is interested. Familiarity with the situation of many companies lends support to this contention. It might be added, however, that a company has nothing to fear if there is economic justification for its activities and also effective, broad-minded administration of its affairs.

For the processing of livestock and the manufacture of numerous products—among them cement, yeast, and corn products—there is little question that the presence of raw materials furnishes ample justification for production activities. On the score of raw-material availability, there is much less justification for the manufacture of radios, victrolas, electric light bulbs, transformers, and automobile tires. But the production of each of these in branch plants may be justified on other grounds. In the case of tires, the chief raw material must be imported, wherever manufacturing facilities are now located. Only in the Dutch East dies would production be close to the source of the chief raw material.

The presence of raw materials cannot be used as a sole criterion of the feasibility of migration. Even when raw materials are available, the advisability of production depends in large measure upon the nature of the production process—more specifically, upon the optimum size of the production unit in relation to market demand. In South America, the demand for most products is limited, and, incidentally, much more limited than numerous migrated companies originally thought. Moreover, population figures alone do not constitute a safe measure of demand, for the purchasing power of a large share of the people is extremely low. Yet some products must be produced in large volume in order to be produced at low cost. These are the products of industries which are of a decreasing-cost nature. For some other products, the nature of the manufacturing process may be such that fairly low unit costs can be attained in a small plant with a comparatively low output.[1] In such circumstances, a small manufacturing plant designed to produce for a limited market, such as that of Brazil or Argentina, can compete without too great disadvantage with large plants located elsewhere. Consequently, if the optimum size of the production unit is small, a much better case can be made for the establishment of branch plants. The significance of this point cannot be overstressed, for the feasibility of establishing branch plants in countries with small populations of limited purchasing power depends very largely upon it.

A closely related question is that of the size of the capital commitment which must be made in order to start manufacturing activities. The uncertainty surrounding migrated companies has been noted frequently. Under such circumstances, it is to the interest of any migrating concern to keep the amount of capital invested as low as possible, perhaps even at the sacrifice of technical efficiencies. A manufac-

[1] See Chap. 3, pp. 51–52.

turing situation in which capital costs are comparatively low and labor costs high is an excellent one, for facilities are costly and labor is cheap in South America. Also, when capital commitment is low, withdrawal is easy. If conditions become such that withdrawal appears to be the only advisable course open, liquidation of investment can be accomplished without undue losses. In any particular case, the likelihood of anything approaching forced withdrawal may seem remote indeed. But knowledge of what has happened to migrated companies previously, and of what is happening today in Japan, precludes any assurance that companies in South America will remain unmolested henceforth, even to the extent of making it unnecessary to consider withdrawal. Therefore, capital investment should be kept at a minimum, particularly if the justification for local production appears none too strong. In all probability, there are concerns which have migrated to South America which would do so on a more modest scale and with a smaller total investment if they could remake their original decisions in the light of their later experience.

Under some circumstances, the simplification of marketing problems has been sufficient justification for the establishment of branch plants. Even without the advantage of lower tariff rates on parts than on completed products, many assembly plants would have been placed in South American countries because of the marketing advantage derived from local assembly. An assembly plant is, in effect, an intermediary production unit within the market of sale. To have such a unit near the consumer is of distinct advantage, particularly for products in which the desires of individual buyers may vary. Automobiles, for example, possess style features which permit a wide range of choice on the part of the purchaser. Elevators are another such product, for they must be adapted to various construction features of buildings. In this product there is also a style element which permits choice. Through partial local production in assembly plants, a product can be more easily adapted to specific consumer needs or desires, transportation costs can be reduced, greater availability can be given to products, and a larger measure of control and supervision can be exercised over distribution. When the nature of a product is such that these marketing factors are of particular importance, a much stronger case can be made for industrial migration. Moreover, marketing advantages are of a permanent character and cannot be summarily withdrawn.

Another factor tending to make the economic situation suitable for migration is the absence of need for high tariff protection. This factor, in contrast to those previously considered, is of an environmental character. Because of nationalistic tendencies throughout the world, and the demands for revenue during the depression, tariff walls have been considerably heightened. Obviously they can likewise be reduced, as was amply illustrated by the tire incident. Thus, it is very questionable whether a high tariff barrier on a product, if the tariff is needed in order to give the local producer a cost advantage, is a factor which lends feasibility to the establishment of branch plants. In many instances, quite the opposite appears to be the case. Of course, it is freely admitted that tariff barriers tend to persist, but they are most likely to do so under two conditions; namely, if a large quantity of labor and raw materials of national origin are used in production, and if native concerns using national rather than foreign capital, and national rather than foreign management, are producing commodities similar to those produced in branch plants.

An illustration of the first condition is afforded by the manufacture of corn products. Argentina, being a large producer and exporter of corn, has practically excluded the importation of corn products, such as corn syrup and corn starch, and reductions in tariffs which will again allow importations are unlikely. Therefore, the branch plant of Corn Products Refining Company is not in a vulnerable position so far as reduced protection is concerned. Other companies are more vulnerable in this respect, for, in a sense, the national stake in local production is less, also the attitude of nationals toward them is different. Industries which use native raw materials are thought of as being more justifiable economically, less parasitical, than those which rely upon imported materials. In most cases, such an attitude has logical bases, but there are instances in which ample justification for production exists even though imported raw materials are used.

The presence of native concerns in the same industry is a favorable condition for migrated companies. Such concerns serve as a buffer against untoward action by the government. A decrease in tariff protection is disadvantageous to both native and foreign producers, and the influence of the former may be important if united action is taken to remedy the situation created by tariff reductions. Native concerns are in a much better position to protect themselves against unfavorable action than are foreign companies, for they do not bear the stigma of foreign origin, and by protecting themselves they protect other concerns as well. In the packing industry the presence of both British and native companies has been distinctly helpful to the American concerns in overcoming, or at least mitigating, unfriendly action.

Branch plants should not be established if the success of their operations depends too heavily upon the maintenance of tariffs, favorable port charges, or other artificial conditions. Such factors should not be the primary incentives behind migration. Even though they may have been operative for many years, still they are of an artificial nature and therefore subject to change at the will of individuals. The assumption frequently made in the past that existing tariff rates would be continued, or at least would not be lowered, is not a safe one. Before migration is decided upon, a company should make sure that there is a reasonable opportunity for profitable operations, even under substantially reduced tariff protection. More dependence can be placed on the maintenance of tariff charges if the presence of native industry of like type or the extensive use of locally produced raw materials furnishes a protective influence.

Other environmental conditions are of a more general nature. They can be listed under two general headings; namely, (1) the economic development of the country in which the branch plant is located, and (2) tendencies of a political and social nature which may be subversive to the security of private enterprise, particularly that of foreign origin. It is not an overstatement to say that the success of branch plants now operating in South America, likewise of those which may be located there in the future, depends very largely on these two factors. Upon the first, operations of branch plants may have some effect, but necessarily a limited one. In regard to the second, however, there is nothing which can be done to stem the tide if it appears to be flowing in the wrong direction. Two decades ago Uruguay was considered to be one of the best countries in South America, if not the best, in which to do business. During the past five to ten years it has been a hotbed of social experiment, and the result has been a large measure of government ownership and administration of business formerly owned and operated by independent entrepreneurs. Furthermore, it would have been very difficult to foresee that such a change would take place. After the World War, and even in the early years of the 1921–1930 decade, foreign companies located in Uruguay were reasonably profitable and felt reasonably secure. Now they are neither. The change has been a product, not of the depression, but rather of social and political developments.

First, our attention will be directed toward the economic development of the countries under consideration. From the point of view of any particular concern, there is little interest in economic changes as such. Rather, interest is centered in the growth of the market for the company's products. If total demand is likely to increase, then profits are likely to increase, also. To a branch plant, increases in demand are of particular importance, for it may be the only producer of a certain commodity and thus the recipient of all new demand, at least until new producers enter the field. Usually the branch organization is stronger, both in its financial resources and in its administrative personnel, than are its competitors, and thus it may secure more than its proportionate share of any new demand that appears. Moreover, an increase in demand may serve to correct initial errors made in the establishment of branch plants. Many concerns overestimated the size of the market when they built their plants, or built with too much optimism as to future increases in demand. At any rate, overcapacity in relation to the volume of business now being done is evident in many cases, and additional business would materially reduce excessive overhead costs.

Companies which are contemplating the establishment of factories in these countries should make as careful and comprehensive an analysis of the potentiality of the market as the data and information available permit. Presumably, if a branch is established, production will be continued indefinitely, and therefore the results of its operation will be determined largely by major economic trends. Trends in population, national income, the diffusion of income, the relationship of industrial to agricultural and raw-material-producing countries—all should command the interest of those who are called upon to make analyses regarding branch plants, for obviously, if there is to be demand, there must be individuals or institutions who desire the product sufficiently to purchase it and who have the wherewithal to make their desires effective.

It is not our purpose here to present a detailed account of economic and social developments in South American countries, but merely to indicate their importance to branch plants and the need for including them in investigations prior to migration. Some brief comments may, however, be given on the various questions as they arise. In a consideration of population growth, both the trend of immigration and emigration and that of the birth and death rates are of significance. Until the past few years, the populations of these countries were increasing with some rapidity. Immigration was considerably heavier than emigration. Before the World War, the net gain for Argentina was about 150,000 people annually, and between 1920 and 1930, about 80,000 annually. As a result of this influx of foreign people in addition to a high birth rate, the Argentine population has nearly trebled since 1900. Other countries have had much the same population tendencies, but the changes have not been so noticeable as in Argentina. Immigration has been interrupted in the past few years, but it is likely to be resumed in view of the overcrowding that exists in those countries which have constituted the chief sources of immigrants. Italians, in particular, appear to have been successful in these countries, and more of them are likely to come in the future.

Qualitative changes in the populations of these countries are likewise taking place. Northern Europeans, also northern Italians, bring to the country of their adoption industrial training, skills, and habits which are invaluable to economic activity. And not only is the work of these people highly productive; they constitute a training nucleus which serves to raise the productivity of others. The level of training in South America is also being raised by the greater attention and financial support which are being given to formal education. While this is not so directly contributory to increased economic output, still, in time, a better trained and more intelligent populace will gain for itself a higher standard of living.

Of major importance is the trend in the national income of a country and in the diffusion of income among the population. To speak with authority on this point, or even to present detailed information in support of any assertions made, would require careful research. Some evidence is presented in an earlier part of the study upon the value of exports from Chile and Argentina.[2] Increased exports of nitrates and copper from Chile, of grains and meat products from Argentina and Uruguay, and of coffee and numerous other products from Brazil, coupled with increased output for internal consumption and a measure of industrial expansion, could have had no other result than to increase the national income. This increase in national income has recently been retarded by the growth of nationalism and by the economic breakdown which started in 1929. Moreover, the retardation has been serious, as foreign trade statistics will amply prove. But whether income will be permanently depressed and held to the proportions of the past few years is open to question. In the case of agricultural exports, there was no serious curtailment of quantity; the drop in value was due primarily to price declines. With better prices, the part of the national income which is derived from these products will rebound rapidly. A revival has already occurred in the exports of Chilean mineral products. Furthermore, in time the world may need the iron ore deposits of Brazil. While technological progress is causing the iron ore deposits of Europe and the United States to last much longer than prognosticators have stated, sooner or later Brazil's iron "mountain" may be of material aid in raising that country's national income.

For all branch plants, with the exception of those which are relying heavily upon tariff protection, a tendency away from nationalism toward free trade would be of distinct advantage. That this is the case for those companies which are engaged in the processing of materials for export—the packing plants for instance—is evident. The automobile assembly plants and those which produce construction materials would also benefit considerably. Of course, a strong tendency away from nationalism would curb industrial expansion to some extent, for tariffs in these countries would be reduced as a necessary complement of reductions

[2] See Tables 4 and 5, p. 34.

elsewhere. Still, it is doubtful whether the branch plants now located there, or at least the great majority of them, would be harmed. Most of them have sufficient economic justification so that the protection which they needed would be retained. Branch plants would be benefited from more active world trade because the national income of South American countries would in all probability be appreciably increased. For certain plants, the lowering of tariffs might mean additional competition in the form of imports, but for all plants taken as a group, the effect of increased national income upon demand would far outweigh any negative factors.

The basis for this statement is fairly obvious. With a reversion toward free trade, Chile, Argentina, and the other countries would be allowed to concentrate their efforts upon those commodities in which they have the greatest comparative advantage. Argentina is probably the world's lowest-cost producer of meats and cereals. Chile has a comparative advantage in nitrates and copper. If industrial nations would permit these countries to supply them to a greater extent with meats, cereals, nitrates, and many other products, national incomes would rise, and not only in the food and raw-material-producing countries, but in the industrial nations as well. Whether nationalism, with its necessary concomitant of stifled world trade, will continue with the intensity which has marked the past decade is open to question. With a return of more prosperous conditions, trade barriers may be relaxed. In this country, some noteworthy steps are now being taken through reciprocal trade agreements.

The extent of the demand for the products of branch plants depends also on the diffusion of national income. South America has always been characterized by concentration of wealth. The economic system which prevails—the *latifundia*—is of a feudal nature. In each of the countries on the eastern seaboard, extremely large tracts of land are held by a few wealthy families. They are either cultivated by hired labor or rented to individuals on a share basis. There are relatively few small individual land holdings, such as we have in this country. This system is one which tends to increase production for export, and the system itself is endangered if there be a drying up of export demand. Large *estancia* owners in Argentina and Uruguay have been hard hit by the reduction in meat exports and by price reductions on cereals.

There is some evidence of a slow disintegration of the *latifundia* system. During the past few years, many large landholders have been forced to sell small tracts from the edges of their estates. Furthermore, as the estates pass to descendants, of whom there are usually many, a natural breaking-up process takes place. Both the governments and certain private enterprises have attempted to colonize the unoccupied land by arranging easy purchase terms and material aid during the first trying years. At the present time the most active colonizing agents in Argentina are the British-owned railroads. While colonization has been none too successful, still it has had some effect, and there is slowly developing in these countries a group of small agriculturists who own the land and depend upon general agriculture rather than upon exportable crops. Admittedly, no rapid change can be expected in the economic system under which these countries operate, but there is evidence of the gradual development of a middle-class group. The result of this diffusion of the national income will be a higher standard of living, and with it will come a larger demand for many consumers' goods.

The industrial advances which have been made in South America in the past two decades have also tended to bring about a diffusion of income. An industrial economy is more productive of a middle-class group than is an agricultural one, for income depends more upon individual and less upon group effort. There is a wider range of skills into which individuals may fit themselves. Greater aptitude and diligence on the part of some will result in higher productivity and higher earning power. Moreover, in industry there is more likelihood of group action among workers to increase their earnings and to improve the conditions under which they labor. Industrial expansion is likely to bring about—in fact, has brought about—increased incomes and moderate capital accumulations by many people. Particularly when the land is closely held, as it has been in South America, there is little opportunity for the mass of the people to earn higher incomes or to accumulate wealth, but to the extent that the *latifundia* system breaks down and industrial activity increases, a middle class will tend to appear, and with it an increased demand for many products.

Thus a trend away from nationalism would have a mixed effect upon the economic development of South America. Immediately, it would increase national incomes, for other countries would purchase agricultural, pastoral, and mineral products more freely. On the other hand, it might arrest industrial growth and the redivision of the land among many smaller agriculturists—tendencies which foster the creation of a middle class and the diffusion of income. If we consider national economy from a long-run point of view, the diffusion of income is perhaps more to be desired than an increase in total income. But, even with some reversion from nationalism, industry in South America is likely to grow, although less rapidly than it has during the past decade under the stimulus of self-sufficiency. It must be remembered that the rapid industrial advance of the past decade has created vested interests and that these have gained strength and authority. Industrial advances will not be relinquished by these interests without bitter struggle, for their capital commitment is at stake. While there is little likelihood that temperate South America will become a great industrial area in view of its lack of essential raw materials, still many items can be produced there economically, and their production will probably continue.

SUMMARY

Enough has been said to show the type of economic analysis which is needed before decisions to migrate are made. Tendencies in population, the national income, the diffusion of that income, and the relationships between industrial and agricultural countries are among the factors that must be taken into account in any careful and comprehensive analysis. Here a cursory consideration of these factors leads to the conclusion that the demand for consumers' goods can be expected to increase appreciably in the future. If branch plants are allowed to continue operations without undue restrictions and to supply the demand for their products as it appears, profitable operations should result.

Thus, so far as economic conditions and tendencies are concerned, the future seems reasonably bright for migrated companies. But social and political conditions and tendencies, in so far as they can be divorced from those of an economic character, make the situation appear less hopeful. Political instability in Brazil and Chile appears to be chronic in nature. Currency depreciation is another questionable element. Neither is conducive to long-continued, effective operations by migrated companies. Furthermore, the parties of the Left are strong, and they are the chief instigators of anti-foreign-capital activities. Agitation against foreign interests is their stock in trade, and no opportunity is neglected to injure companies of foreign origin. Since the revolution of 1930, the Union Civica Radical party has not been in power in Argentina, but it is the party with the most numerous adherents and eventually is likely to regain power. When we recall that the control acts directed at the packing industry and the petroleum reserve acts were passed during the time that this party was in power, there appears to be sufficient basis for apprehension. Even under the present conservative government, certain parts of the Packers Control Law have been enforced for the first time, also the petroleum reserves have been extended to new areas. From the events of the past few years, it seems likely that a badgering policy will persist whatever the political make-up of the government may be.

It thus appears that the future of branch plants depends in no small degree upon the extent of adverse governmental action specifically directed at foreign capital investments. This in turn depends upon the strength of socialistic tendencies. The depressed economic conditions of the past few years have strengthened those groups which are opposed to foreign interests, but perhaps this effect is only temporary. After the recession of 1920, adverse action against the packing companies was particularly strong, and again in the years after the 1929 recession.

While such action is a usual phenomenon of depression years, it is not based solely upon the reaction to lower prices and reduced incomes. Rather, it is based upon a certain distrust of foreign companies—a feeling that there is a measure of exploitation in whatever they do. Productive enterprise financed and managed by foreign concerns is desired and apparently welcomed, but it is also resented. There is a feeling that economic opportunities should be reserved for nationals and that foreigners who take advantage of such opportunities are intruders. These people wish to own and control their own industries and to acquire whatever profits are realized therefrom. But as yet they do not have the technical abilities, the experience, nor the capital which are necessary for conducting many industrial enterprises. Moreover, no thorough technical training is being offered by their educational institutions. Nor is thorough training in economics and business administration available. Major attention is given to the arts, medicine, and law. Until there are more individuals who are prepared for technical positions and for those in which executive capacity is needed, certain industries must necessarily remain in the hands of foreign concerns, if they are to be effectively administered.

Because foreign concerns have taken advantage of economic opportunities and have profited thereby, they will continue to be resented and, very probably, hampered in their activities. In this connection, obscurity will be a virtue, for the small, relatively unimportant companies will be the least molested. Those which are most affected with a wide public interest and are of greatest importance in the national economy will be most subject to governmental control and supervision, and, furthermore, they may be subjected to direct competition from government-owned and operated organizations, such as the YPF in Argentina and the national packing plant of Uruguay. The extent to which the activities of branch plants will be circumscribed in the future is entirely conjectural, but the events of the past few years surely do not promise immunity from prejudicial action.

As yet, most migrated concerns have operated with a reasonable degree of security. There have been many threats of unfavorable action which have failed to mature. Again, such action as the government has taken against foreign concerns has frequently been ineffective and has later been rescinded. In still other cases, protection has been afforded by the legal decisions of the supreme courts of these countries. For these higher courts the migrated companies have a great deal of respect. Furthermore, in each of these countries there is a considerable body of sound public opinion which realizes that the benefits from industrial migration are mutual and that the migrated companies must be given a reasonable opportunity for profitable operation in view of the capital invested and the risk assumed. This sound public opinion may be of sufficient strength to counteract the efforts of those who are opposed to foreign capital.

From a long-run point of view, the greatest protection which branch organizations have is the efficiency of their operations, the service which they give. Whether it be in meat packing, the extraction and processing of petroleum, the production of cement, or the production or assembly of many other products, the effectiveness with which the foreign concerns handle economic resources and perform needed economic services will constitute an element of protection against unfavorable governmental acts. Brazil, Uruguay, and Argentina cannot afford to do without the North American packing companies. Argentina needs the capital and experience of the foreign oil companies. The automobile concerns and the International Cement Corporation have performed a real service for the South American republics. Native concerns have not been so effective, for they have lacked the needed capital and, above all, experience and technical abilities. It has often been remarked that these countries cannot get along with foreign concerns, and that neither can they get along without them. Some truth and some error are involved in this statement, as is usually the case in such generalizations. The South American countries could get along without the foreign concerns which have made investments and operate within their borders, but not without unnecessary sacrifices. Moreover, they can get along with them, and in the majority of instances they are doing so. Their economic well-being calls for amicable adjustments and not a policy of obstruction which can have no legitimate purpose.

Appendix I

NORTH AMERICAN COMPANIES WHICH HAVE MIGRATED TO VARIOUS SOUTH AMERICAN COUNTRIES

Argentina:
  American & Foreign Power Company, Inc.
  Armco International Corporation
  Armour & Company
  Bates Valve Bag Corporation
  Blaw-Knox Company
  Brunswick-Balke-Collender Company
  Colgate-Palmolive-Peet Company
  Consolidated Chemical Industries, Inc.
  Corn Products Refining Company
  E. I. du Pont de Nemours & Company
  Firestone Tire & Rubber Company
  Ford Motor Company
  General Motors Corporation
  Goodyear Tire & Rubber Company
  Intercontinents Power Company
  International Business Machines Corporation
  International Cement Corporation
  International Harvester Company
  International Printing Ink Corporation
  International Telephone & Telegraph Corporation
  Johnson & Johnson
  Lambert Pharmacal Company
  Lehn & Fink Company
  National Lead Company
  Otis Elevator Company
  Parke, Davis & Company
  Pond's Extract Company
  R. C. A. Victor Company, Ltd.
  Scott & Bowne Company
  Singer Sewing Machine Company
  Standard Oil Company
  Swift International Company

Texas Corporation
Truscon Steel Company
United Shoe Machinery Corporation
Utah Radio Products Company
Wilson & Company, Inc.

Brazil:
American & Foreign Power Company, Inc.
Armco International Corporation
Armour & Company
Bates Valve Bag Corporation
Brazilian Traction, Light & Power Co., Ltd.
Colgate-Palmolive-Peet Company
Columbia Phonograph Company, Inc.
Corn Products Refining Company
Daggett & Ramsdell
Ford Motor Company
General Electric Company
General Motors Corporation
Intercontinents Power Company
International Cement Corporation
Otis Elevator Company
Parke, Davis & Company
Pullman Standard Car Export Corporation
R. C. A. Victor Company, Ltd.
Singer Sewing Machine Company
Standard Brands, Inc.
Swift International Company
United Shoe Machinery Corporation
United States Steel Corporation
White (S. S.) Dental Manufacturing Company
Wilson & Company, Inc.

Uruguay:
Armour & Company
Ford Motor Company
General Motors Corporation
International Cement Corporation
International Telephone & Telegraph Corporation
Swift International Company

Chile:
American & Foreign Power Company, Inc.
Anaconda Copper Mining Company
Curtiss-Wright Corporation
E. I. du Pont de Nemours & Company
Ford Motor Company

APPENDIX I

Grace (W. R.) & Company
Guggenheim Brothers
Intercontinents Power Company
International Bitumen Emulsions Corporation
International Telephone & Telegraph Corporation
Kennecott Copper Corporation
Otis Elevator Company
Parke, Davis & Company
R. C. A. Victor Company, Ltd.
Singer Sewing Machine Company
Standard Oil Company
United States Steel Corporation
Warren Brothers Company

APPENDIX II

CLASSIFICATION BY ACTIVITIES OF NORTH AMERICAN COMPANIES WITH PRODUCTION FACILITIES IN SOUTH AMERICA

I. Activities primarily related to the extraction and processing of mineral products and other raw materials
  A. For export
    Anaconda Copper Mining Company
    Guggenheim Brothers
    Kennecott Copper Corporation
    United States Steel Corporation (Brazil)
  B. For domestic use
    E. I. du Pont de Nemours & Company
    International Bitumen Emulsions Corporation
    International Cement Corporation
    National Lead Company
    Standard Oil Company
    Texas Corporation
    Warren Brothers Company

II. Processing products of agricultural or pastoral origin
    Armour & Company
    Consolidated Chemical Industries, Inc.
    Swift International Company
    Wilson & Company, Inc.

III. Furnishing services (public utilities)
    American & Foreign Power Company, Inc.
    Brazilian Traction, Light & Power Co., Ltd.
    Intercontinents Power Company
    International Telephone & Telegraph Corporation

IV. General manufacturing
  A. Production by the North American company
    1. Complete production of a commodity in the branch plant
      Bates Valve Bag Corporation
      Brunswick-Balke-Collender Company
      Columbia Phonograph Company, Inc.
      Corn Products Refining Company
      E. I. du Pont de Nemours & Company
      Firestone Tire & Rubber Company

General Electric Company
Goodyear Tire & Rubber Company
Grace (W. R.) & Company
International Printing Ink Corporation
Parke, Davis & Company (some products)
R. C. A. Victor Company, Ltd.
Scott & Bowne Company
Standard Brands, Inc.
Truscon Steel Company
White (S. S.) Dental Manufacturing Company

2. Production of some assembly units, importation of others, and assembly in the branch plant
    Curtiss-Wright Corporation
    General Motors Corporation
    Otis Elevator Company
    Pullman Standard Car Export Corporation (Brazil)
    Utah Radio Products Company

3. Minor production, assembly, and service operations in subsidiaries of public utility companies
    Brazilian Traction, Light & Power Co., Ltd.

4. Assembly of parts imported from abroad
    Ford Motor Company (in some countries)
    General Motors Corporation (in some countries)

5. Minor assembly and service operations in subsidiaries primarily devoted to merchandising operations
    Armco International Corporation
    International Business Machines Corporation
    International Harvester Company
    National Cash Register Company
    Pullman Standard Car Export Corporation (Argentina)
    Singer Sewing Machine Company
    United Shoe Machinery Corporation
    United States Steel Corporation (Chile)

6. Packaging of commodities imported in bulk
    Johnson & Johnson
    Parke, Davis & Company (some products)

B. Production by native concerns through contractual relationship
    Blaw-Knox Company
    Colgate-Palmolive-Peet Company
    Daggett & Ramsdell
    General Electric Company (Argentina)
    Lambert Pharmacal Company
    Lehn & Fink Company
    Pond's Extract Company

Appendix III
AVERAGE ANNUAL EXCHANGE RATES BETWEEN VARIOUS SOUTH AMERICAN MONETARY UNITS AND THE DOLLAR, 1900–1932*

Year	Argentine paper peso	Brazilian milreis	Chilean peso	Uruguayan peso
1900		$0.1927	$0.3407	$1.0470
1901		0.2307	0.3219	1.0480
1902		0.2427	0.3080	1.0464
1903		0.2434	0.3372	1.0489
1904		0.2478	0.3321	1.0487
1905	$0.4338	0.3223	0.3169	1.0481
1906	0.4372	0.3280	0.2915	1.0499
1907	0.4372	0.3105	0.2586	1.0522
1908	0.4347	0.3074	0.1952	1.0486
1909	0.4319	0.3071	0.2186	1.0468
1910	0.4326	0.3247	0.2186	1.0463
1911	0.4310	0.3228	0.2155	1.0456
1912	0.4328	0.3236	0.2053	1.0501
1913	0.4325	0.3216	0.1977	1.0482
1914	0.4241	0.2926	0.1833	1.0428
1915	0.4132	0.2467	0.1634	0.9970
1916	0.4278	0.2351	0.1878	1.0406
1917	0.4463	0.2501	0.2522	1.1111
1918	0.4441	0.2534	0.2890	1.2019
1919	0.4357	0.2674	0.2256	1.0989
1920	0.3991	0.2251	0.1845	0.8627
1921	0.3212	0.1312	0.1206	0.6861
1922	0.3600	0.1295	0.1222	0.7940
1923	0.3457	0.1023	0.1224	0.7906
1924	0.3438	0.1094	0.1054	0.8227
1925	0.4021	0.1220	0.1160	0.9840
1926	0.4055	0.1444	0.1208	1.0147
1927	0.4237	0.1184	0.1207	1.0134
1928	0.4245	0.1197	0.1215	1.0266
1929	0.4186	0.1181	0.1206	0.9863
1930	0.3674	0.1071	0.1208	0.8586
1931	0.2937	0.0703	0.1207	0.5536
1932	0.2571	0.0712	0.079	0.4706

* Data from U.S. Department of Commerce, *Commerce Yearbook*, Vol. II, Foreign Countries, for 1928 (pp. 23, 95, 146, 655), 1932 (pp. 353, 373, 388, 488), and 1933 (pp. 172, 181, 186, 238).

INDEX

A

American Economic Review, 25n., 237n.
American & Foreign Power Company, Inc., 54, 110–112
Amuchastegui, Judge, 118
Anglo-Argentine commercial treaty (1933), 177–179
Anglo company, 175, 185–188
Armco International Corporation, 73
Armour & Company, 47, 297
Asociación De Industriales Del Caucho, 130
Asociación Importadores De Neumaticós, 130–139
Automobile assembly plants, 66–67, 72, 74–75, 133–135
 effect of local assembly on price of finished product, 60–61

B

Bankruptcy laws, 117–119
 of Argentina, 117–119
 of Chile, 117–119
Boletin Official (Argentina), 18n., 195n.
Branch plants, investment in, 16–25
 management of, 95
 mortality among, 289–290
 number of employees in, 25–26
 overcapacity of, 93, 315
 (*See also* Migrating companies)
Brazilian Traction, Light & Power Co., Ltd., 5, 21, 53–54, 162, 251
British meat quotas, 175–179
Buenos Aires Herald, 177n., 181n., 228n.

C

Cameron, C. R., 104n.
Canada, migration to, 30, 32
Cattle, classification of, Argentina, 187–189
Cía. Argentine Sydney Ross, Inc., 8
Colgate-Palmolive-Peet Company, 7
Comments on Argentine Trade, 118n., 123n., 209n.
Commerce Reports, 119n., 121n.
Commerce Yearbook, 17n., 128n.
Commercial law, inadequacy of, 114–126
 bankruptcy under, 117–119
 conditional sales, 115–117
 trade-marks, 119–126
Companies, with branch plants (*see* Migrating companies; Branch plants)
Competition, effect on decision to migrate, 57–62
 with native concerns, 61
Concessions by governments (*see* Favors)
Consolidated Chemical Industries, Inc., 47–48
Corn Products Refining Company, 63–65, 113, 312
Currency depreciation, 17, 39–41, 108–110
Curtiss-Wright Corporation, 85
Customs administration, 103, 153–156

D

De Marval, J. A. & E., 115n., 123n.
De Valle, Ltd., 8–9
Diario del Plata, 22n.

331

Diario Official (Paraná, Brazil), 112n.
Difficulties in migration, 90–126, 231–270
　differences in nationality, 98–103
　distance from home office, 95–97
　language, 265
Distribution, control over, 81–85

E

Economic development of South American countries, 32–37, 315–321
　effect of migration upon, 303–306
Employee benefits, 275–278
　education, 276
　health, 276–277
　insurance, 276–277
Employees in branch plants, number of, 25–26
　(*See also* Labor)
Employees' Holidays Law, Brazil, 217
Exchange control, 39–41
Exchange rates, 17, 109, 330
Executive personnel, 260–270
　Europeans for, 262–266
　selection of, 98, 267–268
　source of, 260
　(*See also* Managers of branch plants)
Exports, from Argentina, 34
　from Chile, 34

F

Favors extended by governments, 282–285
Firestone Tire & Rubber Company, 58, 128
Ford Motor Company, 5, 254, 259
Foreign Affairs, 195n.
Foreign capital, prejudice against, 97–98, 137–138, 147
Frigorífico-Anglo, S. A., 175, 185–188

G

General Electric Company, 81, 275
General Motors Corporation, 5, 254, 259
Gold clauses in public utility contracts, Brazil, 111–112
Goodyear Tire & Rubber Company, 58, 128, 302
Government ownership, of industry in Uruguay, 213–214
　of oil industry in Argentina, 195–205
Governmental control of business, 165–231
Governmental instability, 103–108

H

Heyman Rinder and Company, 8
Hinds, A. S., Company, 9

I

Immigration, to Argentina, 34, 105, 316
　to Brazil, 104, 105
International Cement Corporation, 49–50, 215, 275–276, 297
International Telephone & Telegraph Corporation, 252
Investment of migrated companies, 16–25
　in Argentina, 18
　in Brazil, 20
　in Chile, 22
　by industries, 24
　in Uruguay, 21
Iron and steel industry (Argentina), 132

L

La Nacion, 181n., 282n.
La Prensa, 175n., 177n., 180n., 198n., 200, 203n.
Labor, 238–260
　abilities of, 238–240

INDEX 333

Labor, nationalities of, 239–241
  productivity of, 245–252
  supervisory, 241–245
  training of, 244–245
Labor costs, 252–253, 273–275
Labor disturbances, 253–260
Labor legislation, 207–226
Labor Legislation in Argentina, 209n.
Labor Legislation in Uruguay, 211n.
Language difficulties, 265
Latifundia system, 318–319
Laws of Argentina, 115n., 119n., 209n.
Laws in South America (*see* Commercial law; Social legislation)
Live Weight Law, Argentina, 171

M

Machinery and equipment, branch plants, 232–235
Managers of branch plants, responsibilities of, 95
  (*See also* Executive personnel)
Manufacturing, extent of, by branch plants, 4
  by native concerns, 8
Market, extent of in South America, 92–93
Marketing inducements to migration, 70–85
Mata, Carlos Garcia, 200–201
Michigan Business Studies, 44n.
Migrating companies, activities of, 328–329
  in Argentina, 13, 325
  in Brazil, 13, 326
  in Chile, 13, 327–328
  classification of, 3, 328–329
  difficulties encountered by, 90–126
  policies of, 271–287
  profits of, 290–301
  in Uruguay, 13, 326
Migration, background of, in South America, 32–37
  background of, in United States, 28–32

Migration, effect of, on South America, 303–306
  on United States industry, 301–303
  extent of, 1–26
  by industries, 15
  marketing inducements to, 70–85
  number of companies, 13, 325–328
  production incentives to, 51–57
  reasons for, 43–89
  time of, 11–16
Minimum Price Law, Argentina, 168–171
Monthly Bulletin of the British Chamber of Commerce in Brazil, 216n., 217n., 218n.
Monthly Labor Review (U.S.), 104n.

N

National income, 316–318
  diffusion of, 318–320
Nationalism, influence of, 37–42, 83–85, 317–320

O

Oil industry (*see* Petroleum industry)
Operating differences and difficulties, 231–270
Otis Elevator Company, 4
Ottawa Conference, 38, 174–175

P

Packers Control Act, Argentina, 171–172, 180–187
  Supreme Court decision upon, 184
Packing industry, 44–47, 166–193
Petroleum industry, 19, 21, 62–63, 193–205
  assumptions behind regulation of, 194–195
  competition with YPF, 196–199
  investment of United States companies, 21
  regulation of, 193–205
  reserves in Argentina, 197

Pharmaceutical industry, 7–11, 65–66, 75
Political uncertainty, 321–324
Population, Brazil, 92
Port charges, 133–137
Prenda Agraria, Argentina, 115–117
Prices, 60, 76–77
  for automobiles, 60
  force of customary, 77–78
  paid for manufacturing facilities, 94
  and policy of single price, 279
Productivity of workers, 245–252
Profits of branch plants, 290–301
  all branch plants, Argentina, 293–295
  in Brazil, Uruguay, and Chile, 297–298
  compared with other types of investment, 298–301
  difficulty of determining, 290–292
  meat-packing plants, Argentina, 294
  other (meat-packing excluded), Argentina, 295
Public utilities, investment in, 20, 21, 23, 93
Public utility contracts, Brazil, 111–112
Pullman Standard Car Export Corporation, 12
Purchasing power of South American countries, 34–35, 92–93
Putnam, George E., 45

R

Racial characteristics, 98–106
Raw material resources, as influence causing migration, 44–51
  use of, in branch plants, 235–236
Regulation and control, 165–207, 226–230
  of packing industry, 166–193
  of petroleum industry, 193–205
  of other industries, 205–207
  protection against, 226–230

Reserve decrees, Argentine petroleum, 197
Retirement and Pension Funds Act, Brazil, 217–218
Retirement and Pension Law, Uruguay, 212–213
Review of the River Plate, 168n., 170n., 172n., 179n., 182n., 183n., 184n., 185n., 186n., 187n., 188n.
Revista de Economia Argentina, 200n.
Revolutionary disturbances, 103–104
Roca, Dr. Julio A., 177, 186

S

Sabotage, in strikes, 257
Sales practices, 99–101
Salta-Standard Oil Company agreement, 202–204
Schilling, Hillier and Company, 8
Service policies, 279
Single price policy, 279
Social legislation, 160, 207–226
  in Argentina, 208–211
  in Brazil, 216–219
  in Chile, 219–225
  in Uruguay, 211–216
  summary of, 225–226
Sociedad Rural Argentina, 167
Standard Brands, Inc., 79
Standard Oil Company, 201–202
Statistical data, lack of, 91–95
Strikes (*see* Labor)
Sunday Rest Law, Argentina, 208
Supervisory labor, 241–245
  lack of, 241
  nationalities for, 243
Swift and Company, 12
Swift International Company, 46–47, 251, 297

T

Tariffs, changes in, 40, 63, 127–157
  customs administration of, 103, 153–156

Tariffs, exemptions from, 69
  illogical classifications, 149–153
  as incentive to migration, 63–70
  interstate, 156
Taussig, F. W., 253
Taxation, 107, 157–164
  discrimination in, 161
  evasion of, 162
  exemption from, 163, 284
  extent of, 160
  for social legislation, 160
Texas Corporation, 49
Tire industry, 52, 56, 58–60, 128–131, 139–145
Trade-marks, 119–126
  Argentine law, 123
  basis of rights, 119–120
  Brazilian law, 123
  bulletins of Department of Commerce on, 121n.
  imitations of, 124–125
  protection of rights in Latin America, 121
Trading under the Laws of Argentina, 115n.
Transportation costs, as reason for migration, 72–73

U

Union Industrial Argentina, 144
United Shoe Machinery Corporation, 11
United States industry, effects of migration upon, 301–303

V

Vestey, Sir Edmund, Bart., 175

W

Wages, 273–275
Wilson & Company, Inc., 12, 47
Wilson, Sir Arnold, 194
Winkler, Max, 23n.
Workmen's Compensation Law, Argentina, 208
World Peace Foundation Pamphlets, 23n.

Y

Yacimientos Petrolíferous Fiscales (YPF), 62, 196–205
  competition with private companies, 196–199